THE LULU PLAYS
and other sex tragedies

D1385723

Also by Wedekind

Spring Awakening

Caricature by Bruno Paul

THE LULU PLAYS
& OTHER SEX TRAGEDIES

Earth-Spirit
Pandora's Box
Death and Devil
Castle Wetterstein

FRANK WEDEKIND

Translated from the German by
Stephen Spender

Calder Publications
London

Riverrun Press
New York

Originally published by Vision Press 1952. Republished by
John Calder (Publishers) Ltd 1972. Reprinted 1977, 2000

ISBN 07145 0868 3

A catalogue record for this book is available from the
British Library.
Library of Congress Cataloging in Publication Data is avail-
able.

Typeset by Action Publishing
Printed and bound by MPG Books, Bodmin, Cornwall

CONTENTS

EARTH-SPIRIT

A Tragedy in Four Acts

I was created out of coarser stuff
By nature, and desire draws me earthwards.
For to the spirit of evil, not of good,
The earth belongs. What the immortals send
Us from above are but the common goods;
Their light gives joy, but it makes no one rich,
And in their realm are no possessions gained.
For precious stones and gold treasured by all
From the deceitful powers must be wrested
Who evil-natured dwell deep underground.
Not without sacrifice their favour is won
And there is no one who from serving them
Has extricated undefiled his soul.

(From Wallenstein's Death by Schiller)

CHARACTERS

DR. GOLL

DR. SCHÖN Editor-in-chief

ALWA his son

SCHWARZ an artist

PRINCE ESCERNY an African explorer

SCHIGOLCH

RODRIGO an acrobat

HUGENBERG a schoolboy

ESCHERICH a reporter

LULU

COUNTESS GESCHWITZ an artist

FERDINAND a coachman

HENRIETTE a chamber-maid

A FOOTMAN

The part of Hugenberg should be played by a girl

PROLOGUE

(The curtain rises to disclose the entrance to a tent from which emerges
to the sound of cymbals and the beating of drums an animal tamer
dressed in a vermilion red frock-coat, white tie, he has long black curly
hair, white breeches and top-boots; in his left hand he carries a riding
whip, in his right a loaded revolver)

ANIMAL TAMER
> Proud gentlemen and ladies who are gay
> Step right inside to look around the zoo
> With burning pleasure, icy shudders too,
> Here where the soulless brute creations play.
> The show is just beginning, come and see
> How to each pair a child's admitted – free.
>
> Here beast and man fight in the narrow cage,
> Where the one sways his whip disdainfully,
> The other with a roar of thunderous rage
> Jumps up against the man's neck murderously;
> First cleverness and later strength proves more
> First man then beast lies stretched out on the floor.
> The beast rears up, and on all fours the man,
> A single, ice-cold domineering look,
> The beast, abased, bends low the stricken neck,
> Tamely beneath the heel now placed thereon.
>
> The times are bad. Ladies and gentlemen
> Who once would crowd before my cage's show,
> They honour farces, dramas, operas, Ibsen,
> With their most estimable presence now –
> And all my pensioners are short of fodder
> So at the moment they devour each other.
> How well off is an actor in the theatre,
> He can be sure the flesh covers the bone
> However hunger makes his colleague moan,

And be his belly never emptier.
But if you seek for greatness in the arts
Don't think that work and wage have equal parts.

What do these plays of joys and griefs reveal?
Domestic beasts, well-bred in what they feel,
Who vent their rage on vegetarian fare
And then indulge in a complacent tear,
Just like those others – down in the parterre.
This hero cannot hold his liquor in,
This one's uncertain if his love is genuine.
You hear the third despair of this earth-ball
(For five long acts he groans about it all),
None gives the coup de grace to do him in.
The wild and lovely animal, the true,
Ladies and gentlemen, only I can show you.
You see the tiger, whose habit it is
To strike down all that comes across his path,
You see the bear begin with gluttonies,
After night's meal fall down dead to earth.
You see the little entertaining monkey
Fritter away his strength through sheer ennui.
Talent he has, but lacks all sense of greatness,
And so coquets with his own nakedness.
In my own tent, you see – upon my soul –
Just behind the curtain, there stands a camel.
The beasts are meekly fawning round my feet,
When (He fires into the audience) my revolver thunderously I pull
The creatures tremble round me. I stay cool –
The man stays cool! – respectfully to greet you.
Wake up? You hang back? No one budges?
Well then, you yourselves can be the judges.
Reptiles you may behold, of all devices,
Also chameleon, snake and crocodile
Dragon and salamander in crevices.
Of course I know you sit back there and smile
And don't believe a single word I say.

(He raises the curtain in front of the door and calls into the tent)

Hey, August, bring our snake this way!

(A navvy with a big stomach carries the actress taking the part of LULU
out of the tent and sets her down in front of the ANIMAL TAMER)

She was created for every abuse,
To allure and to poison and seduce,
To murder without leaving any trace.

(Tickling LULU under the chin)

Sweet creature, now keep in your proper place,
Not foolish nor affected nor eccentric,
Even when you fail to please the critic.
You have no right with miaows and spits inhuman
To distort for us the primal form of woman,
With clowning and with pulling stupid faces
To ape for us the childlike simple vices.
You should – I discuss this today lengthily –
Speak naturally and not unnaturally.
For since the earliest time the basic element
Of every art is that it be self-evident.

(To the audience)

There's nothing now especial to be seen
But wait and see what happens later on.
She coils herself with strong squeeze round the tiger,
He howls and groans. Who finally wins the wager?
Hopla! August! Carry her to her place.

(The NAVVY takes her across his arms; the ANIMAL TAMER strokes
her hips)

Sweet innocence. My treasure all of grace!

(The NAVVY carries her back into the tent)

But now the best of all is still before us.
My head placed in a beast of prey's jaws.
Walk up! It is a sight one often sees
And yet it's one which never fails to please.
I'll tear his jaws apart . I'm not afraid.
And he'll not dare to close them on my head.
So lovely, wild, and varied in his aspect
And yet he holds my head in such respect.
Trustfully I put my head under the teeth.
One joke – and both my temples crack beneath.
Yet I forgo to use my eyes' brightness.

Against my life I set a joke's lightness.
I throw away my whip and all these weapons
And appear harmless as God made me once.
Do you know the name of this wild beast? –
Honoured spectators, do step inside please!

(The ANIMAL TAMER steps back into the tent to the sound of cymbals and the beating of drums)

ACT ONE

Scene One

(A spacious studio. Backstage right the main door, downstage right a side door into a bedroom. In the centre a model's throne. Behind the throne a screen. In front of the screen a Smyrna carpet. Downstage left two easels. On the further one a half-length portrait, on the nearer one a canvas, face down. In front of the easels, approximately in the centre of the stage, an ottoman. Over it a tiger-skin. Against the wall, right, two armchairs. In the background a step-ladder.

SCHWARZ and SCHÖN)

SCHÖN. (seated on the end of the ottoman, examines the portrait on the further easel) Do you know, I'm getting to know the lady from quite a different angle?

SCHWARZ. (stands behind the ottoman with brushes and palette in his hand) I've never painted anyone whose facial expression changed more often – I was hardly able to fix a single feature.

SCHÖN. (indicating the picture – looking at him) Do you think it comes out in this?

SCHWARZ. During the sittings I did everything I could think of in my conversation to produce to some extent at least a restful atmosphere.

SCHÖN. Then I can understand the difference.

(SCHWARZ dips his brush into the oil-tin and passes it over the features)

SCHÖN. Do you think that makes it more like?

SCHWARZ. In art one can do no more than be as conscientious as one knows how.

SCHÖN. Tell me ...

SCHWARZ. (stepping back) The colours had got rather dull again, too.

SCHÖN. (looking at him) Have you ever in your life loved a woman?

SCHWARZ. (goes up to the easel, touches up a colour and steps back on the other side) The material still doesn't stand out enough. One still doesn't have the feeling that there's a living body underneath it.

SCHÖN. I don't doubt the work is excellent.

SCHWARZ. If you'd care to come over here ...

SCHÖN. (rising) You must have told her real horror stories.

SCHWARZ. As far back as possible.

SCHÖN. (stepping back knocks over the canvas on the nearer easel) I'm sorry.

SCHWARZ. (picking it up) It doesn't matter.

SCHÖN. (taken aback) What's this ...

SCHWARZ. Do you know her?

SCHÖN. No.

SCHWARZ. (puts the picture back on the easel. It shows a woman dressed as a pierrot, with a tall shepherd's crook in her hand) A costume picture.

SCHÖN. You've certainly made a success of her.

SCHWARZ. You know her, then?

SCHÖN. No. And in that costume?

SCHWARZ. It lacks the finishing touches.

SCHÖN. Well, yes.

SCHWARZ. What can you expect. While she sits for me I have the pleasure of conversing with her husband.

SCHÖN. Tell me ...

SCHWARZ. About art, of course, to perfect my happiness.

SCHÖN. How did you come to make this charming acquaintance?

SCHWARZ. The way one does. A little man, tottering and old as the hills, appears suddenly and asks if I can paint his wife. But of course, even if she were as wrinkled as Mother Earth. Next morning punctually at ten o'clock the door flies open and the pot-belly comes in driving this angelic creature before him. I can still feel my knees shaking. A footman in green, stiff as a poker, with a parcel under his arm: could I tell them where the dressing-room was? Imagine my position. I open this door here. (Pointing to the right) Luckily everything was already tidy. The sweet creature glides in and the old man plants himself as a bulwark in front of the door. Two minutes later she appears dressed in this pierrot costume. (Shaking his head) I've never seen anything like it. (Goes upstage right and stares at the bedroom door)

SCHÖN. And the pot-belly stood sentinel?

SCHWARZ. (turning round) Her whole body was as much in harmony with this impossible costume as if she had been born in it. Her way of burying her arms in the pockets up to the elbows, of lifting her feet off the carpet – the blood sometimes rushes to my head ...

SCHÖN. One can see that from the picture.

SCHWARZ. People like us, you know ...

SCHÖN. In this case the model directs the conversation.

SCHWARZ. So far she hasn't opened her mouth.

SCHÖN. You don't say so!

SCHWARZ. Allow me to show you the costume. (Exit right)

SCHÖN. (in front of the pierrot, alone) A diabolic beauty. (In front of the half-length portrait) There's more substance here. (Coming downstage) He's still rather immature for his age.

SCHWARZ. (comes back with a white satin costume) What sort of material might this be?

SCHÖN. Satin.

SCHWARZ. And all in one piece.

SCHÖN. However is one supposed to get into it?

SCHWARZ. I can't tell you.

SCHÖN. (holding the costume up by the legs) What enormous trousers.

SCHWARZ. She hitches the left one up.

SCHÖN. (looking at the picture) Above the knee!

SCHWARZ. She does it enchantingly.

SCHÖN. And transparent stockings?

SCHWARZ. They take some painting, I can tell you.

SCHÖN. Oh, you can manage that.

SCHWARZ. And so flirtatious!

SCHÖN. How did you arrive at such a shocking suspicion?

SCHWARZ. There are things which are not dreamt of in our philosophy. (Takes the costume back into the bedroom)

SCHÖN. (alone) When one sleeps ...

SCHWARZ. (coming back, looks at the clock) By the way, if you'd like to make her acquaintance ...

SCHÖN. No.

SCHWARZ. She'll be here immediately.

SCHÖN. How many more times will the lady have to sit for you?

SCHWARZ. I suppose I shall have to endure these torments of Tantalus for another three months.

SCHÖN. I meant the other one.

SCHWARZ. Forgive me. Another three times at the most. (Accompanying him to the door) If the lady could leave me her blouse –

SCHÖN. With pleasure. come and see me again soon. (At the door collides with DR. GOLL and LULU) In the name of God!

Scene Two

(DR. GOLL, LULU. The others as before)

SCHWARZ. Allow me to introduce ...

GOLL. (to SCHÖN) What are you doing here?

SCHÖN. (kissing LULU's hand) Mrs. Goll.

LULU. Surely you aren't going already?

GOLL. What wind blows you here?

SCHÖN. I was inspecting the picture of my fiancée.

LULU. (advancing) Your fiancée is here?

GOLL. So you're having work done here too?

LULU. (looking at the half-length portrait) But look! Enchanting! Delightful!

GOLL. (looking about him) I suppose you have her hidden about here somewhere?

LULU. So this is the sweet infant prodigy who has transformed you into a human being ...

GOLL. And you tell no one anything about it?

LULU. (turning round) Is she really so serious?

SCHÖN. Probably the aftermath of finishing school, Madame.

GOLL. (looking at the portrait) One can see that you've undergone a profound change.

LULU. Now you really can't keep her waiting any longer.

SCHÖN. I intend to announce our engagement in fortnight's time.

GOLL. (to LULU) Let's waste no more time. Buck up!

LULU. (to SCHÖN) Imagine, we went across the new bridge at a trot. I was driving myself.

(SCHÖN tries to take leave)

GOLL. No, no. You and I must have a word together later. Go on, Nelli. Hurry up!

LULU. Now it's my turn.

GOLL. Our Apelles is already licking his brushes.

LULU. I imagined it would be much more amusing.

SCHÖN. At the same time you have the satisfaction of knowing that you afford us a rare pleasure.

LULU. Just wait. (Walks over to right)

SCHWARZ. (standing by the bedroom door) If Madame would be so kind ... (Closes the door behind her and stands in front of it)

GOLL. I called her Nelli in our marriage contract.

SCHÖN. Really? I see.

GOLL. How do you like it?

SCHÖN. Why don't you call her Mignon instead?

GOLL. That would be an idea too. It hadn't occurred to me.

SCHÖN. Do you think a name can make so much difference?

GOLL. Hm – I have no children, you know.

SCHÖN. (taking his cigarette case out of his pocket) But you've only been married a few months.

GOLL. Thank you; but I don't want any.

SCHÖN. Do you smoke?

GOLL. (helping himself) One is quite enough for me. (To SCHWARZ) Tell me, what became of that little dancer of yours?

SCHÖN. (turning to SCHWARZ) You, and a dancer?

SCHWARZ. The lady sat for me as a favour. I got to know her at an outing of the St. Cecilia Society.

GOLL. (to SCHÖN) Hm. I think we're going to have a change in the weather.

SCHÖN. The business of dressing-up doesn't seem to be going so briskly?

GOLL. It's going like lightning. A woman must be a virtuoso in her own sphere. So must we all be in our spheres, if our lives aren't to be reduced to beggary. (Calls out) Hurry up, Nelli!

SCHWARZ. (at the door) Madame!

LULU. (from within) Coming, coming.

GOLL. (to SCHÖN) I can't understand these cold fish.

SCHÖN. I envy them. They think there is something sacred in being on the point of starvation. They feel themselves richer than the likes of us with our 30,000 marks in dividends. Anyhow it's impossible to have an opinion about a man who has lived from palette to mouth since childhood. Make it your business to finance him. It's a problem in arithmetic. I lack the moral courage. It's easy to get one's fingers burnt.

LULU. (coming out of the bedroom dressed as a pierrot) Here I am.

SCHÖN. (turning round, after a pause) Superb!

LULU. (coming nearer) Well?

SCHÖN. You put the most daring imagination to shame.

LULU. How do you like me?

SCHÖN. A picture before which Art must despair.

GOLL. You think so too?

SCHÖN. (to LULU) I suppose you don't realise what you're doing.

LULU. I'm perfectly aware of myself.

SCHÖN. Then you might be a little more circumspect.

LULU. But I'm only doing my duty.

SCHÖN. Have you powdered?

LULU. What a suggestion!

GOLL. I've never seen a skin as white as hers. And I told our Raphael here to concern himself as little as possible with the flesh tones. The fact is I can't feel any enthusiasm for this modern daubing.

SCHWARZ. (at the easels, preparing his colours) At least contemporary Art owes it to Impressionism that it's able to take its place beside the old masters without blushing.

GOLL. Well, I daresay it's suitable enough for a head of fat stock.

SCHÖN. For heaven't sake don't excite yourself!

LULU. (throws her arms round GOLL's neck and kisses him)

GOLL. Your chemise is showing. You must pull it down.

LULU. I wish I could have taken it off altogether. It only gets in the way.

GOLL. He'd be quite capable of putting it in the picture.

LULU. (takes up the shepherd's crook which has been leaning against the screen and mounts the throne. To SCHÖN) What would you say now if you had to stand on parade for two hours?

SCHÖN. I'd sell my soul to the devil for the chance of changing places with you.

GOLL. (sitting down, right) Come over here. This is my observation post.

LULU. (hitching her left trouser-leg up to the knee. To SCHWARZ) Is that all right?

SCHWARZ. Yes ...

LULU. (hitching it a little higher) Like this?

SCHWARZ. Yes,yes ...

GOLL. (to SCHÖN, who has sat down in the chair next to him, with a wave of the hand) I think she shows to even better advantage from here)

LULU. (without moving) I beg to differ. I look equally well from all sides.

SCHWARZ. (to LULU) The right knee a little forward, please.

SCHÖN. (with a gesture) The lines of the body may appear finer, perhaps ...

SCHWARZ. At least the light is halfway tolerable today.

GOLL. You must get her down quickly. Hold your brush a little longer.

SCHWARZ. Certainly, Doctor.

SCHÖN. Treat her as a still-life.

SCHWARZ. Certainly, Doctor. (to LULU) You usually hold your head a little higher, Madame.

LULU. (raising her head) Paint my lips a little parted.

SCHÖN. Paint snow on top of ice. If you get warm in the process your art will immediately become inartistic.

SCHWARZ. Certainly, Doctor.

GOLL. Art, you know, must reproduce Nature in such a way that one derives at least spiritual enjoyment from it.

LULU. (opening her mouth slightly, to SCHWARZ) Like this, you see. I'm keeping them half open.

SCHWARZ. As soon as the sun gets round, the wall opposite will cast warm reflections.

GOLL. (to LULU) In your position you must conduct yourself as if our Velasquez here were not present at all.

LULU. A painter isn't a real man, anyhow.

SCHÖN. I don't think you can draw conclusions about the whole tribe from one illustrious exception.

SCHWARZ. (stepping back from the easel) It would have been better if I'd had to rent a new studio last autumn.

SCHÖN. (to GOLL) What was it I wanted to ask – have you seen little O'Morphi as a Peruvian pearl-fisher?

GOLL. I'm going to see her tomorrow for the fourth time. Count Polossow is taking me. His hair has gone quite blond again with rapture.

SCHÖN. So you think she is so marvellous too?

GOLL. Who would wish to judge of that in advance.

LULU. I think there was a knock.

SCHWARZ. Excuse me a moment. (Goes to the door and opens it)

GOLL. It would be quite safe for you to smile at him a little more freely.

SCHÖN. That would make absolutely no difference to him.

GOLL. And even if it did! – What are we sitting here for!

Scene Three

(ALWA SCHÖN. The others as before)

ALWA. (from behind the screen) May I come in?

SCHÖN. My son.

LULU. Why, it's Mr Alwa!

GOLL. Come right in!

ALWA. (advancing, gives his hand to SCHÖN and GOLL) Dr. Goll. (turns to LULU) Do I see aright? If only I could engage you as my leading lady.

LULU. I imagine I'd hardly dance well enough for your piece.

ALWA. But you have such a dancing-master as is not to be found on any stage in Europe.

SCHÖN. What brings you here?

GOLL. Can you secretly be having someone painted too?

ALWA. (to SCHÖN) I wanted to fetch you for the dress rehearsal.

(SCHÖN rises)

GOLL. Are you having them dance in full costume today?

ALWA. Of course. Won't you come too? I must be on stage in five minutes. (To LULU) Unluckily for me!

GOLL. I've quite forgotten what your ballet is called?

ALWA. Dalai Lama.

GOLL. I thought he was in a lunatic asylum.

SCHÖN. You're thinking of Nietzsche, Doctor.

GOLL. You're right. I always confuse the two.

ALWA. I've put Buddhism onto its legs.

GOLL. One recognises a playwright by his legs.

ALWA. Corticelli dances the youthful Buddha as if she had first seen the light of day on the Ganges.

SCHÖN. While her mother was alive she danced with her legs.

ALWA. Then when she was on her own she danced with her brain.

GOLL. Now she dances with her heart.

ALWA. Would you like to see her?

GOLL. Thank you, no.

ALWA. Oh, do come.

GOLL. Out of the question.

SCHÖN. Incidentally we've no time to lose.

ALWA. Come with us, Doctor. In the third act you can see the Dalai Lama in his monastery with his monks.

GOLL. I'm interested only in the youthful Buddha.

ALWA. Then what's keeping you?

GOLL. Impossible, impossible.

ALWA. We're going on to Peter's afterwards. You'll have the opportunity of putting your admiration into words.

GOLL. Don't go on urging me, please.

ALWA. You'll see the tame monkeys, the two Brahmins, the little girls . . .

GOLL. For God's sake keep your little girls to yourself.

LULU. Reserve us a stage box for Monday, Mr. Alwa!

ALWA. How could Madame have any doubts about that?

GOLL. When I get back I'll find this devil of a Brueghel has made a mess of the whole picture.

ALWA. That wouldn't be such a disaster. It could easily be painted over.

GOLL. If one doesn't prescribe every stroke of the brush to this Caravacci ...

SCHÖN. As a matter of fact, I think your apprehensions are unfounded.

GOLL. Next time, gentlemen.

ALWA. The Brahmins are getting impatient. The daughters of Nirvana are shivering in their tights.

GOLL. Wretched daub!!

SCHÖN. We shall get a scolding for not bringing you with us.

GOLL. I shall be back in five minutes. (Places himself downstage left behind SCHWARZ and compares the picture with LULU)

ALWA. (to LULU) Alas, duty calls me, Madame.

GOLL. (to SCHWARZ) You need a little more modelling here. The hair isn't good. You're not putting your heart into it properly ...

ALWA. Come along.

GOLL. Well, let's get on then. Wild horses won't drag me to Peter's.

SCHÖN. (following ALWA and GOLL) We can take my carriage – it's below.

Scene Four

(SCHWARZ, LULU)

SCHWARZ. (leans over to the left, spits) What scum! If my life were only at an end! – my nose-bag – nose-bag and muzzle at the same time! My pride as an artist balks at it. (After a glance at LULU) What a collection! – (He rises, goes backstage right, surveys LULU from all sides and sits down at the easel again) It would be a difficult choice to make ... Might I ask Madame to hold her right hand a little higher?

LULU. (grasping the crook as high up as possible, aside) Who would have thought it possible!

SCHWARZ. I suppose you think I'm quite ridiculous?

LULU. He'll be back soon.

SCHWARZ. All I can do is paint.

LULU. Here he is.

SCHWARZ. (getting up) Already?

LULU. Don't you hear anything?

SCHWARZ. Someone is coming ...

LULU. I told you so.

SCHWARZ. It's the caretaker; he's sweeping the stairs.

LULU. Thank God.

SCHWARZ. I suppose you accompany the doctor on his rounds?

LULU. That would be the last straw.

SCHWARZ. But you're not used to being alone.

LULU. We have a housekeeper at home.

SCHWARZ. And she keeps you company?

LULU. She has very good taste.

SCHWARZ. In what way?

LULU. She dresses me.

SCHWARZ. I suppose you go to a great many balls?

LULU. Never.

SCHWARZ. Then why do you need so many clothes?

LULU. To dance in.

SCHWARZ. So you really do dance?

LULU. Czardas – Samaqueca – Skirtdance.

SCHWARZ. Doesn't that disgust you?

LULU. You think I'm ugly?

SCHWARZ. You misunderstand me. Who teaches you?

LULU. He does.

SCHWARZ. Who?

LULU. He does.

SCHWARZ. He?

LULU. He plays the violin.

SCHWARZ. One gets to know a new side of life every day.

LULU. I studied in Paris. I took lessons from Eugénie Fougère. She let me copy her costumes too.

SCHWARZ. And what are they like?

LULU. One has a green lace skirt, down to the knee, all in flounces, décolleté of course, very décolleté, and horribly tight-laced. A pale green underskirt, then a paler one, and so on. Snow white pantaloons with a handsbreadth of lace on them.

SCHWARZ. I can't bear it.

LULU. You must go on painting.

SCHWARZ. (scraping with his palette knife) Aren't you cold?

LULU. Good heavens, no! Whatever makes you ask? Are you so cold yourself?

SCHWARZ. Not today, no.

LULU. Thank God at least one can breathe!

SCHWARZ. What do you mean?

(LULU breathes deeply)
Stop doing that, please! (Jumps up, throws down brush and palette, walks up and down) At least the boot-black only has to deal with their feet. And his materials don't eat into his money either. If I go without my supper tomorrow there'll be no lady of fashion to ask me if I know how to swallow oysters.

LULU. What a brute he is!

SCHWARZ. (resumes his work) And why did the fellow have to go to that rehearsal!

LULU. I'd rather he'd stayed, too.

SCHWARZ. We are really martyrs to our profession!

LULU. I didn't mean to hurt your feelings.

SCHWARZ. (hesitantly, to LULU) If you could ... the left hand ... trouser-leg ... a little higher ...

LULU. Like this?

SCHWARZ. (steps up to the throne) If you'll allow me ...

LULU. What are you trying to do?

SCHWARZ. I'll show you what I mean.

LULU. You mustn't.

SCHWARZ. You're nervous. (Tries to take her hand)

LULU. (throws the crook at his hand) Leave me alone. (Hurries to the front door) You can't catch me!

SCHWARZ. You can't take a joke.

LULU. Yes I can. I see it all. Just leave me alone. You won't get anywhere with me by force. Get on with your work. You have no right to molest me. Go and sit down at your easel.

SCHWARZ. (tries to get round the ottoman) I will as soon as I've punished you for your capriciousness.

LULU. But you must catch me first for that. Go away. You won't catch me, anyhow. – In long clothes I'd have fallen into your hands long ago – but not in this pierrot costume.

SCHWARZ. (throwing himself across the ottoman) Got you!

LULU. (throws the tiger-skin over his head) Good night! (Jumps over the throne and climbs the step-ladder) I can see all the cities of the world.

SCHWARZ. (unwinding himself from the rug) The baggage!

LULU. I can reach up into the sky, and stick the stars in my hair.

SCHWARZ. (climbing after her) I shall shake it till you fall down.

LULU. (climbing higher) If you don't stop, I'll knock the ladder over. Will you let go of my legs! – God save Poland! (She causes the ladder to fall, jumps onto the throne and as SCHWARZ picks himself up from the floor, throws the screen at him. Dashes downstage towards the easels) I told you you wouldn't get me.

SCHWARZ. (coming downstage) Let's make peace. (Tries to embrace her)

LULU. Keep your hands off me, or ... (She throws the easel with the half-length portrait at him, so that both easel and picture crash to the ground)

SCHWARZ. (shouts) Merciful heavens!

LULU. (backstage left) You made the hole in it yourself.

SCHWARZ. I'm ruined! Ten weeks' work. My trip, my exhibition. There's nothing more to lose now. (Rushes after her)

LULU. (leaps over the ottoman, over the fallen step-ladder, walks across the throne and comes downstage) A ditch! Mind you don't fall into it. (Stamps on the portrait) So she'd made a new man of him, had she! (Falls forward)

SCHWARZ. (stumbling over the screen) I shall have no mercy now.

LULU. (backstage) Leave me alone. – I feel faint. Oh God, Oh God . . . (Comes downstage and sinks onto the ottoman)

(SCHWARZ bolts the door. Then sits down at her side, seizes her hand and covers it with kisses, then stops short; one can see he is going through an inward struggle)

(Opens her eyes) He might come back.

SCHWARZ. How do you feel?

LULU. As if I'd fallen into the water . . .

SCHWARZ. I love you.

LULU. I loved a student once.

SCHWARZ. Nelli . . .

LULU. With twenty-four duelling scars.

SCHWARZ. I love you, Nelli.

LULU. My name isn't Nelli.

  (SCHWARZ kisses her)

  It's Lulu.

SCHWARZ. I shall call you Eve.

LULU. Do you know what time it is?

SCHWARZ. (looking at the clock) Half past ten.

  (LULU takes the clock and opens the case)

  You don't love me.

LULU. Yes I do. It's five minutes after half past ten.

SCHWARZ. Give me a kiss, Eve.

LULU. (takes him by the chin and kisses him; throws the clock in the air and catches it) You smell of tobacco.

SCHWARZ. Why don't you call me by my Christian name?

LULU. It would embarrass me.

SCHWARZ. You're being hypocritical!

LULU. It seems to me it's you who's the hypocrite. Me hypocritical? How did you get that idea? I've never had any reason to be.

SCHWARZ. (gets up, disconcerted, passing his hand across his forehead) God Almighty! I know nothing of the world ...

LULU. (screams) Don't kill me!

SCHWARZ. (turning swiftly round) You have never loved.

LULU. (half rising) You have never loved ...!

GOLL. (outside) Open the door!

LULU. (has leapt to her feet) Hide me! Oh God, hide me!

GOLL. (beating on the door) Open the door!

(SCHWARZ makes a move to open the door)

LULU. (restrains him) He'll kill me.

GOLL. (beating on the door) Open the door!

LULU. (has sunk down in front of SCHWARZ and embraces his knees) He'll kill me. He'll kill me.

SCHWARZ. Stand up ... (The door falls with a crash into the studio)

Scene Five

(GOLL. The others as before)

GOLL. (with bloodshot eyes rushes at SCHWARZ and LULU with raised stick) You dogs! – You ... (Gasps, struggles a second or two for breath and then falls headlong to the floor)

(SCHWARZ shakes at the knees)

(LULU has run to the door. A pause)

SCHWARZ. (goes up to GOLL) D-Dr. – Dr. – G-Goll.

LULU. (at the door) Please tidy up the studio first.

SCHWARZ. Dr. Goll. (Bends down) Dr ... (Steps back) He's scratched his forehead. Help me to get him onto the ottoman.

LULU. (recoils) No, no ...

SCHWARZ. (tries to turn him over) Dr. Goll.

LULU. He can't hear.

SCHWARZ. Won't you please help me?

LULU. We couldn't lift him even together.

SCHWARZ. (straightening up) We must send for the doctor.

LULU. He's terribly heavy.

SCHWARZ. (picking up his hat) While I'm away could you be so kind as to put my things a little to rights. (Exit)

Scene Six

(LULU, GOLL)

LULU. Suddenly he'll get up. (With urgency) Bussi! – He gives no sign. (Comes downstage in a wide circle) He's looking at my feet and watching every step I take. He doesn't take his eyes off me. (She touches him with the point of her shoe) Bussi! (Recoiling) It's serious ... the ball is over ... He's going to leave me in the lurch ... What shall I do? ... (Bends down to the ground) An utterly strange face! (Straightening up) And no one to perform the last offices for him. How cheerless ...

Scene Seven

(SCHWARZ. The others as before)

SCHWARZ. Hasn't he come round yet?

LULU. (downstage left) What shall I do?

SCHWARZ. (bending over GOLL) Dr. Goll.

LULU. I almost think he means it.

SCHWARZ. Don't be so common.

LULU. He wouldn't have talked to me like that. He used to have me dance for him when he didn't feel well.

SCHWARZ. The doctor ought to be here at any moment.

LULU. Medicine won't help him now.

SCHWARZ. But at such times one does what one can.

LULU. He doesn't believe in it himself.

SCHWARZ. Don't you think you ought at least to change your clothes.

LULU. Yes. In a minute.

SCHWARZ. What are you waiting for?

LULU. Please ...

SCHWARZ. Well, what is it?

LULU. Close his eyes.

SCHWARZ. You are horrible.

LULU. Not half as horrible as you!

SCHWARZ. Why am I horrible?

LULU. You have the nature of a criminal.

SCHWARZ. Doesn't the occasion move you in the least?

LULU. It's going to happen to me too one of these days.

SCHWARZ. Once and for all, will you be quiet!

LULU. It's going to happen to you, too.

SCHWARZ. It really isn't necessary to say that just at this moment.

LULU. Please ...

SCHWARZ. You must do what you think necessary. I know nothing of these things.

LULU. (to the right of GOLL) He's looking at me.

SCHWARZ. (to the left of GOLL) And at me.

LULU. You're a coward.

SCHWARZ. (closes GOLL's eyes with his handkerchief) It's the first time in my life I've been compelled to do this.

LULU. Didn't you do it for your mother?

SCHWARZ. (nervously) No.

LULU. I suppose you were away from home?

SCHWARZ. No!

LULU. Or perhaps you were afraid?

SCHWARZ. (violently) No.

LULU. (recoils) I didn't mean to offend you.

SCHWARZ. She's still alive.

LULU. Then you still have someone.

SCHWARZ. She's as poor as a church mouse.

LULU. I know all about that.

SCHWARZ. Don't mock me.

LULU. Now I shall be rich.

SCHWARZ. It's enough to make one's flesh creep. (Walks off to the left) It's not her fault.

LULU. (to herself) What am I going to do now?

SCHWARZ. (to himself) Completely wild. (SCHWARZ right, LULU left, look at each other suspiciously)

(Goes up to her, grasps her hand) Look me in the eyes!

LULU. (fearfully) What are you after?

SCHWARZ. (steers her to the ottoman, forces her to sit down at his side) Look me in the eyes!

LULU. I can see myself as a pierrot in them.

SCHWARZ. (pushes her away) This damned dancing!

LULU. I must go and change.

SCHWARZ. (restraining her) There's one thing I want to ask ...

LULU. But I mustn't answer.

SCHWARZ. (sitting down on the ottoman again) Can you speak the truth?

LULU. I don't know.

SCHWARZ. Do you believe in a creator?

LULU. I don't know.

SCHWARZ. Is there anything you can swear by?

LULU. I don't know. Leave me alone. You're mad.

SCHWARZ. What do you believe in, then?

LULU. I don't know.

SCHWARZ. Have you no soul, then?

LULU. I don't know.

SCHWARZ. Have you ever been in love?

LULU. I don't know.

SCHWARZ. (rises, walks over to the left. To himself) She doesn't know!

LULU. (without moving) I don't know.

SCHWARZ. (with a glance at GOLL) He knows.

LULU. (going up to him) What is it you want to know?

SCHWARZ. (indignantly) Go and get dressed!

(LULU goes into the bedroom)

Scene Eight

(SCHWARZ, GOLL)

SCHWARZ. I'd like to change places with you, you corpse. I'd be glad to give her back to you. And I'd give you my youth as well. I have neither faith nor courage. I've had to wait too long, and now it's too late for me. I'm not equal to being happy. I'm hellishly frightened of it. Wake up! I haven't touched her. He's opening his mouth. – Mouth open and eyes shut, like children. It's the other way about with me. Wake up! Wake up! (Kneels down and binds his handkerchief round the other's head) I call upon Heaven to let me be happy. May Heaven give me the strength and freedom of soul to be just a little happy. For her sake, only for her sake.

Scene Nine

(LULU. The others as before)

LULU. (comes out of the bedroom, fully dressed, her hat on, her right hand under her left arm, raising her left arm to SCHWARZ) Could you hook me up here? My hand is trembling.

ACT TWO

Scene One

(An extremely elegant drawing-room. Main door backstage right. Downstage left and right portières. A few steps leading up to those on the left. On the back wall over the chimney-piece, in a magnificent brocade frame the portrait of LULU as pierrot. Left a tall mirror. In front of it a chaise longue. Right an ebony writing-desk. In the middle a few armchairs around a small Chinese table.

LULU, SCHWARZ. Later HENRIETTE.

LULU in a green silk negligee stands motionless in front of the mirror, frowns, passes her hand across her brow, feels her cheeks, moves away from the mirror with a discontented, almost angry expression, walks over to the right, turning round several times; opens a box on the writing desk and lights a cigarette, examines the books which are lying on the table, selects one, lies down on the chaise longue facing the mirror, lets the book fall after reading for a moment, nods solemnly to herself and resumes her reading)

SCHWARZ. (brush and palette in hand enters from the right, bends over LULU, kisses her on the forehead, goes up the steps left, turns round at the portières) Eve!

LULU. (smiling) At your service!

SCHWARZ. I find you're looking exceptionally attractive today.

LULU. (with glance in the mirror) That depends on one's expectations.

SCHWARZ. Your hair breathes a morning freshness . . .

LULU. I've just come from my bath.

SCHWARZ. (going up to her) I've a terribly busy day today.

LULU. You just think you have.

SCHWARZ. (lays brushes and palatte down on the carpet and sits down on the edge of the chaise longue) What are you reading?

LULU. (reads) 'Suddenly she heard a sheet-anchor calling up the stairs.'

SCHWARZ. Who in the world is it that writes so movingly?

LULU. (reads) 'It was the postman with a money-order.'

HENRIETTE. (enters through the main door with a hat-box on her arm and sets down a salver with letters on it on the table) The post. – I'm going to take the hat to the milliners. Does Madame require anything else?

LULU. Nothing.

(SCHWARZ signs to her to withdraw)

(HENRIETTE exit, with a knowing smile)

SCHWARZ. What did you dream about last night?

LULU. You've asked me that twice today already.

SCHWARZ. (rises, takes the letters from the salver) I'm terrified of what the news may be. Every day I fear the world may come to an end. (Coming back to the chaise longue, gives LULU a letter) For you.

LULU. (puts the letter to her nose) La Corticelli. (Hides it in her bosom)

SCHWARZ. (skimming through a letter) My Samaqueca dancer, sold for 50,000 marks.

LULU. Who writes that?

SCHWARZ. Sedelmeier in Paris. That's the third picture since our marriage. I scarcely know where to turn with all this good fortune.

LULU. (pointing to the letters) and there's more of it to come.

SCHWARZ. (opening an engagement announcement) Look at this!

(Gives it to LULU)

LULU. (reads) Heinrich Ritter von Zarnikow has the honour to announce the engagement of his daughter Charlotte Marie Adelaide to Dr. Ludwig Schön.

SCHWARZ. (opening another letter) At last! He seems to have spent an eternity trying to get to the point of an official engagement. I can't understand it, a ruthless despot like him, with the influence he has. What can it be that's holding up his marriage!!

LULU. What's that you're reading?

SCHWARZ. An invitation to take part in an international exhibition in St. Petersburg. – I don't know what to paint.

LULU. Some attractive girl, of course.

SCHWARZ. I suppose you wouldn't sit to me for it?

LULU. There are other pretty girls in plenty, God knows.

SCHWARZ. With any other model, even if she's as piquant as hell, I don't seem able to make the most of my abilities.

LULU. Then I suppose I must. Wouldn't it do lying down?

SCHWARZ. I'd really prefer to leave the pose to you. (Folding up his letters) Don't let us forget to get off a letter of congratulation to Schön today.

LULU. We did that long ago.

SCHWARZ. I mean for the benefit of his bride.

LULU. You can write to him once again if you like.

SCHWARZ. And now to work. (Picks up brushes and palette, kisses LULU, goes up the steps left and turns round in the portières) Eve!

LULU. (lowers her book, with a smile) At your service!

SCHWARZ. (coming close to her) Everyday I feel as if I were seeing you for the first time.

LULU. You're terrible.

SCHWARZ. (falls on his knees by the chaise longue, fondles her hand) You're to blame for that.

LULU. (stroking his hair) You're wasting me.

SCHWARZ. Well, you belong to me. And you're never more fascinating than when it would be better if you could be really ugly for an hour or two! Since I've had you I've had nothing else. I've utterly lost myself.

LULU. Don't get so excited.

(A bell rings outside in the passage)

SCHWARZ. (with a start) Damn!

LULU. Nobody at home!

SCHWARZ. Perhaps it's the picture dealer.

LULU. It can be the Emperor of China for all I care.

SCHWARZ. Just a minute. (Exit)

LULU. (as one seeing a vision) You? – You? – (Closes her eyes)

SCHWARZ. (coming back) A beggar, who says he was in the wars. I haven't got any change on me. (Taking up brush and palette) And it's high time I got to work. (Exit left)

(LULU tidies her clothes in front of the mirror, smooths her hair. Exit)

Scene Two

(LULU. SCHIGOLCH)

SCHIGOLCH. (shown in by LULU) I'd imagined him to be a little more courtly. A little more out of the ordinary. He's a bit awkward. He gave a little at the knees when he saw me in front of him.

LULU. (pulling up a chair for him) How can you beg from him?

SCHIGOLCH. That's just what I dragged my seventy-seven summers here to do. You told me he devoted his morning to painting.

LULU. He hadn't all the sleep he wanted. How much do you need?

SCHIGOLCH. Two hundred, if you've got as much in cash; make it three hundred for all I care. One or two of my clients have vanished into thin air.

LULU. (goes to the writing-desk and rummages in the drawers) I'm so tired.

SCHIGOLCH. That's something else that weighed with me. I'd long been curious to see what sort of a place you'd got.

LULU. Well, what do you think of it?

SCHIGOLCH. It's overwhelming. (Looks upwards) It's like my own house fifty years ago. Instead of all these hangings, in those days we had rusty old swords. By old Harry! You have got on in the world! (Shuffling his feet) The carpets ...!

LULU. (hands him two notes) What I like best is to walk barefoot on them.

SCHIGOLCH. (examining LULU's portrait) Is that meant to be you?

LULU. (winking at him) Good, isn't it?

SCHIGOLCH. Even if it's the best that can come of it all.

LULU. Would you care for something sweet?

SCHIGOLCH. What have you got?

LULU. (gets up) Elixir de Spaa.

SCHIGOLCH. That's no good. Does he drink?

LULU. (takes glasses and a decanter out of the cupboard by the chimney-piece) Not yet. (Coming downstage) These stimulants have such different effects on different people.

SCHIGOLCH. Does he hit out?

LULU. No, he goes to sleep.

SCHIGOLCH. When he's drunk you can examine his entrails.

LULU. I'd rather not. (Sits down opposite SCHIGOLCH) Now tell me all about yourself.

SCHIGOLCH. The road gets longer and longer and my legs shorter and shorter.

LULU. And your concertina?

SCHIGOLCH. It's broken-winded, like me with my asthma. But I feel it's not worth doing anything about it. (Clinks glasses with her)

LULU. (empties her glass) I almost thought you were done for.

SCHIGOLCH. ... Done and gone? I thought so too. But even though the sun has gone down, one isn't allowed to rest. I'm pinning my hopes on the winter. Then (Coughing) I expect my asthma will know how to find a way out.

LULU. (filling the glasses) You think they've forgotten about you on the other side?

SCHIGOLCH. It's not impossible. After all, it doesn't go in turns. (Stroking her knee) Now let's hear about you – haven't seen you for a long time – my little Lulu.

LULU. (drawing away from him, with a smile) Life really is incomprehensible!

SCHIGOLCH. What can you know about that? You're so young.

LULU. That you call me 'Lulu'.

SCHIGOLCH. It is 'Lulu', isn't it? Have I ever called you anything else?

LULU. I haven't been called 'Lulu' for ages.

SCHIGOLCH. Is there some other way of addressing you?

LULU. 'Lulu' sounds completely out of date.

SCHIGOLCH. Well, well!

LULU. I'm called ...

SCHIGOLCH. As if the principle wasn't always the same.

LULU. What do you mean?

SCHIGOLCH. What is it now?

LULU. Eve.

SCHIGOLCH. It all boils down to the same thing!

LULU. That's what I answer to.

SCHIGOLCH. (looks about him) This is how I used to dream of it for you. You're cut out for this. What might that be?

LULU. (spraying herself with a scent bottle) Heliotrope.

SCHIGOLCH. Does it smell better than you do?

LULU. You don't have to worry about that any more!

SCHIGOLCH. Who could have foreseen this regal luxury?

LULU. When I think back ... ugh!

SCHIGOLCH. (stroking her knee) What do you do all day? Are you still learning French?

LULU. I lie and sleep.

SCHIGOLCH. That's genteel. It makes a good impression. Well, and then?

LULU. I stretch myself – till my bones crack.

SCHIGOLCH. And when they've finished cracking?

LULU. Why should you care?

SCHIGOLCH. Why should I care? – Why should I care? I'd rather live till the last trump and renounce all heavenly bliss than leave my Lulu behind here below in penury. Why should I care? It's my fellow-feeling. I'm quite transfigured by my better self but I'm still alive to the needs of this world.

LULU. I'm not.

SCHIGOLCH. You're too well off.

LULU. (with a shudder) Idiot ...

SCHIGOLCH. Better than with your old dancing-bear?

LULU. (sadly) I don't dance any more.

SCHIGOLCH. High time he stopped too.

LULU. Now I'm ... (Stops short)

SCHIGOLCH. Speak your mind freely, my child. I had faith in you when all there was to see of you was your two big eyes. What are you now?

LULU. An animal ...

SCHIGOLCH. The devil you are! And what an animal! A fine animal, an elegant animal – a splendid animal! – Now they can bury me. I'm finished with prejudices, even the one against the woman who is to lay me out.

LULU. You needn't be afraid they'll wash you again.

SCHIGOLCH. It doesn't matter anyhow. One only gets dirty again.

LULU. (spraying him) It would bring you back to life.

SCHIGOLCH. We are dust.

LULU. Indeed we're not. I rub myself every day with oil, and then comes powder on top of that.

SCHIGOLCH. Worth the trouble, I suppose, for that young puppy's sake.

LULU. It makes the skin like satin.

SCHIGOLCH. As if it were any the less filth for that.

LULU. Thank you so much. I want to be good enough to eat.

SCHIGOLCH. We're all that, anyhow. There'll be a big dinner down below in the near future, open house.

LULU. Your guests will hardly have an opportunity to overeat themselves.

SCHIGOLCH. Patience, my girl. Your admirers aren't going to preserve you in alcohol either. She's 'fair Melusine', as long as there's any go left in her. And after that? They wouldn't have her in the zoo. (Getting up) She'd give the precious animals a stomach ache.

LULU. (rising) Have you had enough too?

SCHIGOLCH. There'll be enough to plant a turpentine tree on my grave. – I'll find my own way out. (Exit)

(LULU goes out with him and comes back with DR. SCHÖN)

Scene Three

(LULU, SCHÖN)

SCHÖN. What's your father doing here?

LULU. What's the matter with you?

SCHÖN. If I were your husband that man wouldn't cross the threshold.

LULU. You can call me 'Lulu' if you want to. He's not here.

SCHÖN. Thank you for the honour.

LULU. I don't understand.

SCHÖN. I know. (Waving her to a chair) That's what I very much want to speak to you about.

LULU. (sitting down uncertainly) Why didn't you tell me yesterday?

SCHÖN. Don't let's have any talk of 'yesterday'. I told you two years ago.

LULU. (nervously) Oh, I see.

SCHÖN. I must ask you to stop your visits to me.

LULU. May I offer you a drink?

SCHÖN. Thank you, no drink for me. Do I make myself clear?

(LULU shakes her head)

Very well. You have the choice. You force me to extreme measures. Either you behave yourself as becomes your position ...

LULU. Or?

SCHÖN. Or – you yourself compel me to it – I shall have to apply to the person who is responsible for your conduct.

LULU. How do you think you'd do that?

SCHÖN. I'd ask your husband to supervise your comings and goings.

(LULU rises and goes up the steps, left)

Where are you going?

LULU. (at the portières, calls out) Walter!

SCHÖN. (jumping up) Are you mad?

LULU. (turning back) Aha!

SCHÖN. I'm making the most superhuman efforts to advance you in society. You can be ten times prouder of your name than of your intimacy with me.

LULU. (comes down the steps, puts her arm around SCHÖN's neck) What can you still be afraid of, now that you've reached the goal of all your hopes?

SCHÖN. None of that nonsense! The goal of all my hopes? At last I am engaged. My one wish now is to bring my bride back to a respectable home.

LULU. (sitting down) She has blossomed enchantingly in these two years.

SCHÖN. She no longer looks through one quite so solemnly.

LULU. She's only just become wholly a woman. We can meet each other whenever you think fit.

SCHÖN. We won't meet each other anywhere, save in the company of your husband.

LULU. You don't believe in what you're saying yourself.

SCHÖN. Then he will have to believe in it. Call him. It's through his marriage with you, through what I did for him, that he's become my friend.

LULU. (rising) Mine too.

SCHÖN. Then I can cut down the sword that's hanging over my head.

LULU. You've got me on a chain. I owe my happiness to you. You'll have a whole host of friends once you have a pretty young wife again.

SCHÖN. You judge other women by yourself. He has the disposition of a child. Otherwise he'd have found out your infidelities long ago.

LULU. I could ask nothing better. He'd have outgrown his baby shoes at last. He presumes on the fact that he has the marriage contract in his pocket. The necessary effort has been made, so now let's let ourselves go and make ourselves at home. He is **not** like a child. He is banal. He has had no education, he notices nothing, he sees neither me nor himself. He is blind, blind, blind ...

SCHÖN. (half to himself) But when his eyes **are** opened!

LULU. You must open his eyes! I'm going to pieces. I neglect myself. He knows nothing about me. What do I mean to him? He calls me 'treasure' or 'little devil'. He'd call any little piano teacher the same thing. He makes no pretensions. Everything is all right for him. And that's because he's never in his life felt the need to go with women.

SCHÖN. Can that be true?

LULU. He admits it quite openly.

SCHÖN. Someone who's been painting any rag tag and bobtail since he was fourteen?

LULU. He's afraid of women. He trembles for his health. But he's not afraid of me!

SCHÖN. God knows how happy some girls would think themselves in your place.

LULU. (wheedlingly) You must lead him astray. You're an expert in such things. Bring him into bad company. You know the right people. I'm his wife, his wife, and nothing but his wife. I feel such a fool. He will be all the prouder of me. He doesn't know the difference. I rack my brains, day and night, how I can shake him up. In my despair I dance the can-can; he yawns and mutters some nonsense about indecency.

SCHÖN. Nonsense. After all, he's an artist.

LULU. At any rate he thinks he is.

SCHÖN. Which is the main thing!

LULU. When I sit for him. And he believes he's a famous man.

SCHÖN. We've made him one!

LULU. He believes anything. He's as suspicious as a thief, and yet he lets himself be lied to so that one loses all respect for him. When we first met I made him believe I'd never been in love.

(SCHÖN falls into an armchair)

If I hadn't he'd have thought of me as an abandoned creature!

SCHÖN. God knows you make exorbitant demands enough on **legitimate** relationships.

LULU. I don't make exorbitant demands. I often dream of Goll, even.

SCHÖN. He certainly wasn't banal.

LULU. He's here as if he'd never been away. Only he walks about as if he were in stocking feet. He's not angry with me. He's just terribly sad. And then he's worried, as if he were here without permission of the police. Otherwise he feels quite comfortable with us. Only he can't get over the fact that I've thrown so much money about lately.

SCHÖN. You're pining for the cash.

LULU. Perhaps I am. I don't dance any more.

SCHÖN. Educate him up to it.

LULU. It would be wasted effort.

SCHÖN. Ninety out of every hundred women have to educate their husbands.

LULU. He loves me.

SCHÖN. That's awkward, I must admit.

LULU. He loves me.

SCHÖN. That's awkward, I must admit.

LULU. He loves me.

SCHÖN. That's an unbridgeable gulf.

LULU. He doesn't know me, but he loves me. If he had anything approaching an accurate picture of me he'd tie a stone round my neck and sink me in the ocean where it's deepest.

SCHÖN. (rising) Let's make an end of this.

LULU. As you wish.

SCHÖN. I married you off. I've married you off twice. You live in luxury. I've contrived a position for your husband. If that's not enough for you and he's laughing up his sleeve too, well, I'm not making any idealistic demands, but – leave me out of it!

LULU. (in a decided tone) If I belong to anyone in the world, I belong to you. Without you I should be – I wouldn't care to say where. You took me by the hand, gave me food and clothing when I tried to steal your watch. Do you think I can forget a thing like that? Anyone else would have called a policeman. You sent me to school and taught me how to behave. Who in the world apart from you has ever thought anything of me? I danced and was a model and was glad to be able to earn my keep in that way, but to love to order is beyond me!

SCHÖN. (raising his voice) Leave me out of the picture. Do what you like. I haven't come to make a scandal, I've come to put an end to one. My connection with you has cost me sacrifice enough! I expected that with a healthy young man, than whom a young woman of your age could wish no better, you would at last be satisfied. If you feel yourself under an obligation to me, then don't throw yourself at my head for the third time. Must I wait even now before I can bring my harvest safely home? Must I risk all that I have gained by my concessions in the past two years? What good does your being married do me when you're to be seen going in and out of my house at all hours of the day? Why the devil couldn't Dr. Goll have stayed alive for one year more? You were in safe keeping with him. And I'd have brought my wife home long since.

LULU. And then what would you have? The child gets on your nerves. The child is too unspoilt for you. The child has been much too carefully brought up. Why should I have any objection to your marriage? But you deceive yourself if you think your impending marriage entitles you to express your contempt.

SCHÖN. Contempt? I shall be able to make what I want of the child. If anything is contemptible it's your intrigues.

LULU. (laughing) Do you think I'm jealous of the child? It simply wouldn't occur to me ...

SCHÖN. Why 'the child'? 'The child' is less than a year younger than you. Leave me free to live what life is left to me. However the child may have been brought up, she has her five senses just as much as you have ...

Scene Four

(SCHWARZ. The others as before)

SCHWARZ. (a brush in his hand, comes through the portières, left) What's going on?

LULU. (to SCHÖN) Well, speak up.

SCHWARZ. What's the matter with you both?

LULU. Nothing that concerns you.

SCHÖN. (quickly) Be quiet!

LULU. People have had enough of me.

(SCHWARZ takes LULU out, left)

SCHÖN. (turns the pages of one of the books lying on the table) It had to come out ... I must have my hands free at last.

SCHWARZ. (coming back) Is this your idea of a joke?

SCHÖN. (pointing to a chair) Please sit down.

SCHWARZ. What's the matter?

SCHÖN. Sit down.

SCHWARZ. (sitting down) Well?

SCHÖN. (sitting down) You married half a million ...

SCHWARZ. Has it gone?

SCHÖN. Not a penny of it.

SCHWARZ. Explain this strange scene.

SCHÖN. You married half a million ...

SCHWARZ. There's nothing criminal in that.

SCHÖN. You've made a name for yourself. You are free to work undisturbed. You need deny yourself nothing ...

SCHWARZ. What have you two got against me?

SCHÖN. For the past six months you have been basking in the seventh heaven of delight. You have a wife, whose qualities the world envies you, and who deserves a husband whom she can respect ...

SCHWARZ. Doesn't she respect me?

SCHÖN. No.

SCHWARZ. (uneasily) I am from the murky depths of society. She comes from the top. I have no more burning desire than to be worthy of her. (giving SCHÖN his hand) Thank you.

SCHÖN. (half embarrassed, pressing his hand) Don't mention it, don't mention it.

SCHWARZ. (with decision) Speak!

SCHÖN. Keep her somewhat more under supervision.

SCHWARZ. I – her?

SCHÖN. We're not children – this isn't a game. It's life. She demands to be taken seriously. Her qualities fully entitle her to it.

SCHWARZ. What has she been up to, then?

SCHÖN. You married half a million!

SCHWARZ. (gets up, beside himself) You ...

SCHÖN. (taking him by the shoulder) No, that isn't the way. (Forces him to sit down) We've got a very serious matter to discuss with each other.

SCHWARZ. What is she up to?

SCHÖN. Count off on your fingers exactly what you have to thank her for, and then ...

SCHWARZ. What is she up to, man!!

SCHÖN. And then hold yourself responsible for your mistakes and not anyone else.

SCHWARZ. With whom? With whom?

SCHÖN. If you think we ought to have a duel –

SCHWARZ. How long as this been going on?

SCHÖN. (evading him) I've not come to cause a scandal but to save myself from one.

SCHWARZ. (shaking his head) You have misunderstood her.

SCHÖN. (embarrassed) That's no good to me. I can't bear to see you living in such blindness. The girl deserves to be a decent woman. She has changed for the better since I've known her.

SCHWARZ. Since you've known her? How long have you known her then?

SCHÖN. Since she was about twelve.

SCHWARZ. (bewildered) She didn't tell me anything about it.

SCHÖN. She sold flowers outside the Alhambra Café. She used to squeeze her way barefoot through the guests every evening between twelve and two.

SCHWARZ. She told me nothing about it.

SCHÖN. She was quite right not to. I'm telling you to show you that it's not a question of moral depravity. On the contrary, the girl has quite exceptional gifts.

SCHWARZ. She told me she'd been brought up by an aunt.

SCHÖN. That was the woman to whom I entrusted her. She was her best pupil. The mothers used to hold her up as an example to their children. She has a sense of duty. It's your fault and yours alone if you've failed hitherto to bring out the best in her.

SCHWARZ. (sobbing) Oh God ...'

SCHÖN. There's no 'Oh God' about it. Nothing can detract from the happiness you've tasted. What's done is done. You overestimate yourself against your own better judgment if you persuade yourself that you are the loser. You must gain. And nothing is gained by saying 'Oh God'. I've never done you a greater service than this. I'm speaking openly and offering to help you. Don't show yourself unworthy of it.

SCHWARZ. (from now on going more and more to pieces) When I got to know her she told me she'd never been in love before.

SCHÖN. For a widow to say such a thing! It's to her credit that she chose you for a husband. Make the same demands on yourself and your happiness is unalloyed.

SCHWARZ. He's supposed to have made her wear short frocks.

SCHÖN. He married her, after all. That was her master-stroke, How she brought him to the point is beyond me. But you must know yourself. You are enjoying the fruits of her diplomacy.

SCHWARZ. How did Dr. Goll get to know her?

SCHÖN. Through me! It was after the death of my wife, when I was establishing my first connections with my present fiancée. She came between us. She had made up her mind that she was going to be my wife.

SCHWARZ. (as if seized by a terrible suspicion) And when her husband died?

SCHÖN. – You married half a million!!

SCHWARZ. (groaning) If only I'd stayed where I was. If only I'd died of hunger.

SCHÖN. (in a superior tone) Do you think I am making no concessions? Is there anyone who makes no concessions? You married half a million. Today you're one of our leading artists. One doesn't get as far as that without money. You're not the one to sit in judgment on her. It's impossible to apply the standards of bourgeois society to such a background as Mignon has had.

SCHWARZ. (utterly bewildered) Who are you talking about?

SCHÖN. I'm talking about her father. You're an artist, as I say. Your ideas lie in a different sphere than those of a day labourer.

SCHWARZ. I don't understand a word you're saying.

SCHÖN. I'm speaking of the conditions, unfit for human beings, out of which, thanks to her upbringing, the girl has developed into what she is today.

SCHWARZ. Who?

SCHÖN. Your wife. Who else?

SCHWARZ. Eve??

SCHÖN. I called her 'Mignon'.

SCHWARZ. I thought she was called 'Nelli'.

SCHÖN. That's what Dr. Goll called her.

SCHWARZ. I called her 'Eve'.

SCHÖN. What her real name is I don't know.

SCHWARZ. (absently) Perhaps she knows.

SCHÖN. With such a father as she had she's nothing short of a miracle, for all her failings.

SCHWARZ. He died in a mad-house, didn't he?

SCHÖN. He's just been here.

SCHWARZ. Who was here?

SCHÖN. Her father.

SCHWARZ. Here, in my house?

SCHÖN. He made himself scarce when I came. Their glasses are still here.

SCHWARZ. She said he'd died in a mad-house.

SCHÖN. (encouragingly) Let her feel your authority. She asks nothing better than to render unconditional obedience. She was blissfully happy with Dr. Goll, and he wasn't a man to stand any nonsense.

SCHWARZ. (shaking his head) She said she'd never been in love.

SCHÖN. But you must begin with yourself. Pull yourself together.

SCHWARZ. She swore to me.

SCHÖN. You can't demand any sense of duty from her as long as you fail to recognise where your own task lies.

SCHWARZ. By her mother's grave!!

SCHÖN. She didn't know her mother, let alone her grave. Her mother has no grave.

SCHWARZ. (despairingly) I don't fit into this society.

SCHÖN. What's the matter with you?

SCHWARZ. I'm suffering horribly.

SCHÖN. (rises and steps back. After a pause) Hang on to her, for she is yours. The moment is decisive. Tomorrow she may be lost to you.

SCHWARZ. (touching his breast) Here, here ...

SCHÖN. You married half a ... (Recollecting himself) She's lost if you let the moment slip.

SCHWARZ. If I could weep! – Oh, if I could scream!

SCHÖN. (lays his arm across the other's shoulder) You are feeling wretched.

SCHWARZ. (rising, with apparent calm) You're right, absolutely right.

SCHÖN. (grasping his hand) Where are you going?

SCHWARZ. To talk to her.

SCHÖN. That's right. (Accompanies him to the door, right)

Scene Five

(SCHÖN. Soon afterwards LULU)

SCHÖN. (coming back) That was a tough job. (After a pause, with a glance to the left) He took her into the studio before, didn't he?

(Terrible groans from off-stage, right)

(Hastens to the door, right, finds it locked) Open the door! Open the door!

LULU. (stepping out of the portières, left) What is ...?

SCHÖN. Open the door!

LULU. (coming down the steps) This is frightful.

SCHÖN. Have you an axe in the kitchen?

LULU. He'll open it himself.

SCHÖN. I don't like to kick it down.

LULU. When he's cried his eyes out.

SCHÖN. (kicking against the door) Open the door! (To LULU) Fetch me an axe!

LULU. Send for the doctor.

SCHÖN. Are you out of your mind?

LULU. It serves you right.

(A bell rings outside in the passage. SCHÖN and LULU gaze wildly at each other)

SCHÖN. (goes stealthily backstage, stops at the door) I can't let myself be seen here now.

LULU. Perhaps it's the picture-dealer.

(The bell rings again)

SCHÖN. But if we don't answer ...

(LULU creeps up to the door)

(Stops her) Stay where you are. One isn't always immediately available anyhow. (Goes out on tiptoe)

(LULU goes back to the locked door and listens)

Scene Six

(ALWA, the others as before. Later HENRIETTE)

SCHÖN. (showing ALWA in) Please keep calm.

ALWA. (very excitedly) Revolution has broken out in Paris.

SCHÖN. Be quiet.

ALWA. (to LULU) You're pale as death.

SCHÖN. (rattling the door handle) Walter! – Walter! (A choking noise can be heard)

LULU. May God have mercy on you ...

SCHÖN. Haven't you brought an axe yet?

LULU. If there is one ... (Hesitates, goes off backstage right)

ALWA. He's having us on.

SCHÖN. You say revolution has broken out in Paris?

ALWA. At the newspaper office they're running their heads against the wall. No one knows what to write.

(A bell rings in the passage)

SCHÖN. (kicking at the door) Walter!

ALWA. Shall I break it down?

SCHÖN. I'm capable of doing that myself. Who can it be this time? (Straightening himself up) He enjoys life while he can and then leaves us to pick up the pieces!

LULU. (comes back with an axe) It was Henriette coming home.

SCHÖN. Shut the door behind you.

ALWA. Give it to me. (Takes the axe and strikes with it between the lock and the doorpost)

SCHÖN. You must grip it more firmly.

ALWA. It's giving already. (The door flies open. He drops the axe and reels back. A pause)

LULU. (pointing to the door, to SCHÖN) After you.

(SCHÖN shrinks back)

Are you faint?

(SCHÖN wipes the sweat from his forehead and goes in)

ALWA. (on the chaise longue) Horrible!

LULU. (holding on to the doorpost, her hand over her mouth, screams suddenly) Oh! Oh! (Rushes over to ALWA) I can't stay here.

ALWA. Ghastly!

LULU. (taking him by the hand) Come on.

ALWA. Where to?

LULU. I can't bear to be alone. (Exit left with ALWA)

(SCHÖN comes back right, a bunch of keys in his hand; the hand has blood on it; he closes the door behind him, goes to the desk, opens it and writes two notes)

ALWA. (enters left) She's changing.

SCHÖN. She's not here?

ALWA. Upstairs in her room. She's changing.

(SCHÖN rings the bell.

Enter HENRIETTE)

SCHÖN. You know where Dr. Bernstein lives?

HENRIETTE. Of course, Dr. Schön. Right next door.

SCHÖN. (giving her a note) Take this to him.

HENRIETTE. What if the doctor's not at home?

SCHÖN. He is at home. (Giving her the other note) And take this to the police station. Take a cab.

(Exit HENRIETTE)

It's a judgment on me.

ALWA. I'm paralysed by the sight of the blood.

SCHÖN. The crazy fool!

ALWA. I suppose it dawned on him all of a sudden.

SCHÖN. He worried about himself too much.

(LULU on the steps left, in a dust coat and hat)

ALWA. Where are you going now?

LULU. Out. I can see it on the walls.

SCHÖN. Where did he keep his papers?

LULU. In the desk.

SCHÖN. Whereabouts?

LULU. At the bottom on the right. (Kneels down at the desk, opens a drawer and empties the papers onto the floor) Here. There's nothing to be afraid of. He had no secrets.

SCHÖN. Now I might as well withdraw from the world.

LULU. (on her knees) Write an article. Call him a Michelangelo.

SCHÖN. What's the good of that – (Pointing right) There lies my engagement.

ALWA. It's a retribution for the game you've been playing.

SCHÖN. Go shout it in the streets!

ALWA. (pointing to LULU) If you'd done what would have been only right and proper by the girl when my mother died ...

SCHÖN. (walks across right) There's my engagement, bleeding to death.

LULU. (rising) I can't stay here any longer.

SCHÖN. In an hour's time they'll be selling the special editions. I mustn't venture into the streets.

LULU. How can you be blamed for it?

SCHÖN. All the more reason for people to do so! I shall be stoned for it!

ALWA. You'll have to go away.

SCHÖN. And leave the scandal a clear field?

LULU. (on the chaise longue) Ten minutes ago he was lying here.

SCHÖN. This is how he thanks me for what I've done for him! Lays my whole life in ruins inside of a second!

ALWA. Control yourself, please.

LULU. (on the chaise longue) We're among ourselves.

ALWA. We certainly are!

SCHÖN. (to LULU) What are you going to say to the police?

LULU. Nothing.

ALWA. He wanted to give Fate as good as he got.

LULU. He was always quick to think of violence.

SCHÖN. He had what most men can only dream of!

LULU. He paid dearly for it.

ALWA. He had something **we** have not got!

SCHÖN. (flaring up suddenly) I know your motives. I've no cause to be considerate of you. The fact that you leave no stone unturned to avoid having brothers and sisters to me is all the more reason why I should bring up other children.

ALWA. Your understanding of human nature is poor.

LULU. Why don't you bring out a special edition yourself?

SCHÖN. (in tones of violent indignation) He had no conscience! (Suddenly recovering his composure) Revolution in Paris?

ALWA. Our reporters are thunderstruck. Everything is at a standstill.

SCHÖN. Well, that will have to help me to get over it ... If only the police would come. The minutes are more precious than gold.

(A bell rings in the passage)

ALWA. There they are.

(SCHÖN makes for the door)

LULU. (jumping up) Wait, there's blood on you.

SCHÖN. Where?

LULU. Wait; I'll wipe it away. (Sprinkles her handkerchief with scent and wipes the blood from SCHÖN's hand)

SCHÖN. It's your husband's blood.

LULU. It doesn't leave any marks.

SCHÖN. You monster!

LULU. You'll marry me in the end.

(A bell rings in the passage)

Patience, children, patience.

(SCHÖN exits backstage right)

Scene Seven

(ESCHERICH. The others as before)

ESCHERICH. (shown in by SCHÖN, out of breath) Permit me ... to ... to introduce ... to introduce myself ...

SCHÖN. You've been running?

ESCHERICH. (offering his card) All the way from the police station. A suicide, I hear.

SCHÖN. (reads) Fritz Escherich, correspondent of The —— This way, please.

ESCHERICH. One moment. (Fetches out notebook and pencil, looks round the room, writes a few words, bows to LULU, writes again, turns to the broken door, writes again) An axe ... (Tries to pick it up)

SCHÖN. (restraining him) Please leave it alone.

ESCHERICH. (writes) Door broken open with an axe. (Examines the lock)

SCHÖN. (his hand on the door) Prepare yourself, my good fellow.

ESCHERICH. If you'd be so good as to open the door.

(SCHÖN opens the door)

(Drops book and pencil, thrusts his hand through his hair) God in heaven!

SCHÖN. Take a good look at everything!

ESCHERICH. I can't look.

SCHÖN. (with a contemptuous snort) What did you come here for, then?

ESCHERICH. Cut his th ... throat with a ra-ra—razor ...

SCHÖN. Have you seen everything?

ESCHERICH. What must it feel like!

SCHÖN. (closes the door, walks over to the desk) Sit down. Here are pen and paper, now write ...

ESCHERICH. (sitting down mechanically) I can't write ...

SCHÖN. (standing behind his chair) Take this down ... Persecution mania ...

ESCHERICH. (writes) Per-sec-ution-ma-nia.

(A bell rings in the passage)

ACT THREE

Scene One

(A dressing room in a theatre, the walls done up in red cloth. Backstage left the door. Backstage right a screen. In the middle, end on to the audience, a long table on which dancing costumes are laid out. To right and left of the table an armchair. Downstage left a small table with chairs. Downstage right a tall mirror, next to it an old-fashioned armchair, very wide, with a high back. In front of the mirror a pouffe, make-up boxes, etc., etc.

LULU, ALWA. (Soon afterwards SCHÖN)

ALWA. (downstage left, fills two glasses with champagne and red wine) I've never seen the public so beside itself since I began working in the theatre.

LULU. (out of sight behind the screen) Don't give me too much red wine. Is he going to see me today?

ALWA. My father?

LULU. Yes.

ALWA. I don't know if he's in the theatre.

LULU. I suppose he doesn't want to see me at all.

ALWA. He has so little time.

LULU. His fiancée makes demands on him.

ALWA. He's speculating. He gives himself no rest. (As SCHÖN enters) Is that you? We were just speaking of you.

LULU. Is he here?

SCHÖN. Are you changing?

LULU. (looking over the screen, to SCHÖN) You write in all the papers that I'm the most spirited dancer that has ever trod the boards, that I'm a second Taglioni and I don't know what else, yet you don't even find me amusing enough to come and confirm your judgment.

SCHÖN. I've so much writing to do. But you can see I was right. There was scarcely a seat to be had. – You must learn to keep more downstage.

LULU. I must get used to the lights first.

ALWA. She was conforming strictly to her role.

SCHÖN. (to ALWA) You should use your performers to better advantage. You have insufficient grasp of the technique as yet. (To LULU) What are you going on as next?

LULU. As a flower-girl.

SCHÖN. (to ALWA) In tights?

ALWA. No, in an ankle-length skirt.

SCHÖN. You'd have done better to leave symbolism alone,

ALWA. I'm interested in a dancer's feet.

SCHÖN. It's what the public are interested in that matters. Anyone with her looks has no need of this symbolical tomfoolery of yours, thank God.

ALWA. The public doesn't look as if it was bored.

SCHÖN. Naturally. Because I've been working for her success in the papers for the past six months. Was the Prince here?

ALWA. No one was here.

SCHÖN. Who's going to have a dancer appear in a mackintosh for two whole acts?

ALWA. Who is the Prince?

SCHÖN. Shall I see you again tonight?

ALWA. Are you alone?

SCHÖN. With friends. At Peter's?

ALWA. At twelve?

SCHÖN. At twelve. (Exit)

LULU. I'd already given up hope of his coming.

ALWA. Don't let yourself be put off by his grumbling and ungraciousness. Your concern must be that you don't waste your strength before your final appearance.

LULU. (comes out from behind the screen in a classical robe with ankle length skirt, sleeveless, with a red band at the hem; a many-coloured garland in her hair, a basket full of flowers in her hands) He seems not to have noticed the clever use you make of your performers.

ALWA. After all, one doesn't put everything one's got into the first act.

LULU. (her glass to her lips) You reveal me by degrees.

ALWA. I was quite certain you'd be good at changing costumes.

LULU. If I'd tried to sell my flowers outside the Alhambra Café like this, they'd have had me under lock and key the first evening.

ALWA. Why on earth!? You were a child!

LULU. Do you remember how I came into your room for the first time?

ALWA. (with a nod) You were wearing a dark blue dress trimmed with black velvet.

LULU. They had to hide me and they didn't know where.

ALWA. My mother had already been bed-ridden for two years...

LULU. You were playing with a toy theatre and you asked me if I wanted to join you.

ALWA. Of course! Our toy theatre!

LULU. I can still see you pushing the figures to and fro.

ALWA. It became and remained the most terrible memory for me, when I came to see the truth of the situation.

LULU. And then you became icily reserved towards me.

ALWA. My God – I felt you to be so far above me. I think I had a loftier regard for you than for my mother. Imagine – when my mother died – I was seventeen – I went to my father and demanded that he make you his wife on the spot, or I would have to call him out.

LULU. Yes, he told me about it at the time.

ALWA. Now that I'm older I can only pity him. He'll never understand me. He's concocted a little plot in his imagination whereby I'm supposed to be working against his marriage with the countess.

LULU. Does she still survey the world so innocently?

ALWA. She loves him. I'm convinced of that. Her family have done everything they could to get her to withdraw. I believe no sacrifice in the world would be too great for her for his sake.

LULU. (holding her glass out to him) May I have some more, please?

ALWA. (pouring out for her) You're drinking too much.

LULU. He must be made to believe in my success. He doesn't believe in art of any kind. He only believes in newspapers.

ALWA. He doesn't believe in anything.

LULU. He got me into the theatre in the hope that someone might be found who was rich enough to marry me.

ALWA. Oh well! What does it matter to us anyhow!

LULU. I'd be only too happy to dance myself into the heart of a millionaire.

ALWA. God forbid that you should be taken away from us!

LULU. But you composed the music for it.

ALWA. You know I've always wanted to write a play for you.

LULU. But the stage isn't my métier at all.

ALWA. You're a born dancer.

LULU. Why don't you make your plays at least as interesting as real life?

ALWA. Because no one would believe me.

LULU. If I hadn't known more about acting than they do in the theatre I wonder what would have become of me.

ALWA. But I've furnished your part with every conceivable improbability.

LULU. In real life that sort of hocus pocus won't wash at all.

ALWA. I'm quite satisfied if the public sees itself absolutely mad with excitement.

LULU. But I like to see myself absolutely mad with excitement. (Drinks)

ALWA. You don't seem very far off it now.

LULU. How can you wonder at it, since my performance has a higher purpose! Some of the audience are taking council with themselves quite seriously down there – I can sense it without looking.

ALWA. How can you sense it?

LULU. Not one of them has any idea what the others are feeling. Each one thinks he alone is the unhappy victim.

ALWA. But how can you be aware of this?

LULU. A sort of icy thrill runs up one's body.

ALWA. You are incredible ... (An electric bell rings outside the door)

LULU. My scarf ... I must remember to keep well downstage!

ALWA. (placing a wide shawl around her shoulders) Here's your scarf.

LULU. He shall have no further reason to worry about his shameless publicity.

ALWA. You must preserve your self-control.

LULU. May God help me to dance the last spark of sense out of his head.

Scene Two

ALWA. (alone) One could certainly write an interesting play about her. (Sits down left, takes out a notebook and makes notes. Looking up) Act one. Dr. Goll. Bad enough. I can conjure Dr. Goll out of purgatory or wherever he may be expiating his orgies, and people will hold me responsible for his sins. (Prolonged muffled applause and shouts of 'bravo' are audible from outside) – It's as wild as in a menagerie at feeding time. Act Two. Walter Schwarz! More impossible still! How souls are stripped of their last covering under the impact of such thunderbolts. Act Three. Can it really go on like this?

(The dressing-room door opens from outside to admit ESCERNY.

ESCERNY, quite at home, sits down right, next to the mirror, without looking at ALWA)

ALWA. (seated left, without looking at ESCERNY) It can't go on like this in the third act!

ESCERNY. Up to the middle of the third act it didn't seem to be going as well as usual today.

ALWA. I haven't been backstage.

ESCERNY. Now it's in full swing again.

ALWA. She's prolonging her number.

ESCERNY. I had the pleasure of meeting the artiste once at Dr. Schön's.

ALWA. My father brought her before the public by means of interviews in his paper.

ESCERNY. (bowing slightly) I have consulted Dr Schön about publishing the results of my explorations on Lake Tanganyika.

ALWA. (bowing slightly) His observations on the subject leave no doubt that he takes the liveliest interest in your work.

ESCERNY. The way the public simply does not exist for the artiste has a most refreshing effect.

ALWA. She learnt how to change costumes when she was still a child, but I was surprised to discover so considerable a dancer in her.

ESCERNY. When she dances her solo she is intoxicated with her own beauty – seems to be idolatrously in love with it.

ALWA. Here she comes. (Rises and opens the door)

Scene Three

(LULU. The others as before)

LULU. (without wreath and flower basket, to ALWA) They're calling for you. I've been before the curtain three times. (To ESCERNY) Dr. Schön isn't in your box?

ESCERNY. No, not in mine.

ALWA. (to LULU) Didn't you see him?

LULU. He's probably gone again.

ESCERNY. He has the last box on the left.

LULU. He seems to be ashamed of me!

ESCERNY. He couldn't get a better seat.

LULU. (to ALWA) Won't you ask him if he liked me better this time?

ALWA. I'll send him up.

ESCERNY. He did applaud.

LULU. Did he really?

ALWA. Do allow yourself a little rest. (Exit)

Scene Four

(LULU, ESCERNY)

LULU. I'm afraid I must change again.

ESCERNY. But your dresser isn't here.

LULU. I can do it more quickly alone. Where did you say Dr. Schön was sitting?

ESCERNY. I saw him in the last box on the left.

LULU. I've still got five costumes before me: dancing-girl, ballerina, Queen of the Night, Ariel and Lascaris. (Retires behind the screen)

ESCERNY. Would you believe it possible that when we first met I was expecting no more than to make the acquaintance of a young lady of the literary world? (Sits down next to the table, right, where he remains till the end of the scene) Is my judgment of your nature mistaken or have I rightly interpreted the smile which the roars of applause call to your lips –: that you suffer inwardly at having to degrade your art before persons whose interest in it is of a dubious nature? ... (As LULU makes no reply) That you would be ready at any time to exchange the blaze of publicity for quiet, sunny happiness in elegant seclusion? ... (As LULU makes no reply) That you feel there is enough dignity and nobility in you to keep a man at your feet, so that you may enjoy his utter helplessness? ... (as LULU makes no reply) That you would feel yourself more worthily placed in a villa furnished with every comfort, and with unlimited means at your disposal, so that you might live entirely as your own mistress?

LULU. (steps out from behind the screen in a short pleated petticoat, white satin corset, black shoes and stockings, spurs on her heels, and busies herself with the string of her corset) If I don't appear even for one night, I dream that I'm dancing all night long and next morning I feel quite worn out.

ESCERNY. But what a difference it could make if instead of this rabble you had **one** spectator, a **chosen** one!

LULU. It would make no difference at all. I never notice anyone.

ESCERNY. A lighted summer-house, the plash of waves coming up from the shore ... You see, on my voyages of exploration I am forced to exercise a quite inhuman despotism ...

LULU. (fastening a pearl necklace round her neck before the mirror) A good training!

ESCERNY. If I now long to yield myself without reserve into a woman's power, it is from a need for relaxation ... Can you imagine a greater happiness for a woman than to have a man wholly in her power?

LULU. (jingling her spurs) Oh, yes!

ESCERNY. (dazzled) You wouldn't find a single man of education who didn't lose his head over you.

LULU. But no one could meet your wishes without betraying you at the same time.

ESCERNY. It must make one ten times happier to be betrayed by a girl like you than to be loved virtuously by anyone else.

LULU. You've never been loved virtuously in your life! (Placing herself with her back to him, pointing to her corset) Could you undo the knot for me? I've laced myself too tight. I'm always so excited when I'm dressing.

ESCERNY. (after several attempts) I'm sorry, I can't do it.

LULU. Leave it, then. Perhaps I can manage. (Walks over to the right)

ESCERNY. I must confess I lack dexterity. Perhaps I haven't profited enough from intercourse with women.

LULU. I suppose you haven't had much opportunity for it in Africa?

ESCERNY. To you I can frankly admit that my isolation in the world has embittered many an hour for me.

LULU. I've almost got the knot undone.

ESCERNY. It's not your dancing that so attracts me. It is your physical and spiritual distinction, which reveals itself in all your movements. Anyone as interested in works of art as I am could not be mistaken. For ten evenings I have studied the life of your soul as it is expressed in your dancing, until today, when you came on as a flower-girl. I was able to complete my picture. Yours is a generous nature, unselfish. You cannot bear to see anyone suffer. You are the embodiment of mortal happiness. As a wife you would make a man supremely happy ... Your being is all candour ... you would make a poor actress ...

(The electric bell over the door rings)

LULU: (has loosened the strings of her corset slightly, takes a deep breath, jingling her spurs) Now I can breathe again. The curtain's going up. (She takes from the centre table a skirt dance costume of pleated yellow silk, all in one piece, high-necked and having long sleeves reaching to the knuckles – and throws it over her) I must dance.

ESCERNY. (rises and kisses her hand) If you will let me, I'll stay here for a while.

LULU. Please, do stay.

ESCERNY. I should like to be alone for a little.

(Exit LULU)

Scene Five

ESCERNY. What is nobility? Is it eccentricity, as in my case? Or is it bodily and spiritual perfection, as in the case of this girl? (Clapping and shouts of applause are heard) Anyone who restores my faith in human beings restores me to life. Would not this woman's children be more aristocratic in soul and body than children whose mother had no more vitality in her than I have left in myself, till today? (Seating himself downstage left, with enthusiasm) Dancing has ennobled her body . . .

Scene Six

(ALWA, ESCERNY)

ALWA. One can't be sure for a single moment that some wretched accident won't happen to ruin the whole performance. (He throws himself into the armchair on the right of the mirror so that the earlier position of the men is precisely reversed. Their conversation is rather languid and apathetic)

ESCERNY. Yet the public has never been more appreciative.

ALWA. She's finished the skirt-dance.

ESCERNY. I can hear her coming . . .

ALWA. She isn't coming. – She hasn't time. – She changes her costume in the wings.

ESCERNY. She has two ballerina costumes, if I'm not mistaken?

ALWA. I think the white suits her better than the pink.

ESCERNY. I don't.

ALWA. The white tulle is more expressive of the child in her.

ESCERNY. The pink tulle is more expressive of the woman in her!

(The electric bell over the door rings)

ALWA. (jumping up) My God! What can have happened?

ESCERNY. (also getting up) What is the matter?

(The electric bell continues to ring till the end of the scene)

ALWA. Something must have happened ...

ESCERNY. Why are you at once alarmed?

ALWA. There must be the devil of a confusion. (Exit)

(ESCERNEY follows him.

The door remains open. The sounds of a waltz are faintly audible)

Scene Seven

(Lulu enters in a long opera cloak and closes the door behind her. She is wearing a white ballet skirt with garlands of flowers. She goes diagonally across the stage and seats herself in the armchair near the mirror.

A pause)

Scene Eight

(ALWA, LULU. Soon afterwards SCHÖN)

ALWA. You fainted?

LULU. Please close the door.

ALWA. Come out onto the stage, at least.

LULU. Did you see him?

ALWA. See whom?

LULU. With his fiancée?

ALWA. With his ... (To SCHÖN, as he comes in) That's a joke you might have spared her!

SCHÖN. What's the matter with her? (To LULU) Do you really mean to play this scene against me to the end?

LULU. I feel as if I'd been beaten.

SCHÖN. (having bolted the door) You'll dance, as sure as I've taken on myself the responsibility of you!

LULU. In front of your fiancée?

SCHÖN. Have you any right to care whom you dance for? You've been engaged here. You get your pay ...

LULU. Is that any business of yours?

SCHÖN. You'll dance in front of anyone who chooses to buy a ticket. I can sit in my box with whom I like – it's got nothing to do with your activities here.

ALWA. If only you'd stayed in your box! (To LULU) Please tell me what I am to do. (Someone knocks on the door outside) That's the stage manager. (Calls) Coming, coming. One moment. (To LULU) You're not going to make us break off the performance?

SCHÖN. (to LULU) On stage with you!

LULU. Leave me alone for just a moment. I feel terribly ill.

ALWA. Devil take the whole backstage intrigue.

LULU. Put on the next number instead. No one will notice whether I dance now or in five minutes. There's no strength in my feet.

ALWA. But will you dance then?

LULU. As best I can.

ALWA. As badly as you like. (As the knocking is heard again from outside) I'm coming. (Exit)

Scene Nine

(SCHÖN, LULU)

LULU. You are right to show me where I belong. And there could be no better way of doing so than by having me dance the skirt-dance in front of your fiancée. You do me the greatest service in reminding me of my position.

SCHÖN. Considering your origins it's a matchless piece of luck that you should have the opportunity of appearing before respectable people.

LULU. Even when they don't know where to look because of my shamelessness!

SCHÖN. What a stupid way to talk! – Shameless? Don't make a necessity of virtue! Your shamelessness is worth its weight in gold, every step of it. One person shouts 'Bravo', another shouts 'Shame', it's all the same as far as you're concerned. What greater triumph could you desire than when a decent girl can hardly be persuaded to stay in the box? Has your life any other objective? As long as you keep a spark of self-respect you can't be a perfect dancer! The more you shock people, the greater your professional standing.

LULU. I don't care in the least what people think of me. I don't want to be better than I am. It suits me.

SCHÖN. (shocked) There speaks your true nature! I call that honest. – What corruption!!

LULU. I shouldn't have thought I'd ever had a spark of self-respect.

SCHÖN. (suddenly suspicious) No tricks now!

LULU. Oh God – I know very well what would have become of me if you hadn't saved me from it.

SCHÖN. Are you anything else today, then?

LULU. No, thank God.

SCHÖN. That's just like you!

LULU. (with a laugh) And how wildly happy I am!

SCHÖN. (spits) Are you going to dance now?

LULU. In any way and in front of anyone you like!

SCHÖN. On stage, then!!

LULU. (pleading childishly) Just a little longer. Please. I still can't stand up. They'll ring for me.

SCHÖN. This is what you've come to, in spite of all I have sacrificed for your education and well-being.

LULU. (ironically) Possibly you overestimated your ennobling influence.

SCHÖN. Spare me your witticisms.

LULU. – The Prince was here.

SCHÖN. Really?

LULU. He's going to take me to Africa with him.

SCHÖN. To Africa?

LULU. And why not? You made a dancer of me so that someone should come and take me away.

SCHÖN. But not to Africa.

LULU. Then why didn't you just let me faint and secretly thank your stars for it?

SCHÖN. Because unfortunately I had no reason to believe your faint was genuine.

LULU. (contemptuously) Or because you couldn't stand it down there any longer?

SCHÖN. Because I must make you realise who you are, and to what you may not aspire!

LULU. Were you afraid my limbs might have been seriously damaged?

SCHÖN. I know only too well that you're indestructible.

LULU. So you do know that?

SCHÖN. (flaring up) Don't look at me so impudently!

LULU. No one is keeping you here.

SCHÖN. I'm going as soon as the bell rings.

LULU. As soon as you have the energy, you mean. What's become of your energy? You've been engaged for three years. Why don't you marry? Nothing stands in your way. Why should you want to put the blame on me? You told me to marry Dr. Goll. I made Dr. Goll marry me. You told me to marry the painter, and so I made the best of a bad job. – You create artists, you're the patron of princes – Why don't you marry?

SCHÖN. (angrily) You don't by any chance think you're standing in my way?

LULU. (from now till the end of the scene exultantly) If you only knew how happy your anger makes me! How proud I am that you will do anything to humiliate me! You degrade me as deep as a man can degrade a woman, in the hope that then you'll find it easier to ignore me. But you hurt yourself unspeakably by what you just said to me, I can see it in your face. You're almost at the end of your self-control. Go! For your sweet innocent fiancée's sake, leave me alone! In another minute your mood will change and you'll make another scene, one that you won't find it easy to justify at the moment!

SCHÖN. I'm no longer afraid of you.

LULU. Of me? – You should be afraid of yourself! – I don't need you. Please go. Don't hold *me* responsible. You know I didn't have to faint in order to upset your future. You have an unbounded faith in my integrity. You believe not only that I'm an enchanting creature, but one with a heart of gold. I'm neither the one nor the other. It's unfortunate for you that you think I am.

SCHÖN. (in despair) Leave my thoughts alone! You've got two husbands underground. Take your prince and dance him to destruction! I'm finished with you. I know where the angel in you stops and the devil takes over. I may take life as it comes, but the Creator is responsible for it, not I! I don't regard life as an entertainment.

LULU. Yet no one could make greater demands on life than you do ... Tell me, which of us is the more exacting, you or I?

SCHÖN. Be quiet! I no longer know how or what I'm thinking. When I listen to you I cease to think at all. I'm to be married in eight days' time, and I appeal to you, by the angel there is in you, to keep out of my sight meanwhile!

LULU. I'll lock my doors.

SCHÖN. Still so pleased with yourself! – As God is my witness, I've never, in all my long battle with life, cursed anyone as I curse you!

LULU. That is because of my lowly origins.

SCHÖN. Because of your depravity!

LULU. I am delighted, a thousand times delighted, to take the blame! Now you must feel quite pure. You must see yourself as a model of austerity, a puritan of unshakeable principles – you couldn't marry the girl otherwise, in her unfathomable innocence.

SCHÖN. Do you want me to lay hands on you?

LULU. Yes! Yes! What can I say to make you? I wouldn't change places with the child now for all the kingdoms of the world. And yet the girl loves you, as no woman has ever loved you before.

SCHÖN. Be silent! You monster!

LULU. Marry her – then she'll dance in front of me in her childish misery, instead of my dancing in front of her!

SCHÖN. (raises his fist) God forgive me ...

LULU. Strike me! Where is your whip? Strike me across the legs ...

SCHÖN. (his hands to his temples) Away! I must get away! (Rushes to the door, pulls himself together, turns back) Can I appear before the child like this? – I must go home. – If only I could escape from the world itself!

LULU. Be a man. – Look yourself in the face for once. – You haven't a scrap of conscience. – You stop at nothing however shameful. Quite coldbloodedly you mean to make this girl who loves you unhappy. – You take half the world by storm. – You do just as you please – and you know as well as I do – that ...

SCHÖN. (has sunk down utterly exhausted into the chair on the left of the centre table) Stop!

LULU. That you're too weak – to free yourself from me ...

SCHÖN. (groaning) Oh! Oh! You're hurting me!

LULU. I can't tell you what satisfaction this moment gives me!

SCHÖN. The evening of my life! My world!

LULU. He's crying like a child, the terrible despot! – Now go to your fiancée and tell her what a wonderful girl I am – not a bit jealous!

SCHÖN. (sobbing) The child! The innocent child!

LULU. How can the devil incarnate suddenly become so soft. – But please go now! You're nothing to me any more.

SCHÖN. I can't go to her.

LULU. Away with you! Come back to me when you've recovered your strength.

SCHÖN. For God's sake, tell me what I am to do.

LULU. (gets up. Her cape remains on the chair. She pushed aside the costumes on the centre table) Here is writing paper ...

SCHÖN. I couldn't write ...

LULU. (standing behind him, her hand on the arm of his chair) Write: 'My dear Countess' ...

SCHÖN. (hesitating) I call her Adelaide ...

LULU. 'My dear Countess' ...

SCHÖN. My death-sentence!

LULU. 'You must take back your word. I cannot reconcile it with my conscience' – (As SCHÖN puts down the pen and looks at her imploringly) write 'reconcile' it with my *conscience*, to link you with my unhappy existence' ...

SCHÖN. You're right. You're right.

LULU. 'I give you my word that I am unworthy of your love'. (As SCHÖN again turns aside) Write 'of your love. These lines will prove it to you. I have been trying to break away for three years; I have not the strength. I am writing to you at the side of the woman who dominates me. You must forget me. – Dr. Ludwig Schön'.

SCHÖN. (groaning aloud) Oh God!

LULU. (half frightened) Don't say that! (With emphasis) 'Dr Ludwig Schön'. – Postscript: 'Do not attempt to rescue me'.

SCHÖN. (collapses as he finishes writing) Now – for the – execution ...

ACT FOUR

Scene One

(Magnificent room in German Renaissance style, with a heavy ceiling in carved oak. Dark wood-carvings half way up the walls. Above them, on each side of the stage, faded tapestries. The upper half of the room back-stage is filled by a gallery hung with drapery from which a massive staircase descends on the left to half way downstage. Under the gallery in the centre the door with twisted columns and a pediment. On the right hand side wall a wide, high chimney-piece. Further downstage a French window behind heavy curtains. On the left hand side wall, below the foot of the staircase, a portière of Genoese velvet.

In front of the fireplace a Chinese screen. Close to the final column of the outer bannister-rail LULU's portrait as Pierrot, in a reproduction antique frame. Downstage left a deep sofa, in front of which, right, an armchair. In the centre of the stage a square table with a heavy cloth on it, around which stand three upholstered chairs with high backs. On the table an arrangement of white flowers.

SCHÖN, LULU, COUNTESS GESCHWITZ)

GESCHWITZ. (seated on the sofa in a hussar's jacket trimmed with fur, a high stand-up collar, enormous cuff-links, a veil over her face, her hands tightly clasped inside her muff. To LULU) You cannot imagine how happy I am to think I shall see you at our ball for women artists.

SCHÖN. (downstage left) Is there really no way for any of our sort to smuggle ourselves in?

GESCHWITZ. It would be high treason for any of us to lend ourselves to such a scheme.

SCHÖN. (walks round behind the sofa and up to the centre table) What glorious flowers.

LULU. (in a flowered negligée, her hair in a simple knot fastened by a gold clasp) Countess von Geschwitz brought them to me.

GESCHWITZ. Pray don't mention it. – Anyhow, you will dress as a man, won't you?

LULU. Do you think it will suit me?

GESCHWITZ. (pointing to the portrait) You're a fairy-tale in this.

LULU. My husband doesn't like it.

GESCHWITZ. Is it by someone from here?

LULU. You would hardly have known him.

GESCHWITZ. Is he no longer alive?

SCHÖN. (downstage, right, in a deep voice) He'd had enough.

LULU. You're in a bad mood.

(SCHÖN controls himself)

GESCHWITZ. I must go, Madame. I mustn't stay any longer. Tonight I have a life-class and I still have preparations to make for the ball. – (With a bow) Dr. Schön. (Exit through centre, escorted by LULU) ·

Scene Two

SCHÖN. (alone, looking about him) The Augean stables pure and simple. So this is the evening of my life. I'd like to be shown a corner that is still uncontaminated. The plague is in the house. The poorest labouring man has a clean nest to come back to. Thirty years of hard work, and this my family circle, the circle of my near and dear ... (Looking about him) God knows who may be eavesdropping! (He pulls a revolver from his breast-pocket) One can't be sure of one's own safety! (With the revolver held cocked in his right hand, he walks over to the right and speaks into the drawn curtains) My family circle! – The fellow still has courage! – Might I not better put a bullet through my own brain? – One fights one's mortal enemies, but this ... (He pulls the curtains aside; as he finds no one concealed behind them) Filth – filth ... (He shakes his head and walks over to the left) Either madness has already taken possession of my reason, or – exceptions prove the rule! (As he hears LULU coming he replaces the revolver)

Scene Three

(LULU, SCHÖN. Both downstage left)

LULU. Couldn't you make yourself free this afternoon?

SCHÖN. What did the Countess want?

LULU. I don't know. She wants to paint me.

SCHÖN. Misfortune in human form, come to pay its respects.

LULU. Couldn't you make yourself free? I should like to go for a drive with you in the Park.

SCHÖN. Just the day when I must be at the Exchange. You know I'm not free today. All that I have is drifting on the seas of chance.

LULU. I'd rather be dead and buried than let my life be so embittered by my possessions.

SCHÖN. He who takes life lightly dies easily.

LULU. Even as a child I had this terrible fear of death.

SCHÖN. That's why I married you.

LULU. (her arms round his neck) For weeks and months I've seen nothing of you.

SCHÖN. (stroking her hair) Your gaiety ought to cheer my old age.

LULU. You didn't marry me at all.

SCHÖN. Whom else should I have married?

LULU. I married you!

SCHÖN. What difference does that make?

LULU. I'm always afraid it may make a lot of difference.

SCHÖN. It's certainly trodden a good deal beneath its feet.

LULU. There's one thing it hasn't, thank God!

SCHÖN. I'd be curious to know what it is.

LULU. Your love for me.

(SCHÖN winces, makes a sign for her to precede him. Exeunt downstage, left)

Scene Four

COUNTESS GESCHWITZ. (cautiously opens the centre door, ventures forward and listens. Is startled to hear voices in the gallery) My God, there's someone there ... (Hides behind the firescreen)

Scene Five

(SCHIGOLCH, RODRIGO, HUGENBERG)

SCHIGOLCH. (emerges from behind the curtains above the steps, turns back) I suppose the lad has left his heart behind in the 'Lantern Café'.

RODRIGO. (between the curtains) He's still too small for the big world, he can't walk as far as this yet. (Disappears)

SCHIGOLCH. (comes down the steps) Thank God we're at home again at last! Some fiend has waxed these stairs again! If I'm to have my bones put in plaster again before I'm called home, she can stick me between these palms here and show me off to her relations as the Medici Venus. Shoals and pitfalls everywhere!

RODRIGO. (comes down the stairs carrying HUGENBERG in his arms) He has a police-chief for a father and not as much guts as the seediest beggar!

HUGENBERG. If it were a matter of life and death you'd soon see what I'm made of.

RODRIGO. The little chap weighs no more than eight stone, with the weight of his lover's sorrow thrown in. – I'll stake my life on it any day.

SCHIGOLCH. Throw him up to the ceiling and catch him by the feet. That'll set his blood flowing in the right direction.

HUGENBERG. (kicking his legs about) Oh dear, oh dear, I'll be expelled from school!

RODRIGO. (setting him down at the foot of the stairs) You haven't been to a proper school yet!

SCHIGOLCH. There's not a few have won their spurs in this house. No need to be shy! But first I'll give you a drop of something worth more that its weight in gold. (He opens a small cupboard under the stairs)

HUGENBERG. But if she doesn't dance in pretty quick I'll give you both such a hiding that you'll still be rubbing your backs in the next world.

RODRIGO. (has sat down at the table, right) The little chap's going to beat up the strongest man in the world? (to HUGENBERG) Get your father to put you into long trousers first.

HUGENBERG. (sitting down at the table, left) I'd rather have you lend me your moustache.

RODRIGO. Do you want to have her throw you out of the house at once?

HUGENBERG. Damn it, if I only knew what to say to her!

RODRIGO. She knows that best herself.

SCHIGOLCH. (places two bottles and three glasses on the table) I opened one of them yesterday. (He fills the glasses)

RODRIGO. (covering HUGENBERG's glass) Don't give him too much, or you and I will only have to answer for it.

SCHIGOLCH. (supporting himself with both hands on the table) Do the gentlemen smoke?

HUGENBERG. (opening his cigar-case) These are Havanas.

RODRIGO. (helping himself) From your police-chief papa?

SCHIGOLCH. (sitting down) I have everything in the house. You only have to ask.

HUGENBERG. I wrote her a poem yesterday.

RODRIGO. What did you write her?

SCHIGOLCH. What did he write her?

HUGENBERG. A poem.

RODRIGO. (TO SCHIGOLCH) A poem.

SCHIGOLCH. He promised me a Taler if I could find out where he could meet her alone.

HUGENBERG. Who actually lives here?

RODRIGO. We live here!

SCHIGOLCH. At Home, every Stock Exchange day. Your health! (They touch glasses)

HUGENBERG. Do you think I ought to read it aloud to you first?

SCHIGOLCH. What's he talking about?

RODRIGO. His poem. He wants to stretch her on the rack a little first.

SCHIGOLCH. (staring at HUGENBERG) His eyes! His eyes!

RODRIGO. Yes, his eyes! They've robbed her of her sleep for the past eight days.

SCHIGOLCH. (to RODRIGO) You might as well have yourself pickled.

RODRIGO. We can both have ourselves pickled! Your health, Grandpa Death!

SCHIGOLCH. (touching glasses with him) Your health, clown! If there's anything better in store for us, I'm ready to pack up at any moment, but ... but ...

Scene Six

(LULU. The others as before. Later on FERDINAND)

LULU. (enters from the left, in an elegant Parisian ball-gown deeply décolleté, with flowers at her bosom and in her hair) But children, children, I'm expecting a visitor.

SCHIGOLCH. Well, I must say, they certainly throw the money about over there!

(HUGENBERG has risen to his feet)

LULU. (sitting down on the arm of his chair) This is a fine company for you to have got yourself into. I'm expecting a visitor, children.

SCHIGOLCH. I think I must stick something on myself too. (Searches among the flowers on the table)

LULU. Do I look nice?

SCHIGOLCH. What are those things you've got out in front?

LULU. Orchids. (Inclining her bosom towards HUGENBERG) Smell them.

RODRIGO. I suppose you're expecting Prince Escerny.

LULU. (shaking her head) God forbid!

RODRIGO. Someone new already?

LULU. The Prince has gone away.

RODRIGO. To put his kingdom up for auction?

LULU. He's exploring a new tribe somewhere in Africa. (Rises, hastens up the stairs into the gallery)

RODRIGO. (to SCHIGOLCH) At one time he wanted to marry her, you know.

SCHIGOLCH. (fastening a lily onto himself) I wanted to marry her at one time myself.

RODRIGO. You wanted to marry her at one time?

SCHIGOLCH. Didn't you want to marry her at one time?

RODRIGO. Of course I wanted to marry her at one time!

SCHIGOLCH. Who hasn't wanted to marry her at one time?

RODRIGO. I couldn't have done better.

SCHIGOLCH. She's never let anyone regret not having married her.

RODRIGO. So she's not your child?

SCHIGOLCH. It never crossed her mind.

HUGENBERG. Then what's her father's name?

SCHIGOLCH. What did he say?

RODRIGO. He asked what her father's name was.

SCHIGOLCH. She never had one.

LULU. (comes down from the gallery and sits down again on the arm of HUGENBERG's chair) What did I never have?

ALL THREE. A father.

LULU. Why yes, of course, I'm a freak. (To HUGENBERG) How do you like *your* father?

RODRIGO. He smokes a decent cigar at any rate, does Mr. Police Chief.

SCHIGOLCH. Did you lock the door upstairs?

LULU. Here's the key.

SCHIGOLCH. You should have left it in the lock.

LULU. Why?

SCHIGOLCH. So it can't be opened from the outside.

RODRIGO. Isn't he at the Exchange?

LULU. Oh yes. But he suffers from persecution mania.

RODRIGO. I'll just take him by the feet and hoopla! he'll be sticking to the ceiling.

LULU. He can chase you into a mousehole with one quarter of a look out of the corner of his eye.

RODRIGO. What's that about chasing me? When is he going to chase me? Just look at these biceps.

LULU. Let's see them. (Over to right)

RODRIGO. (striking himself on the arm) Granite. – Cast iron.

LULU. (feeling first RODRIGO's arm and then her own) If only you hadn't got such long ears ...

FERDINAND. (enters at centre) Dr. Schön.

RODRIGO. (jumping up) The bastard. (Goes to hide behind the firescreen, recoils) God preserve us! (Hides downstage right, behind the curtains)

SCHIGOLCH. Give me the key. (Takes the key from LULU and drags himself upstairs)

(HUGENBERG gets out his chair and slides under the table)

LULU. I'm ready to receive him. (Exit FERDINAND)

HUGENBERG. (looks out from under the tablecloth and listens. Aside) Perhaps he won't stay – then we shall be alone ...

(LULU touches him with the toe of her shoe.

HUGENBERG goes out of sight)

Scene Seven

(ALWA. The others as before.

FERDINAND shows ALWA in. Exit)

ALWA. (in evening dress) I believe the matinée is going to take place by artificial light. I have ... (Noticing SCHIGOLCH, who is dragging himself laboriously upstairs) What's that?

LULU. An old friend of you father's.

ALWA. A complete stranger to me.

LULU. They were in the war together. He's in a bad way ...

ALWA. Is my father here, then?

LULU. He had a drink with him. Then he had to go to the Exchange. – But we're going to have luncheon first?

ALWA. When does it begin?

LULU. After two o'clock. (As ALWA follows SCHIGOLCH with his eyes) How do you think I'm looking?

(SCHIGOLCH exits through gallery)

ALWA. I think it would be better for me to be silent on that subject.

LULU. I only meant my gown.

ALWA. Your dressmaker is obviously more familiar with you than I – can allow myself to be.

LULU. When I looked at myself in the mirror I wished I were a man ... my own husband! –

ALWA. You seem to envy your husband the happiness you give him.

(LULU on the left, ALWA on the right at the centre table. He looks at her with bashful pleasure)

(FERDINAND enters at centre with crockery, lays the table for two, sets out a bottle of Pommery, Hors d'oeuvres)

Have you got the toothache?

LULU. (to ALWA) Please don't.

ALWA. He strikes me as so miserable today.

FERDINAND. (through his teeth) I'm only human. (Exit. The others seat themselves at the table)

LULU. What I've always respected most about you is your firmness of character. You're always so sure of yourself. Even though it meant a risk of falling out with your father, you've always taken my part like a brother.

ALWA. Don't let us talk about that. It's simply my lot in life. (Tries to lift up the tablecloth)

LULU. (hastily) That was I.

ALWA. Impossible – Well, it is my lot to have the most reckless ideas and the best intentions.

LULU. You deceive yourself when you make yourself out to be so bad.

ALWA. Why do you flatter me like this? It's true – there's no wickeder man alive – who has at the same time brought about so much good.

LULU. At all events you're the only man in the world who has protected me without debasing me in my own eyes.

ALWA. Do you think that has been so easy ...?

Scene Eight

(SCHÖN. The others as before)

SCHÖN. (appears in the gallery between the two central pillars, parts the curtains cautiously and speaks out over the stage) My own son!

ALWA. With such heaven-sent gifts as yours people make criminals of those around them without dreaming what they're doing. – Even I am no more than human, and if we hadn't been brought up as brother and sister ...

LULU. That's why you're the only man I can be quite unreserved with. From you I have nothing to fear.

ALWA. I assure you, there are moments when one realises one is experiencing the disintegration of one's innermost being. The more self-denial one has imposed on oneself the more easily one goes to pieces. There's no way out save ... (He makes as if to look under the table)

LULU. (quickly) Are you looking for something?

ALWA. Please, let me keep my confessions of faith to myself. As an inviolable shrine you have been more to me than you have ever been to anyone else, with all your natural gifts.

LULU. In that respect your view is very different from your father's!

(FERDINAND enters at centre, changes the plates, serves roast chicken and salad)

ALWA. (to FERDINAND) Are you ill?

LULU. (to ALWA) Do leave him alone.

ALWA. He's shivering as if he had a fever.

FERDINAND. I'm not exactly used to waiting at table.

ALWA. You ought to get the doctor to give you something.

FERDINAND. I'm really the coachman ... (Exit)

SCHÖN. (in the gallery, speaking out across the stage) So he's another of them. (Takes up his position at the balustrade, hiding behind the curtain when necessary)

LULU. What sort of moments are those you spoke of, when one experiences the disintegration of one's innermost being?

ALWA. I spoke of it against my will. I shouldn't care to make light of it over a glass of champagne. It's been the supreme joy of my life for the last ten years.

LULU. I've hurt you. I won't speak of it again.

ALWA. Will you promise me that for always?

LULU. I'll give you my hand on it. (Stretches out her hand to him across the table)

ALWA. (takes it hesitantly, holds it in his own, presses it long and fervently to his lips)

LULU. What are you doing?

(RODRIGO sticks his head out between the curtains, right.

LULU gives him an angry look over ALWA's head.

RODRIGO withdraws)

SCHÖN. (speaking out over the stage) And there's another of them!

ALWA. (holding her hand) A soul – rubbing the sleep out of its eyes in the next world ... Oh, this hand ...

LULU. (innocently) What is there to that?

ALWA. An arm.

LULU. And what is there to that?

ALWA. A body ...

LULU. (without comprehension) And what is there to that?

ALWA. (passionately) Mignon! Mignon!

LULU. (throws herself down on the ottoman) Don't look at me like that, for goodness sake. We'd better go before it's too late. You're a wicked wretch!

ALWA. But I told you myself that I was vile, a scoundrel ...

LULU. So I see!

ALWA. I have no sense of honour – no pride ...

LULU. And you take me for one of the same sort!

ALWA. You? – you are as high above me as the sun over the abyss...
(Kneeling) Destroy me! I beg you, make an end of me – Make an end
of me!

LULU. Do you *love* me, then?

ALWA. I'll give everything I own for you!

LULU. Do you love me?

ALWA. Do you love me – Mignon!

LULU. I? Not a soul!

ALWA. I *love* you. (Buries his head in her lap)

LULU. (both hands in his hair) – I poisoned your mother ...

(RODRIGO sticks his head out between the curtains, right; sees
SCHÖN in the gallery and draws his attention by signs to LULU and
ALWA.

SCHÖN points his revolver at RODRIGO.

RODRIGO signs to him to point the revolver at ALWA.

SCHÖN cocks the revolver and aims it at RODRIGO.

RODRIGO darts back behind the curtains)

LULU. (sees RODRIGO as he withdraws, sees SCHÖN sitting in the
gallery, rises to her feet) His father!

(SCHÖN stands up, lets the curtain fall in front of him.

ALWA remains motionless on his knees.

A pause)

SCHÖN. (a newspaper in his hand, takes ALWA by the shoulder)

Alwa!

(ALWA stands up as if half asleep)

SCHÖN. Revolution has broken out in Paris.

ALWA. To Paris ... let me go to Paris ...

SCHÖN. At the office they're running their heads against the wall. No one knows what to write ... (Unfolds the newspaper and leads ALWA out by the centre door)

(RODRIGO bursts out from behind the curtains and makes for the stairs)

LULU. (barring the way) You can't get out this way.

RODRIGO. Let me pass!

LULU. You'll run straight into his arms.

RODRIGO. He'll put a bullet through my head.

LULU. He's coming.

RODRIGO. (staggering back) Holy smoke! (Lifts the tablecloth)

HUGENBERG. No room!

RODRIGO. Damn and blast! (Looks about him and hides behind the portières)

SCHÖN. (enters centre, shuts the door, goes, the revolver in his hand, to the window downstage right, lifts the curtain) Where's *he* got to?

LULU. (on the bottom step) He's got away.

SCHÖN. Down from the balcony?

LULU. He's a professional acrobat.

SCHÖN. That's something one couldn't foresee – (Turning to LULU) You wretched creature, dragging me through the gutter to a martyr's death!

LULU. Why didn't you bring me up better?

SCHÖN. You avenging angel! You inexorable fate! To turn murderer, or drown in filth, run away to sea like a discharged convict, or string myself up over the morass. You joy of my old age! You hangman's noose!

LULU. Shut up and kill me!

SCHÖN. I made over all my goods and chattels to you and asked nothing in return but the respect for my house which any servant might be expected to show. Your credit is exhausted!

LULU. I can be your security for that account for years to come. (Advancing from the stairs) How do you like my new dress?

SCHÖN. Out of my sight or I may be out of my mind by tomorrow and my son will swim in his own blood. You have fastened on me like some incurable disease from which I must groan and suffer till my last breath. I want to heal myself. Do you understand? (Thrusting the revolver at her) And here is the medicine. No giving at the knees! – You should turn it on yourself. It is you or I – let us measure our strength.

LULU. (has sunk down on the divan as her strength threatens to desert her; turns the revolver this way and that) This won't go off.

SCHÖN. Do you remember when I snatched you from the clutches of the police?

LULU. How trusting you are ...

SCHÖN. Because I'm not afraid of a whore? Must I guide your hand? Have you no pity for yourself? (As LULU points the revolver at him) No false alarms, now!

(LULU fires a shot at the ceiling.

RODRIGO leaps out from behind the portières, up the stairs, and exits)

SCHÖN. What was that?

LULU. (innocently) Nothing.

SCHÖN. (raising the portières) Something came fluttering out – what was it?

LULU. You suffer from persecution mania.

SCHÖN. Have you got any more men hidden in here? (Snatching the revolver from her) Have you any other visitors? (Over to the right) I'd like to entertain your men. (Raises the curtains, throws aside the firescreen, seizes GESCHWITZ by the collar and drags her downstage) Did you come down the chimney?

GESCHWITZ. (terrified, to LULU) Save me from him.

SCHÖN. (shaking her) Or are you an acrobat too?

GESCHWITZ. (whimpering) You're hurting me.

SCHÖN. (shaking her) Now you simply must stay to dinner. (Drags her over to the left, pushes her into the next room, locks the door behind her) We don't need any publicity. (Sits down beside LULU, shoves the revolver at her) There's enough in it for you too. – Look at me! I can't be expected to help my coachman fix the horns on me in my own house. Look at me! I pay my coachman. Look at me! Am I doing him a favour in not being able to bear the foul stable smell myself?

LULU. Please order the carriage. We'll drive to the opera.

SCHÖN. We'll drive to the devil! I'm coachman now. (Turning the revolver in LULU's hand away from himself and aiming it at LULU's breast) After being abused the way you have been abusing me, do you expect me to pause to weigh the disgrace of going to prison in my old age against the public service I should perform in ridding the world of *you*? (Holds her down by the arm) Let's finish if off. It will be the happiest moment of my life. Fire!

LULU. – You could get a divorce.

SCHÖN. (rising) That would be the finishing touch! So that my successor may find his amusement where once I had shuddered from abyss to abyss, a suicide like a millstone round my neck and **you** before my eyes. I wonder you dare speak such a thought aloud. Am I to see the part of my life which I made part of your life thrown to the wolves? Can you see your bed, with the sacrificial victim upon it? The boy is longing for you. – Did you get a divorce? You trampled on him, beat his brains out, collected his blood in gold-pieces. Me get a divorce? Does one divorce when one has grown so together that half of oneself goes too? (Reaching for his revolver) Give it to me.

LULU. Spare me!

SCHÖN. I want to spare you the effort.

LULU. (wrenches herself away from him; holding down the revolver, in a firm, confident tone) If men have done away with themselves for my sake, that doesn't reduce my value. – You were just as well aware of your motives in making me your wife as I was of my own motives in taking you as my husband. – You had betrayed your best friends with me, you couldn't very well betray yourself as well. – You may have sacrificed the evening of your life to me, but you've had my whole youth in exchange. You know ten times better than I do which is of greater value. I've never in the world wanted to be anything but what I've been taken for, and no one has ever taken me for anything but what I am. You're trying to make me put a bullet through my heart. I'm no longer sixteen years old, but I think I'm still too young to put a bullet through my heart!

SCHÖN. (rushing at her) Down, murderess! Down! On your knees, murderess! (He forces her back to the stairs; raises his hand) Down, and don't dare rise again!

(LULU has sunk to her knees)

Ask God to give you the strength, murderess! Implore Heaven to give you the strength for it!

HUGENBERG (jumping up from under the table, pushing the chair aside) Help!

(SCHÖN turns towards HUGENBERG, presenting his back to LULU.

LULU fires five shots at SCHÖN, and continues to pull the trigger)

SCHÖN. (falling forward, is caught by HUGENBERG, who lowers him into an armchair) And – there – is – another – of them ...

LULU. (rushing at SCHÖN) Merciful God ...

SCHÖN. Out of my sight! – Alwa!

LULU. (on her knees) The only man I ever loved!

SCHÖN. Whore! Murderess! – Alwa! Alwa! – Water!

LULU. Some water; he's parched. (Fills a glass with champagne and holds it to SCHÖN's lips)

ALWA. (crosses the gallery and comes down the stairs) My father! Good God! My father!

LULU. I shot him.

HUGENBERG. She is innocent!

SCHÖN. (to ALWA) You are the winner. I have failed.

ALWA. (tries to lift him) You must get to bed. Come.

SCHÖN. Don't take hold of me like that. – I am parched with thirst –

(LULU approaches with the champagne glass)

(to LULU) You remain true to yourself. (When he has drunk, to ALWA) Don't let her escape. – You are the next one ...

ALWA. (to HUGENBERG) Help me to get him to bed.

SCHÖN. No, no, please! Champagne, murderess!

ALWA. (to HUGENBERG) Take hold with me. (Pointing left) Into the bedroom. (Between them they raise SCHÖN and lead him off, right. LULU remains by the table, glass in hand)

SCHÖN. (groaning) Oh God! Oh God!

(ALWA finds the door locked, turns the key and opens it. COUNTESS GESCHWITZ walks out)

(Drawing himself up stiffly at the sight of her) The devil – (Falls backwards onto the carpet)

LULU. (throws herself down beside him, takes his head on her lap, kisses him) It's all over. – (Gets to her feet, goes towards the stairs)

ALWA. Don't move!

GESCHWITZ. (to LULU) I thought it was you.

LULU. (throwing herself at ALWA's feet) You can't hand me over to the police. It'll be *my* head they'll cut off. I shot him because he wanted to shoot me. I have loved no one in the world but him. Alwa, you can ask what you please. Don't let me fall into the hands of the law. It would be such a pity! I'm still so young. I'll be true to you all my life. Look at me, Alwa, look at me, man! Look at me! (Knocking is heard outside)

ALWA. The police. (Goes to open the door)

HUGENBERG. I shall be expelled from school.

PANDORA'S BOX

**A Tragedy in Three Acts
with a Prologue**

CHARACTERS

LULU

ALWA SCHÖN a writer

RODRIGO QUAST an acrobat

SCHIGOLCH

ALFRED HUGENBERG an inmate of a reformatory

COUNTESS GESCHWITZ

MARQUIS CASTI-PIANI

BANKER PUNTSCHU

HEILMANN a journalist

MAGELONE

KADIKJA DI SANTA CROCE her daughter

BIANETTA GAZIL

LUDMILLA STEINHERZ

BOB a groom

A POLICE INSPECTOR

MR. HUNIDEI

KUNGU Imperial Prince of Uahubee

DR. HILTI a university lecturer

JACK

The first act takes place in Germany, the second in Paris, the third in London.

FOREWORD

I was at work on the drama which follows for nine years between 1892 and 1901. I have submitted every subsequent edition to a thorough revision until it attained its present form which it is my purpose to regard as definitive. The following words are those which I added to the book in 1906 just after it had been annihilated by a judicial ban.

The prosecution having characterised the drama as an incompetent piece of work devoid of any moral or artistic merits, its moral and artistic qualities were precisely those picked out for recognition by all three courts whose task it was to pronounce judgment on the play. These courts were: the 'Königliche Landgericht I', in Berlin, the 'Reichsgericht' in Leipzig, and the 'Königliche Landgericht II' in Berlin.

On the strength of this recognition the 'Landgericht I' found in favour of acquitting the accused and releasing the book. The Reichsgericht took the stand that moral and artistic qualities were not in themselves enough to redeem a play from the reproach of indecency and on this basis reversed the original judgment. The 'Landgericht II' associated itself with the opinion of the Reichsgericht and, while acquitting the accused, ordered the suppression of the book in its original form, at the same time, however, rendering a much more careful appreciation of its moral and artistic merits than had hitherto fallen to its lot in open discussion.

It is the purpose of this edition to preserve the moral and artistic qualities of the book, to cleanse it of any impurities which may have crept into it through artistic exuberance and the joy of creation during the first by no means easily accomplished subjugation of the material. I cannot take upon myself the responsibility of suppressing or destroying values declared to be present by twenty German judges, mature and serious men. I am therefore permitting myself here no more than a few purely factual observations.

The tragic central figure of the play is not Lulu, as the justices mistakenly assumed, but Countess Geschwitz. Apart from an intrigue here and there, Lulu plays an entirely passive role in all three acts; Countess Geschwitz on the other hand in the first act furnishes an example of what one can justifiably describe as super-human self-sacrifice. In the second act the progress of the plot forces her to summon all her spiritual resources in the attempt to conquer the terrible destiny of abnormality with which she is burdened; after which, in the third act, having borne the most fearful torments of soul with stoical composure, she sacrifices her life in defence of her friend.

That I chose the fate of a human being burdened with the curse of abnormality as the theme of a serious dramatic creation was not pronounced inadmissible in any of the three judgments. It is a matter of fact that the chief protagonists in the old Greek tragedies are almost always beyond the pale of normality. They are of the race of Tantalus; the gods have forged an iron band around their brows. That is to say: in spite of a spiritual development inspiring enough to transport their audience to the summit of human happiness, they are unable to shake off the unholy inheritance by which they are dominated; instead, unfit for human society and in extreme torment they succumb to their fate. As far as the audience are concerned abnormality as such could scarcely be more tellingly stigmatised. If at the same time the spectator derives aesthetic pleasure from this presentation as well as unqualified spiritual gain, then the presentation is lifted out of the realm of morality into that of art.

Nevertheless the curse of abnormality would not by itself have tempted me to select it as the theme for dramatic creation. I did so rather because I had never found this affliction as we encounter it in our contemporary culture handled as tragedy. I was animated by the desire to rescue the powerful human tragedy of exceptional but wholly fruitless spiritual struggles from its fate of ridicule and bring it home to the sympathy and compassion of those not themselves affected by it. As one of the most effective means to this end I thought it necessary to personify in the most telling possible form the vulgar mockery and shrill derision which is the uneducated man's reaction to this tragedy. For this purpose I created the figure of the acrobat Rodrigo Quast. Rodrigo Quast is the counterpart of Countess Geschwitz. While I worked I was fully aware that the more brutal the pleasantries put into the mouth of this brutal man, the greater by contrast must be shown to be the spiritual exertions to which the Countess is driven by her misfortune. I was fully aware that I must over and over neutralise and outdo his mockery by my serious treatment of the Countess's fate, and that in the end this tragic seriousness must have emerged as unconditional victor if the work was to have fulfilled its purpose.

That I was successful in achieving this effect in the last act of the play has been confirmed by every performance. Moreover the judgments pronounced on the drama in its original form recognise this fact. The judgments of the Reichsgericht and the Landgericht II dispute only whether the 'normal' reader would be susceptible to this intended effect of tragedy. Not without exception, must of course be the answer. For to the great mass of normal readers belongs above all the uneducated person who appears in the drama itself as a strong man and against whose strident mockery the piece is directed. The intended victim of my satirical shafts naturally cannot be made sensible of their sting by the *written* word alone, but only when to his great surprise he notices that cultivated persons find his counterpart on the stage both contemptible and ridiculous. Incidentally the indecencies which I have put into the mouth of this strong man do not compete with those of a Falstaff, Mephistopheles, or Spiegelberg.

When I published this play in its original form I was permeated to the depths of my soul by the conviction that I was thereby satisfying a claim of the highest human morality. I was equally aware that its publication could provoke a charge of offence against public morals or of dissemination of indecent literature. That this expected consequence did indeed come to pass is proof neither for nor against this conviction of mine. But it has always been of the very essence of our spiritual evolution that a man who makes a decisive step forward in one sphere or another should be hailed into court for violation in that very sphere. A doctor who on the strength of his own researches undertakes a hitherto unknown operation, deliberately and from the outset exposes himself to the risk of being charged with wounding or manslaughter. Experience shows that things which appear diametrically opposed to each other in their everyday form come almost to overlap if carried to extremes. Poison and physic thus differ from each other only in the method of their application. The world in general can seldom be relied upon to distinguish between the sublime and the ridiculous. The truly sublime has always been regarded as ridiculous at first, and conversely behaviour felt by all concerned to be sublime has revealed itself from one moment to the next as the greatest absurdity. *Summum jus* and *summa injuria* are concepts which will forever overlap each other till the end of time. The archetype to which our culture has conformed for two thousand years in respect of the facts mentioned in the foregoing train of thought, and which presumably will preserve its validity to all eternity, is the fate of the Founder of our religion, who was sentenced to death by the Sanhedrin in Jerusalem for *blasphemy*. Moreover, as the Gospel account reveals, the Sanhedrin concerned itself with the case only after lengthy hesitation and with extreme reluctance, compelled by a challenge which left them no alternative, that is to say, the parable, uttered in the forecourt of the Holy of Holies, of the destruction of the Temple and the rebuilding of it in no more than three days. It is equally evident from the Gospels that the Sanhedrin discharged its judicial function with a dignity which could not be surpassed by any tribunal of the present day. Nonetheless in such cases to judge will always remain a severer fate than to be judged.

My final reason for mentioning this case, which I describe as archetypal, in connection with the judgments passed on my play is the difference between bourgeois morality which the courts are called upon to uphold, and human morality which transcends all earthly justice. In all three judgments commercial love was condemned out of hand as immoral and its practice designated as obscene. This designation is entirely valid from the point of view of bourgeois morality.

But venerated poets of all ages from King Cudraka (*The Earthen Carriage*) to Goethe (*God and the Dancing-girl*) have felt themselves called upon to defend the unfortunate victims of commercial love against the general ostracism. And Jesus Christ told the priests and judges of his time: 'Verily I say unto you that the publicans and the harlots go into the Kingdom of God before you'. (The Gospel according to St. Matthew, Chapter 21, verse 31.) From his own point of view, Jesus Christ cannot speak more logically or consistently since he builds the Kingdom of Heaven for the weary and the heavily laden, not for the rich; for the sick, not for the healthy; for the sinner, not for the righteous man. This saying, in conjunction with the astonishing authenticity of the legal proceedings against the 'desecrator of the Temple', is to me the most striking refutation of the contemporary Biblical criticism which contends that *Jesus never lived* and that the Gospel story is no more than the pious fabrication of later elders of the Church; for what priest would dare to quote this saying even in the pulpit?

But, I can hear the judge ask, may not our civilisation miserably perish in that the weary, the sick and the sinners find their justification in this morality?

To this question I can think of answers in plenty, enough to allay any anxiety; for if human morality wishes to stand higher than bourgeois then to be sure it must be founded on a profounder knowledge of the nature of the world and of men. But I am not going to take on myself the task of defending the sayings of the Founder of our religion before the tribunal without being invited expressly to do so.

PROLOGUE IN THE BOOKSHOP

Characters

THE NORMAL READER
THE ENTERPRISING PUBLISHER
THE TIMID AUTHOR
THE PUBLIC PROSECUTOR

(The prologue may be spoken by the actors taking the parts of
RODRIGO, CASTI-PIANI, ALWA and SCHIGOLCH, wearing appropriate
outer garments and headgear. RODRIGO in a light-coloured summer
coat and hat of rough felt, CASTI-PIANI in a dressing gown and velvet
cap, ALWA in a grey cape and slouch hat, SCHIGOLCH in robes and
cap. For scenery: A drop-curtain, a primitive book-stall)

THE NORMAL READER. (staggers in)
I'd greatly like to buy a book from you.
What it contains is all the same to me.
That man can't live from drink alone is true.
I want to get it as cheap as can be.
I want it for my eldest daughter in
Commemoration of her first communion.

THE ENTERPRISING PUBLISHER.
Here is a book I warmly recommend
Which makes men's hearts beat high with inspiration
Five million souls now read it to the end,
And every morning there's a new edition.
For everyone it is a lasting gain.
And yet there's not one new thought it contains.

THE TIMID AUTHOR. (slinks in)

I'd like to have you print my book of verse
Ten years out of my life I've set therein.
My strong wish was to embrace the universe
And yet I've scarcely learned to embrace women.
But what I learned of truth in those hard days
I've set down with a sort of clumsy grace.

THE PUBLIC PROSECUTOR. (blusters in)
A book of yours I have to confiscate
Which made each separate hair stand up from me.
The fellow whom one saw was quite without
Shame, exhibits himself now for money.
We'll punish him severely, as the law
Ordains in paragraph one eighty four.

THE TIMID AUTHOR. (with a smile)
Punish me? No. Your cruel chastisement
Can't rob me of creative happiness.
Who will refuse to suffer for his infant?
Your work can never bring you joy like this.
Torture, choke, flay me: hang me, if you will.
You cannot do my words the slightest ill.

THE PUBLIC PROSECUTOR.
Impertinence, let me inform you,
Will gain no victims for damnation now.
I must protect the normal reader from you
Lest, with a grin, you corrupt him to the marrow.
Your sure reward will be two years of jail.
Loss of your civil rights is without fail.

THE NORMAL READER.
I want to buy my book from you at once.
I find that your demeanour's most unseemly.
Were my children baptised at Christian fonts
So that I starve with hunger, thirst consumes me?
Unless you stop your quarrelling, I'll spend
My money on egg-punch, and that's the end.

THE PUBLIC PROSECUTOR. (embraces him, whereupon the
NORMAL READER bursts into tears)
Poor, sorry victim! Sacred modesty
Died murdered in your bosom by this fellow.
If only we could stop his mouth, we'd see

Propriety and piety would grow
Anew. Two years in gaol! I'll take a bet
That they will put an end to his sharp wit.

THE TIMID AUTHOR.
Why should the thought of Law Courts frighten me?
They might be useful too, serve as detector
Of weak spots in my play, as truly
As genuine art must be its own protector.
Everyone must certainly acquit
Me of all blame. I am quite sure of it.

THE PUBLIC PROSECUTOR.
Were you acquitted – from which God preserve us –
On the self-same day I'd lodge an appeal.
Not every judge is so wise as to serve us
But the next one would carry wisdom's seal.
And even if he let you get away
He'd certainly suppress your wicked play.

THE TIMID AUTHOR.
Then I would have it published once again
In a more serious and nobler book
Not in thieves' Latin for the philistine
But in clear German without holding back.
I'm sure of it; and that it must succeed
In winning through by merit of its deed.

THE PUBLIC PROSECUTOR.
Good heavens! Then this world lacks nothing but
That this piece should be put on the stage.
Then let it be so scrubbed and cleaned up that
It doesn't advertise you as the rage.
This poisonous devilish work of yours will only
Reach the theatre over my dead body.

THE TIMID AUTHOR.
What do I care about the stage? Our daring
Realism never reaches there.
The human brain be stage of my appearing
Imagination my favoured producer.

(To the PUBLIC PROSECUTOR)

And your job will be nothing less than this:
To write the Prologue which precedes the piece.

THE ENTERPRISING PUBLISHER. (pushing his way between them)
   The prologue's splendid. Printed in a daily
   It is as good as on the stage already,
   I'll back its circulation eagerly,
   Send advance notices to everybody,
   And even before the public take their places
   I know I won't be left with any copies.

THE NORMAL READER. (likewise pushing to the front)
   Then I shall plant myself in the front row
   With complimentary ticket and loud snore.
   You've no idea how much I love to go
   And hear some chap mouth Schnitzler or Shakespeare.
   Won't it suffice to give my Christian pardon
   Although my horror is observed by no one?

<u>CHORUS</u>

THE PUBLIC PROSECUTOR. (keeping his arm round the
NORMAL READER's shoulder)
   Let us both unitedly encourage
   Promotion of dramatic poeticising.

THE NORMAL READER.
   I prefer filling up my stomach
   But don't think I don't like grand-passionising.

THE ENTERPRISING PUBLISHER. (keeping his arm round the
TIMID AUTHOR's shoulder)
   I'm glad when others are, especially
   Over what strikes them most sensationally.

THE TIMID AUTHOR.
   If need be, I will sacrifice my liberty
   O Muse, O mistress of my soul, for thee.

ACT ONE

(Magnificent drawing-room in German renaissance style with heavy
ceiling in carved oak. Dark wood-carvings half-way up the walls. Above
them on each side of the stage faded tapestries. The upper half of the
room backstage is shut off by a gallery hung with drapery from which a
massive staircase descends on the left to half way downstage. In the
centre, beneath the gallery is the entrance door with spiral columns and
a pediment. On the right-hand side wall a high, spacious chimney-piece.
Further downstage a French window with heavy drawn curtains. On the
left-hand side wall below the foot of the stairs a closed portière.
Standing near the foot of the stairs is an empty ornamental easel.
Downstage left a deep sofa, in the centre of the stage a rectangular table,
around which stand three upholstered chairs with high backs.
Downstage left a small serving-table and next to it a reclining-chair. The
room is softly lit by a shaded oil lamp standing on the centre table.
ALWA SCHÖN is walking up and down in front of the door. On the sofa
sits RODRIGO dressed as a footman. In the reclining-chair sits
COUNTESS GESCHWITZ in a black close-fitting frock, deep in the
cushions with a rug over her knees. Close by her on the table a coffee-
machine and a cup of black coffee)

RODRIGO. He keeps one waiting as if he were a maestro!

GESCHWITZ. I beg you not to talk!

RODRIGO. How can a fellow keep his trap shut with his head as full of
ideas as mine is! What I simply can't make out is how she can have
been changed for the better by it!

GESCHWITZ. She's more exquisite to look at than I've ever seen her!

RODRIGO. Heaven forbid that I should base my life's happiness on your
standards of beauty. If the illness has agreed with her as little as it

has with you, I may as well shut up shop. You've come out of hospital looking like a fat lady at the circus who's been on a hunger-strike. You've hardly the strength left to blow your nose. You take a quarter of an hour to get your fingers sorted out and even then you have to take the greatest care that the tips don't break off.

GESCHWITZ. What puts *us* underground restores her to health and vigour.

RODRIGO. That's all very fine and large. All the same, I dare say I won't go this evening.

GESCHWITZ. You mean to say that in the end you'll let your bride travel alone?

RODRIGO. For one thing the old man is going too, to defend her if the worst comes to the worst. My company would only throw suspicion on her. For another I must stay here till my costumes are ready. – I shall still manage to get over the border in time. Let's hope she puts on a bit of flesh in the meanwhile. Then there'll be the wedding, provided I can produce her before a decent audience. I like women to be useful; I don't care what theories they choose to make up themselves. Don't you agree, Dr. Schön?

ALWA. I didn't hear what you said.

RODRIGO. I'd never have got myself involved in this plot if she hadn't made advances to me even before she went to prison. I only hope she doesn't start over-exercising again as soon as she gets abroad. The best thing would be to take her with me to London for six months and feed her on plum cake. In London the sea air alone makes one swell up. Besides, in London one doesn't feel the hand of fate at one's throat with every mouthful of beer one takes.

ALWA. I've been wondering for the past week whether someone who's been sentenced to penal servitude would be a suitable central figure for a modern drama.

GESCHWITZ. If only the fellow would come!

RODRIGO. And I've still got to get my props out of pawn; six hundred kilos of the best iron. Their transport always costs me three times as much as my own ticket. What's more, the whole outfit isn't worth a trouser-button. And when I reached the pawn-shop dripping with sweat they asked me if the things were real – actually I'd have done better to have had my costumes made abroad. The Parisian for instance spots one's good points at the first glance. And cuts bravely away accordingly. But you can't learn that by sitting back and crossing your legs, one has to study with men of classical education. Here they're as afraid of bare skin as foreigners are of bombs. Two years ago I was fined fifty marks at the Alhambra Theatre for letting people see I had a few hairs on my chest, not enough to make a decent tooth-brush. But the Minister of Culture thought it might make the little schoolgirls lose interest in their knitting. I've had myself shaved once a month ever since.

ALWA. If I didn't need the whole of my intellectual energy for *Ruler of the World* I'd like to test the drawing-power of the problem. That's the curse that weighs on literature today, that it's much too literary. We know nothing about any problems save those that arise among artists and scholars. Our horizon doesn't extend beyond the interests of our profession. To bring about a rebirth of a genuine vigorous art we should go as much as possible among men who have never read a book in their lives, whose actions are dictated by the simplest animal instincts. In my play *Earth-Spirit* I did my utmost to work on these principles. The woman whom I took as model for the central figure has been living and breathing for a full year behind bars. At the same time one must admit that oddly enough the play reached production only through enlightened literary society. As long as my father was alive my plays were welcomed on every stage in Germany. All that is mightily changed.

RODRIGO. I've had tights made in the most delicate shade of grey green. If they aren't a success abroad I'll take to selling mousetraps. The trunks are so scanty that I daren't sit on the edge of a table with them. The flattering effect is spoilt only by the terrible paunch for which I have to thank my active participation in this grand conspiracy. To lie in hospital for three months in perfect health would make a fat hog out of the most broken-down tramp. Since I came out I've done nothing but swallow Carlsbad pastilles. Night and day there's an orchestra rehearsing in my guts. By the time I get across the border I'll be so flushed out that I won't be able to lift as much as a cork.

GESCHWITZ. The way the warders avoided her yesterday was a joy to see. The garden was deserted. For all the glorious midday sun the convalescents didn't dare venture out of doors. Right at the back by the isolation wing she appeared from behind the mulberry trees and did exercises on the gravel. The porter had recognised me, and a house physician who met me in the corridor jumped as if a bullet had struck him. The nursing sisters flitted about in the wards or kept close to the walls. When I came back there wasn't a soul to be seen either in the garden or under the porch. The moment couldn't have been more propitious, if only we'd had those wretched passports. And now the fellow says he isn't going!

RODRIGO. I can understand those poor hospital boys. One has a sore foot, the next a swollen cheek; and then a veritable death-insurance agent appears in their midst. When I spread the news that Sister Theophila had departed this life, in the Hall of the Knights as they call the blessed ward from which I conducted my investigations, you couldn't keep the fellows in their beds. They swarmed up the window bars, carrying their ailments with them by the hundred-weight. I've never heard such language in all my life.

ALWA. Countess Geschwitz, permit me to recur for a moment to my former suggestion. The woman shot my father in this very room. Nevertheless I can't see the murder or the punishment of it as anything but a shocking misfortune which has overtaken her. I even believe that my father, had he lived, would not entirely have withdrawn his support from her. I still doubt whether your plan for her escape will succeed, though I won't wish to discourage you. But I can't find words for the admiration which your self-sacrifice, your pluck, your super-human contempt for death arouse in me. I don't believe any man ever risked as much for a woman, let alone for another man. I don't know how well-off you are, Countess, but the expense involved in putting this plan into effect must have disorganised your finances. May I offer you a loan of twenty thousand marks, the realisation of which in ready money would be a simple matter for me?

GESCHWITZ. How we exulted when the nurses told us Sister Theophila was safely *dead*! From that day forward we were without supervision. We changed beds whenever we wanted to. I did her hair like mine and imitated every inflection of her voice. When the specialist came he addressed her as 'Countess', and said to me: 'It's a better life here than in prison!' When the nurse suddenly disappeared we looked at each other in suspense; we were both ill for five days; now must come the crisis. Next morning the house physician visited us. – 'How is Sister Theophila?' 'Dead'. We signalled to each other behind his back and when he went we fell on each other's necks. 'Thank God! Thank God!' – What a strain it was for my darling not to betray how well she already was. 'You have nine years in prison ahead of you', I kept telling her from morning till night. They won't leave her more than another three days in the isolation hospital.

RODRIGO. I lay in hospital a full three months to spy out the land, having first laboriously acquired the qualities necessary for such a prolonged stay. Now I'm playing the man-servant here, Dr. Schön, so that no strange servants shall come into the house. When has a bridegroom ever done more for his bride? My finances are disorganised too.

ALWA. If you succeed in making a respectable artist of this woman you'll have done a service to the world at large. With the temperament and beauty which are hers to give from the depths of her being she can keep the most jaded audience on the edge of their seats. And in simulating passion she will be protected from becoming a criminal in reality for the second time.

RODRIGO. I'll teach her not to play tricks!

GESCHWITZ. Here he comes!

Steps are heard in the gallery. Then the curtains above the stairs are parted and SCHIGOLCH emerges in a long black frock-coat, a white umbrella in his right hand. During all three acts his speech is interrupted by frequent yawning)

SCHIGOLCH. Confound this gloom! Outside the sun burns one's eyes out.

GESCHWITZ. (painfully disentangling herself from the rug) I'm just coming!

RODRIGO. Your ladyship hasn't seen a gleam of daylight for three days. It's like living in a snuff-box here.

SCHIGOLCH. I've been making the rounds of all the rag-pickers since nine o'clock this morning. I've sent off three brand-new trunks stuffed full of old pairs of trousers to Buenos Aires via Bremerhaven. My legs are dangling from my body like hell-clappers. But from now on it's all going to be quite different.

RODRIGO. Where do you mean to put up tomorrow morning?

SCHIGOLCH. Let's hope it's not at Government expense, wherever it is.

RODRIGO. I can recommend an excellent hotel. I lived there once with a female lion-tamer. The proprietors are Berliners.

GESCHWITZ. (raising herself in her chair) Could you please give me a hand?

RODRIGO. (hastens to her side and supports her) And what's more, you're safer there from the police than if you were on the high wire.

GESCHWITZ. The truth is, he wants you to leave alone with her this afternoon.

SCHIGOLCH. I suppose his chilblains are troubling him!

RODRIGO. Do you expect me to make my debut in my new role in dressing-gown and slippers?

SCHIGOLCH. Hm. Sister Theophila wouldn't have gone to Heaven so promptly if she hadn't taken such a loving interest in our patient.

RODRIGO. If anyone is going to live through a honeymoon with her she'll show herself to quite different advantage. Anyhow it won't do her any harm to air herself a little first.

ALWA. (holding a brief-case in his hand, to GESCHWITZ, who stands at the centre table supporting herself on the arm of a chair) There are ten thousand marks in this case.

GESCHWITZ. Thank you. No.

ALWA. I beg you to take them.

GESCHWITZ. (to SCHIGOLCH) Are you ever coming?

SCHIGOLCH. Be patient, Miss. It's only a stone's throw across Hospital Street. I'll have her here in five minutes.

ALWA. You're bringing her here?

SCHIGOLCH. I'm bringing her here – unless you fear for your health.

ALWA. Can't you see I'm not afraid of anything?

RODRIGO. According to the latest despatches, Dr. Schön is on the way to Constantinople to have his *Earth-Spirit* performed before the sultan by concubines and eunuchs.

ALWA. (opening the door beneath the balcony) This is the quickest way. (SCHIGOLCH and COUNTESS GESCHWITZ leave the room. ALWA locks the door behind them)

RODRIGO. So you even wanted to give that crazy female money?

ALWA. What business is that of yours?

RODRIGO. I'm paid no more than a lamp-cleaner, though I had to bribe every single nurse in the hospital. And then it was the house physicians' turn, and then the honoraries. And then ...

ALWA. Do you seriously expect me to believe the doctors let themselves be corrupted by you?

RODRIGO. In America I could make myself President of the United States with the money those gentlemen cost me.

ALWA. But Countess Geschwitz paid you back every penny you spent. To the best of my knowledge you also receive a monthly allowance of five hundred marks from her. It's sometimes rather difficult to believe in your love for the unfortunate murderess. If I did ask Countess Geschwitz just now to accept my help, I certainly didn't do so in order to stimulate your insatiable lust for money. I am far from entertaining for you the admiration which this affair has taught me to feel for the Countess. Although I'm not quite clear what claims you think you have on me. The fact that you happened to witness my father's murder has by no means forged any ties between us. On the contrary, I am firmly convinced that if this heroic enterprise of Countess Geschwitz' had not turned up for you, you'd be lying drunk in the gutter somewhere without a penny.

RODRIGO. And do you know what would have become of *you* if you hadn't disposed of that wretched little paper your father edited, for two million? – You'd have joined up with the seediest ballet-girl you could find and today you'd be a stable-boy in Humpelmeier's Circus. What work do you do? You wrote a melodrama in which my fiancée's legs were the two main figures and which no respectable theatre will put on. You poor fish! You miserable worm! Two years ago I was balancing two saddled cavalry horses on this chest of mine. I must say it remains to be seen how I'll get on with such a paunch on me. The ladies abroad will get a fine idea of German artistry when they see the beads of sweat oozing through my tights with every kilo more I lift. I'll pollute the whole auditorium with my exhalations.

ALWA. You're a weakling.

RODRIGO. I wish to God you were right! Or did you by any chance mean to insult me? If so I'll apply my toe to the point of your jaw so that your tongue will crawl on the wall-paper over there.

ALWA. Why don't you try it?

(Voices and footsteps are audible outside)

Who's that?

RODRIGO. You can thank God I've no audience in front of me.

ALWA. Who can it be?

RODRIGO. It is my beloved! We have not seen each other for a whole year.

ALWA. How could they be back so soon! Who can have come? I'm not expecting anyone.

RODRIGO. Damn it, aren't you going to open the door?

ALWA. Hide yourself!

RODRIGO. I'll get behind the portières. I stood there once before, a year ago.

(RODRIGO disappears behind the portières downstage left. ALWA opens the centre door, whereupon ALFRED HUGENBERG enters, hat in hand)

ALWA. With whom have I ... You? – Aren't you ...?

HUGENBERG. Alfred Hugenberg.

ALWA. What do you want?

HUGENBERG. I come from Münsterburg. I ran away this morning.

ALWA. My eyes are troubling me. I'm obliged to keep the blinds closed.

HUGENBERG. I need your help. I'm sure you won't refuse me. I've prepared a plan. – Can we be overheard?

ALWA. What are you talking about? What plan?

HUGENBERG. Are you alone?

ALWA. Yes. What is it you want to tell me?

HUGENBERG. I've abandoned two plans already. What I'm about to tell you I've examined against every possible contingency. If I had any money I wouldn't take you into my confidence. I thought about it a long time first, as it is ... Wouldn't you like me to explain my plan to you?

ALWA. I'd like you to explain what you're talking about.

HUGENBERG. You surely can't care so little about the woman that I have to tell you that. The evidence *you* gave before the examining magistrate helped her more than anything her counsel said.

ALWA. I deprecate any such suggestion.

HUGENBERG. You would have to say that, naturally; I understand. All the same, you were the best witness for the defence.

ALWA. So that's who you are! You said my father tried to force her to shoot herself.

HUGENBERG. And so he did. But nobody believed me. I wasn't sworn.

ALWA. Where have you come from?

HUGENBERG. From a reformatory; I broke out of it this morning.

ALWA. What do you mean to do?

HUGENBERG. I'm going to try to win the confidence of one of the turnkeys.

ALWA. What do you propose to live on?

HUGENBERG. I'm lodging with a girl who's had a child by my father.

ALWA. Who is your father?

HUGENBERG. He's a police-inspector. I know that prison though I was never inside it; none of the warders will recognise me as I am now. Not that I'm relying on that. I know of an iron ladder by which one can get from the first court-yard onto the roof and through a skylight into the loft. There's no way of getting there from inside. But in all five wings there are planks and boards lying under the roof, and huge piles of wood-shavings. I shall drag the boards and planks from all five wings together into one place and set fire to them. I've got my pockets full of inflammable material such as incendiaries use.

ALWA. But then you'll burn to death!

HUGENBERG. Of course, unless I'm rescued. But to get into the first court I must have the warder on my side, and for that I need money. Not that I want to bribe him. I shouldn't succeed. I must lend him the money beforehand, so that he can send his three children for a holiday in the country. Then at four o'clock in the morning, when they release prisoners from respectable families, I'll slip inside the door. He'll lock up behind me and ask me what I'm after. I'll ask him to let me out again in the evening. And before daybreak I'll be in the loft.

ALWA. How did you escape from the reformatory?

HUGENBERG. Jumped out of a window. I need two hundred marks so that the fellow can send his family for a holiday in the country.

RODRIGO. (stepping out from behind the portières) Will his lordship have coffee served in the music-room or on the verandah?

HUGENBERG. Where did this man come from? From the same door! He leapt out of the same door!

ALWA. I've taken him into service here. He's quite dependable.

HUGENBERG. (clutching his temples) Fool that I am! Fool that I am!

RODRIGO. Yes, yes, we've seen each other here before. Be off with you to your adopted mamma. Your little brother would like to be an uncle to his brothers and sisters. Make your father a grandfather to his own children. You're the last straw. If you cross my path again in the next fortnight I'll beat your brains to a jelly.

ALWA. Be quiet.

HUGENBERG. Fool that I am!

RODRIGO. What do you think you're up to with this inflammable material of yours? Don't you know the woman's been dead for three weeks?

HUGENBERG. Did they cut off her head?

RODRIGO. No, she's till got *that*. She pegged out from cholera.

HUGENBERG. That's not true!

RODRIGO. What do you know about it? Here, read this! (Pulls out a newspaper and points to a paragraph in it) The murderess of Dr. Schön ... (Hands the paper to HUGENBERG)

HUGENBERG. (reading) 'The murderess of Dr. Schön has mysteriously contracted cholera in prison'. It doesn't say she died.

RODRIGO. What else should she have done? She's been lying in the graveyard for three weeks. In the far left-hand corner behind the rubbish dump where the little crosses are with no names on them – there she lies under the first of them. You'll recognise the place because there's no grass growing there. Hang a tin wreath on it, and then see that you get back to your nursery school or I'll hand you over to the police. I know the female who uses you to sweeten her leisure hours!

HUGENBERG. (to ALWA) Is it true that she's dead?

ALWA. Thank God, yes! I must ask you not to take any more of my time. My doctor has forbidden me to have visitors.

HUGENBERG. My future is of so little value. I'd gladly have sacrificed what little it's still worth for her happiness. Oh, well – I suppose now I'll go to the devil one way or another.

RODRIGO. If you dare to bother me or Dr. Schön or my honoured friend Schigolch in any way I'll report you for attempted arson. Three years' penal servitude is just what you need to teach you not to meddle with things that don't concern you. And now get out!

HUGENBERG. What a fool I am!

RODRIGO. Get out!! (Throws HUGENBERG out of the door. Comes downstage) I'm surprised you didn't put your money-bags at that lout's disposal as well.

ALWA. Please spare me your vulgarities. The boy has more in his little finger than you have in your whole body!

RODRIGO. I've had enough of this Geschwitz woman. If my future wife is going to be a limited liability company someone else can have the leading part. I propose to make a magnificent trapeze artist out of her, and I don't mind risking my life for it. But in that case I shall expect to be master in my own house and have some say in what cavaliers she's to receive.

ALWA. The boy has something our generation lacks. He has the heroic spirit. And of course it will be his undoing. Do you remember how before sentence was passed, he leapt up from the witness bench and called out to the judge 'How can you tell what would have become of you if as a ten-year-old child you'd had to knock about barefoot at night in cafés?!

RODRIGO. I wish I could have dotted him one on the jaw for it then and there! Thank God there are prisons capable of instilling respect for the law into ruffians like that.

ALWA. He is the sort that could be a model for me in my *Ruler of the World*. Literature has produced nothing but half-men for the past twenty years. Men who can't beget children and women who can't bear any. It's what's known as 'The Modern Problem'.

RODRIGO. I've ordered a rhinoceros-hide whip two inches thick. If that doesn't do the trick with her then I've got potato soup where my brains ought to be. Beating or love-making, it's all one to a woman. Keep her amused and she remains firms and fresh. This one is twenty years old, has been three times married, has given satisfaction to an incredible number of lovers, and now at last she's showing signs of having a heart herself. But the fellow will have to have the seven deadly sins written on his forehead or she'll have no respect for him. Let a man look as if he'd been spat out onto the street by a dog-catcher and he need have nothing to fear even from princes, with females like this. I shall rent a garage fifty feet high and there I'll train her and if she brings off her first 'salto' without breaking her neck I'll put on my black frock coat and won't lift another finger for the rest of my life. With her practical turn of mind it's not half as much of an effort for a woman to support her husband as the other way about. So long as the man takes care of the intellectual side and sees that the sense of family doesn't entirely go down the drain.

ALWA. I've learnt to control humanity and drive it four-in-hand – but I can't get that young man out of my head. I really think I could take lessons in cynicism from that schoolboy.

RODRIGO. She can dress herself in thousand-mark notes if she feels like it. I shall extract her wages from the managers with a centrifugal pump. I know that crowd. If they don't need you, you can black their boots; and when they do need an artiste they'll cut her down from the very gallows with their own hands and the most effusive compliments.

ALWA. As far as material things are concerned I have nothing in the world to fear but death – in the realm of feeling I am the neediest beggar! But I can no longer summon the moral courage necessary to exchange my consolidated position for the thrills of a life of adventure.

RODRIGO. She had sent Papa Schigolch and me out on the prowl together to ferret her out some really efficacious cure for insomnia. We each got twenty marks for travelling expenses. And then we see this boy sitting in the 'Lantern' café. He was sitting there like a criminal in the dock. Schigolch sniffed him up and down and said 'He's still a virgin'.

(Up in the gallery dragging footsteps are heard)

Here she is! – The future most magnificent trapeze artist of our time!

(The curtains over the stairs are parted and LULU, in a black frock and supporting herself on SCHIGOLCH's arm, comes slowly downstairs)

SCHIGOLCH. Gee up, old mare! We've still got to get across the border today.

RODRIGO. (staring stupidly at LULU) Great God in heaven!

LULU. (speaks till the end of the act in the most cheerful tone) Gently! You're squeezing my arm!

RODRIGO. Where did you get the nerve to break out of gaol with a wolfish face like that?

SCHIGOLCH. Shut up!

RODRIGO. I shall go straight to the police! I'll denounce you! This scarecrow here wants to show herself in tights. The padding alone would cost two months' pay. You're the biggest imposter that ever spent a night in jug!

ALWA. I must ask you not to be rude to her.

RODRIGO. Rude, you call it? Was it for this bag of gnawed bones that I've eaten myself into my present bloated condition? I'm unemployable! They can make a clown of me if I'm able to lift as much as a broomstick! But may I be struck by lightning on the spot if I don't rake myself in an annuity of ten thousand marks from your swindling. I can tell you that! I wish you a pleasant journey! I'm off to the police. (Exit)

SCHIGOLCH. Get on with you, then!

LULU. He wouldn't dream of it!

SCHIGOLCH. We're well rid of him. – And now, black coffee for the lady!

ALWA. (at the table downstage left) The coffee is here. Help yourselves.

SCHIGOLCH. I've still got to get the sleeping-car tickets.

LULU. (in a loud voice) Oh, freedom! God in heaven!

SCHIGOLCH. I'll come for you in half an hour. We'll celebrate our departure in the station restaurant. I'll order a supper that'll see us through till tomorrow morning. Good day, Dr. Schön!

ALWA. Good evening!

SCHIGOLCH. Sleep well! Thank you, I know every door handle in the place. Good-bye, have a nice time! (Exit by the centre door)

LULU. I haven't seen a room for eighteen months – curtains, armchairs, pictures . . .

ALWA. Don't you want something to drink?

LULU. I've swallowed black coffee enough in the last five days. Haven't you any brandy?

ALWA. I've got Elixir de Spa.

LULU. That brings back old times. (While ALWA fills two glasses she looks round the room) Where has my picture got to?

ALWA. I've got it in my room, so that no one shall see it here.

LULU. Do go and get it.

ALWA. Didn't you lose your vanity even in prison?

LULU. One feels so frightened when one hasn't seen oneself for months. Then one day I got a brand-new dust-pan. When I swept up at seven o'clock in the morning I used to hold the underside up to my face. The tin didn't flatter me, but it did me good all the same. Fetch the picture from your room. Shall I come too?

ALWA. For heaven's sake! You must take care of yourself.

LULU. I've taken care of myself long enough.

(ALWA goes out of the door left, to fetch the picture)

He has a weak heart; but to torture himself for fourteen months with that illusion ... he kisses one in mortal fear, his knees shake like a tramp suffering from exposure. In God's name! – If only I hadn't shot his father in the back in this very room!

ALWA. (comes back with the portrait of LULU in Pierrot costume) It's covered with dust. I had it leaning face-down against the chimney-piece.

LULU. Haven't you looked at it while I was away?

ALWA. I had so many business matters to attend to in connection with the sale of the paper. Geschwitz would have liked to hang it in her house, but she knew the police might search it. (He lifts the picture onto the easel)

LULU. Now the poor monster is getting to know the joys of Government hospitality at first hand.

ALWA. I still don't understand how all these events came about.

LULU. Oh, Geschwitz arranged it very cleverly; I admire her resourcefulness. Apparently there was a raging epidemic of cholera in Hamburg this summer. And around that she formed her plan for my escape. She took a nurse's training course here and when she had the necessary certificates she went to Hamburg and nursed the cholera victims. With the first opportunity that offered she put on the underclothing which belonged to a patient who had just died and which really ought to have been burnt. The very same morning she came back here and visited me in prison. And in my cell, while the wardress was outside, we exchanged underclothes.

ALWA. So that was the reason why you and Geschwitz both fell ill of cholera on the same day?

LULU. Of course. That was the reason. Naturally Geschwitz was immediately taken from her house to the isolation wing of the hospital. And they couldn't find anywhere else to put me, either. So we lay in the same room in the isolation wing behind the hospital and from the very first day Geschwitz employed all her arts to make our faces as alike as possible. Day before yesterday she was discharged as cured. Just now she came back and said she'd forgotten her watch. I put on her clothes, she slipped into my prison overall, and then I came away. (With amusement) So now she's lying there as the murderess of Dr. Schön.

ALWA. As far as outward appearances are concerned, you can still stand comparison with the picture.

LULU. I'm a little thin in the face, but otherwise I've lost nothing. Only one gets incredibly nervous in prison.

ALWA. You looked terribly ill when you came in.

LULU. I had to, to get rid of that clown. – And you, what have you been doing in the past year and a half?

ALWA. I had a succès d'estime in literary society with a piece I wrote around you.

LULU. Who's your sweetheart now?

ALWA. An actress – I've taken an apartment for her in Charles Street.

LULU. Does she love you?

ALWA. How should I know! I haven't seen the woman for six weeks.

LULU. Can you stand that?

ALWA. It's something you'll never understand. With me there's a close reciprocal action between sensuality and intellectual creation. So that, for example, where you are concerned, I have only two alternatives, to exploit you creatively or to love you.

LULU. (as if telling a fairy-story) Every few nights I used to dream that I'd fallen into the hands of a sex-maniac. Come on, give me a kiss!

ALWA. Your eyes shimmer like the surface of a deep pool into which a stone has been thrown.

LULU. Come on!

ALWA. (kisses her) Your lips have got rather thin, I must admit.

LULU. Come on! (She pushes him into a chair and seats herself on his knee) Do I repel you? – In gaol we had a lukewarm bath once every four weeks. As soon as we were in the water the wardress took the opportunity to go through our pockets. (She kisses him passionately)

ALWA. Oh! Oh!

LULU. I suppose now you're afraid you won't be able to write a poem about me when I'm gone.

ALWA. On the contrary, I shall write a dithyramb to your glory.

LULU. The only thing that annoys me is the ghastly footgear I'm wearing.

ALWA. It doesn't detract from your charm. Let us be thankful for what the moment has to offer.

LULU. I don't feel in that sort of mood today at all. – Do you remember the fancy-dress ball when I was dressed like a page? And how the tipsy women all ran after me? Geschwitz crawled round at my feet and begged me to kick her in the face with my cloth shoes.

ALWA. Come, my darling!

LULU. (in the tone with which one calms a troublesome child) Quiet; I
   shot your father.

ALWA. I don't love you any the less for that. One kiss!

LULU. Lean your head back. (She kisses him with deliberation)

ALWA. You keep my ardour in check with expert skill. And your bosom
   breathes so chastely. Yet were it not for your big brown childlike
   eyes, I should be forced to regard you as the most designing bitch
   that ever brought a man to ruin.

LULU. I only wish I were! Come with me over the border today. Then .
   we can see each other as often as we wish, and will have more
   pleasure from each other than we can now.

ALWA. Through this dress your form is like a symphony to my fingers.
   These slender ankles – cantabile; the enchanting roundness of your
   calves, and these knees – capriccio; and the powerful andante of
   voluptuousness. – How peaceably the two slender rivals nestle
   against each other in the knowledge that neither equals the other in
   beauty – till their wayward mistress wakes and the rivals move apart
   like hostile poles. I'll sing your praises till your senses reel!

LULU. (gaily) Meanwhile I shall bury my hands in your hair. (Does so)
   But here we can be disturbed.

ALWA. You've robbed me of my reason!

LULU. Won't you come today?

ALWA. But the old man is going with you!

LULU. We've seen the last of him. – Isn't that the very sofa on which
   your father bled to death?

ALWA. Be quiet ... be quiet ...

ACT TWO

(A spacious drawing-room in white gesso with a wide double-door in the back wall. On either side of it tall mirrors. In each of the side walls two doors. Between them on the left a rococo console with white marble top, above it LULU's picture as Pierrot let into the wall in a narrow gold frame. In the middle of the room a fragile Louis XV sofa in light-coloured upholstery. Wide armchairs in light-coloured upholstery with slender legs and fragile arms. Downstage, right, a small table. Backstage, left, the entrance door. The nearer door leads into the dining-room. The centre door is open and discloses a large baccarat-table in the room beyond, with Turkish upholstered chairs around it. ALWA SCHÖN, RODRIGO QUAST, MARQUIS CASTI-PIANI, BANKER PUNTSCHU, JOURNALIST HEILMANN, LULU, COUNTESS GESCHWITZ, MAGELONE, KADIDJA, BIANETTA, and LUDMILLA STEINHERZ move about the room in lively conversation.

The men are in evening dress. LULU wears a white Directoire gown with enormous sleeves and white lace falling from her waist to her feet, her arms in white kid gloves, her hair dressed high with a small plume of white feathers. GESCHWITZ wears a pale blue hussar's jacket edged with fur, with facings of silver braid, a white bow-tie, close-fitting stand-up collar and stiff cuffs with enormous ivory links – MAGELONE in a rainbow-coloured dress of shot silk with very full sleeves, long tight bodice and on the skirt three spiral flounces of pink ribbon and bunches of violets. Her hair is parted in the middle, looped low over her temples and curled at the sides. In the centre of her forehead she wears a mother-of-pearl ornament held in place by a fine chain drawn through her hair. – KADIDJA, her daughter, twelve years old, in pale green satin boots which reveal the tops of her white silk socks; a bodice of white lace, pale green, close-fitting sleeves, pearl-grey kid gloves, her black hair loose under a large pale green lace hat with white feathers. – BIANETTA in dark green velvet, a wide collar sewn with pearls, bloused sleeves, full skirt without a waist, the hem, studded with imitation topazes set in silver. – LUDMILLA STEINHERZ in a garish, red and white-striped frock such as one might wear at the seaside)

RODRIGO. (a full glass in his hand) Ladies and Gentlemen – pardon me – please be quiet – I drink – permit me to drink – for it is the birthday of our gracious hostess (Taking LULU by the arm) Countess Adelaide d'Oubra – damn and blast! – I drink therefore ... and so on and so on, ladies.

(They all crowd round LULU and clink glasses with her)

ALWA. (to RODRIGO, pressing his hand) Congratulations.

RODRIGO. I'm sweating like a pig.

ALWA. (to LULU) Let's see if everything's in order in the gaming-room. (Exeunt into gaming-room)

BIANETTA. (to RODRIGO) They've just been telling me you're the strongest man in the world.

RODRIGO. And so I am, Miss. Permit me to put my strength at your disposal.

MAGELONE. Personally I prefer sharp-shooters. Three months ago a sharp-shooter appeared at the Casino and every time he went 'Bang!' I went like this! (She wriggles her hips)

CASTI-PIANI. (speaks throughout the Act in a bored, languid tone. To MAGELONE) Tell me, my sweet, how is it that we're seeing your enchanting little daughter here for the first time?

MAGELONE. Do you really think she's enchanting? She's still at her convent. She goes back to school next Monday.

KADIDJA. What did you say, Mamma?

MAGELONE. I was just telling the gentleman that you were top in geometry last week.

JOURNALIST HEILMANN. What pretty hair she has!

CASTI-PIANI. Look at her feet! And the way she walks.

PUNTSCHU. She has breeding, by God!

MAGELONE. Have a heart, gentlemen! She's no more than a child still!

PUNTSCHU. (to MAGELONE) That would trouble me damn little! I'd give ten years of my life to be able to initiate the little lady into the ceremonies of our secret cult!

MAGELONE. You couldn't buy my consent to that with all the money in the world. I won't have the child's youth corrupted as mine was.

CASTI-PIANI. The confessions of a beautiful soul. (To MAGELONE) Wouldn't you even give your consent in return for a *garniture* of real diamonds?

MAGELONE. Don't brag! You know better than anybody else that you're no more likely to give diamonds to my daughter than you are to give them to me.

(KADIDJA goes into the gaming-room)

GESCHWITZ. Isn't anyone going to play this evening?

LUDMILLA STEINHERZ. But of course, Comtesse! I'm absolutely counting on it as a matter of fact.

BIANETTA. Then let's go and take our places at once. The men will come after us soon enough.

GESCHWITZ. I must ask you to excuse me for a moment – I have something to say to my friend.

CASTI-PIANI. (offering BIANETTA his arm) May I have the honour of going fifty-fifty with you? You have such a lucky hand!

LUDMILLA STEINHERZ. And now give your other arm to me and lead us into the gambling-hell.

(Exit CASTI-PIANI into gaming-room with the two women)

MAGELONE. Tell me, Mr. Puntschu, have you any more Jungfrau shares for me?

PUNTSCHU. Jungfrau shares? (To HEILMANN) The lady means shares in the cable-railway up the Jungfrau. The Jungfrau, you understand, is the mountain on which they wish to build a cable-railway. (To MAGELONE) I say this simply to avoid misunderstanding, which might so easily arise in this select company. – Certainly, I still have about four thousand Jungfrau shares, but I would like to keep them for myself. The opportunity may not so quickly come again, to make oneself a small fortune just by the way.

HEILMANN. So far I have only one single one of these Jungfrau shares. But I'd be glad to have more.

PUNTSCHU. I'll do my best to procure you a few, Mr. Heilmann. But I can tell you this much already – you'll have to pay a stiff price for them.

MAGELONE. My fortune-teller forewarned me, so that I was on the look-out for them in good time. All my savings are in Jungfrau shares now. If the thing doesn't come off, Mr. Puntschu, I'll scratch your eyes out!

PUNTSCHU. I know what I am about perfectly, dear lady.

ALWA. (who has returned from the gaming-room, to MAGELONE) I can guarantee that your apprehensions are wholly unfounded. I paid very dear for my Jungfrau shares and haven't regretted it for a moment. They go up every day. There's never been anything like it.

MAGELONE. So much the better, if you're right. (Taking PUNTSCHU's arm) Come, my friend! Now let's try our luck at baccarat.

(MAGELONE, PUNTSCHU, ALWA, HEILMANN go into gaming-room. RODRIGO and COUNTESS GESCHWITZ remain behind)

RODRIGO. (scribbles something on a piece of paper and folds it up. Notices GESCHWITZ) Ah, her ladyship. (As GESCHWITZ gives a start) Do I really look as dangerous as that? (Aside) I must produce some sort of *bon mot*. (Aloud) If I may make so bold?

GESCHWITZ. Go to hell!

CASTI-PIANI. (escorting LULU into the room) Will you permit me a word or two?

LULU. (while RODRIGO surreptitiously passes her his scrap of paper) Please, as many as you wish.

RODRIGO. I have the honour to excuse myself. (Exit into gaming-room)

CASTI-PIANI. (to GESCHWITZ) Leave us alone!

LULU. (to CASTI-PIANI) Have I somehow offended you again?

CASTI-PIANI. (since GESCHWITZ does not stir) Are you deaf?

(Exit GESCHWITZ into gaming-room with a deep sigh)

LULU. Tell me at once, how much do you want?

CASTI-PIANI. You no longer have any money to give me.

LULU. Where do you get the idea that we have no money left?

CASTI-PIANI. You handed over your last penny to me yesterday.

LULU. If you're so certain, I suppose it must be so.

CASTI-PIANI. You're high and dry, you and this writer of yours.

LULU. Why all this talk then? If you want me to come to you, you needn't threaten me with execution first.

CASTI-PIANI. I know. But as I've told you several times already, you're not my type. I haven't fleeced you because I loved you, but loved you in order to fleece you. Bianetta is every inch of her more attractive to me than you are. You set forth the choicest delicacies, and when one has frittered away one's time at them, one finds oneself hungrier than ever. You have loved too long, even by our local standards. All you do for a healthy young man is to ruin his nervous system. But you're all the better qualified for the position I have in mind for you.

LULU. You must be mad! – Have I asked you to find me a job?

CASTI-PIANI. I've already told you that I'm an employment agent.

LULU. You told me you were a police spy.

CASTI-PIANI. One can't make a living by that alone. Originally I was an employment agent, till I slipped up over a clergyman's daughter for whom I'd procured a job in Valparaiso. In her childish dreams the little darling had imagined life to be even more intoxicating than it is and so she complained to her mama. Whereupon I was clapped in gaol. But my exemplary character soon won the confidence of the police. I was sent here with a monthly allowance of a hundred and fifty marks, as they were tripling our local contingent on account of the constant bomb outrages. But who can get along here with a hundred and fifty marks a month? My colleagues let themselves be kept by women. Naturally the more obvious thing for me was to resume my former profession. And from the adventuresses without number who congregate here from the best families in the world I've already despatched more than one young creature with a hunger for life to the place of her natural vocation.

LULU. (firmly) I wouldn't be any good at that profession.

CASTI-PIANI. I'm not interested in your opinion on the subject. The public prosecutor's office will pay a thousand marks to the person who delivers the murderess of Dr. Schön into their hands. I have only to whistle up the policeman who's standing down there on the corner and the thousand marks are mine. On the other hand, the Etablissement Oikonomopoulos in Cairo is offering sixty pounds for you. That is twelve hundred marks – two hundred more than the public prosecutor is paying. And apart from that, I'm enough of a philanthropist that I'd rather make my mistresses happy than hurl them to disaster.

LULU. (as before) Life in such a house could never make a woman like me happy. I might have liked it when I was fifteen. At that time I doubted if I should ever be happy. I bought myself a revolver and at night I walked barefoot through the deep snow over the bridge into the park in order to shoot myself. But after that luckily I was in hospital for three months without even seeing a man. And in that time my eyes were opened and I saw myself for what I was. Night after night in my dreams I saw the man for whom I was created and who was created for me. So when I was let loose among men again I was no longer a silly goose. Since then I can tell in the pitch dark at a distance of a hundred feet whether a man is made for me or not. And if I sin against my knowledge I feel myself next day soiled in body and soul, and it takes me weeks to overcome the disgust I feel for myself. Yet you imagine I'm going to give myself to any Tom, Dick, or Harry.

CASTI-PIANI. You won't find any Toms, Dicks or Harrys at Oikonomopoulos in Cairo. His clientele consists of Scottish lords, Russian dignitaries, Indian rulers and our own prosperous Rhineland industrialists. I need only guarantee that you can speak French. With your outstanding talent for languages, moreover, you'll soon pick up as much English as your activities will demand. And you'll live in a princely apartment overlooking the minarets of the El-Azhar mosque, will stroll all day over Persian carpets inches thick, dress yourself every evening in fabulous Parisian ball-gowns, drink as much champagne as your clients can pay for, and after all up to a point you remain your own mistress. If you don't fancy a man you need show no feeling for him of any kind. You let him leave his visiting-card with you and that's that! If the ladies didn't train themselves to it the whole thing would be utterly impossible, because after the first four weeks they'd all go straight to the devil!

LULU. (her voice trembling) I really believe you've got a screw loose somewhere since yesterday. Do you really expect me to believe that your Egyptian will pay 500 francs for a woman he knows nothing whatsoever about?

CASTI-PIANI. I took the liberty of sending him your pictures.

LULU. You sent him the pictures that *I* gave you?

CASTI-PIANI. You can see that he's better able to appreciate them than I am. Once you're there I expect he'll hang the picture of you as Eve before the looking-glass over the front door. Then there's one other thing for you to take into account. You're safer from your pursuers with Oikonomopoulos in Cairo than if you were to crawl away into one of Canada's virgin forests. They wouldn't be so eager to transfer an Egyptian courtesan to a German prison, in the first place from considerations of economy and secondly from a fear of thereby coming too near to Eternal Justice themselves.

LULU. (proudly, in a clear voice) I don't give a fig for your Eternal Justice. It should be as plain to you as the nose on your face that I'm not going to let myself be locked up in any such place of amusement.

CASTI-PIANI. Shall I whistle up the policeman, then?

LULU. (wonderingly) Why don't you simply ask me for twelve hundred marks, if you need money?

CASTI-PIANI. I don't need money. What's more, I haven't asked you for any because you've run dry.

LULU. We still have thirty thousand marks.

CASTI-PIANI. In Jungfrau shares. I never touch shares. The public prosecutor pays in the currency of the German Reich and Oikonomopoulos pays in English gold. You could be on board by tomorrow. The crossing doesn't last much more than five days. In fourteen days at the most you are in safety. Here you're nearer to prison than anywhere. It beats me, a member of the secret police myself, how you've been able to live here a whole year unmolested. But since I got on the track of your past history I don't see what's to stop one of my colleagues from making the same happy discovery, especially in view of your heavy consumption in men. Then I can wash my hands of you, and you'll spend the most enjoyable years of your life in prison. You must make up your mind at once. The train leaves at half past twelve. If we haven't come to terms by eleven o'clock, then I call the police. On the other hand, I can pack you into a car just as you stand, drive you to the station and take you on board tomorrow evening.

LULU. You're not serious about this, are you?

CASTI-PIANI. Can't you understand that I'm concerned solely for your physical safety?

LULU. I'll go to America with you, or to China, but I can't tell myself. That is worse than prison.

CASTI-PIANI. Just read this effusion. (Taking a letter out of his pocket) I'll read it aloud to you. See, here's the Cairo postmark, in case you think I'm using forged documents. The girl is a Berliner, was married for two years, and to a man whom you'd have envied her, a one time colleague of mine. He's travelling now for some sort of colonial enterprise in Hamburg.

LULU. (lightly) Then I dare say he *visits* her from time to time.

CASTI-PIANI. It's not impossible. But listen to this impulsive expression of her feelings. I don't think any more highly of my traffic in young women than the next best judge, but a cry of joy such as this momentarily permits me to feel a certain moral justification. I am proud to earn a living by scattering happiness with a liberal hand. (Reads) 'Dear Mr. Meier' – that's what I'm called as a white-slave trader – 'When you are in Berlin go at once to the Conservatory on the Potsdamer Platz and ask for Gusti von Rosenkron – the most beautiful woman I have ever seen: enchanting hands and feet, naturally small waist, straight back, full body, large eyes and a retroussé nose, exactly as you like them best. I have already written to her myself. She has no prospects with her singing. Her mother hasn't a penny. Unfortunately she's already twenty-two, but pining away for love. Can't marry, being entirely without dowry. I have already spoken to Madame. Another German would be welcome, provided well brought-up and musical. Italian and French girls can't compete with us, owing to lack of education. If you see Friz ...' – Fritz is the husband – he's getting a divorce of course – '... then tell him it was nothing but boredom. He knew no better, nor did I ...' – now comes a more precise enumeration ...

LULU. (goaded) I cannot sell the one thing I've ever owned.

CASTI-PIANI. Let me go on reading!

LULU. I'll hand over our entire fortune to you this very night.

CASTI-PIANI. You must believe me when I tell you I've already had your last farthing. If we haven't left the house by eleven o'clock the whole pack of you will be deported to Germany tomorrow.

LULU. You can't hand me over!

CASTI-PIANI. Do you think that's the worst thing I've ever been capable of? In case we do leave tonight I must just have a word or two with Bianetta.

(CASTI-PIANI goes into the gaming-room, leaving the door open behind him. LULU stares in front of her, mechanically crumpling the note RODRIGO thrust at her and which she has held in her fingers throughout the foregoing conversation. ALWA gets up from the gaming-table, some scrip in his hand, and comes into the drawingroom)

ALWA. Brilliant! It's going brilliantly! Geschwitz has just staked her last farthing, Puntschu has promised me ten more Jungfrau shares. Steinherz is making her little bit of profit. (Exit downstage right)

LULU. (alone) Me, in a brothel? ... (She reads the note which she holds in her hand and laughs hysterically)

ALWA. (re-enters downstage right, a cash-box in his hand) Aren't you playing?

LULU. Of course, of course, why not?

ALWA. By the way, it says in today's *Berliner Tageblatt* that Alfred Hugenberg has thrown himself over the stairs in prison.

LULU. Is he in prison too?

ALWA. Only in a sort of preventive custody.

(Exit ALWA into gaming-room. LULU makes a move to follow him. COUNTESS GESCHWITZ meets her in the doorway)

GESCHWITZ. Are you going because I'm coming?

LULU. (firmly) Good heavens, no! But when you come I go.

GESCHWITZ. You have defrauded me of all the worldly goods I still possessed. You could at least preserve an outward show of good behaviour in your dealings with me.

LULU. (as before) I am as well-behaved towards you as to any other woman. All that I ask is that you should be equally so toward me.

GESCHWITZ. Have you forgotten the passionate assurances by which as we lay in hospital together you induced me to let myself be locked up in prison for your sake?

LULU. Then why did you plant the cholera on me first? During the trial I swore quite different things from what I had to promise you. I shudder with disgust at the thought of it ever becoming reality.

GESCHWITZ. Then you deliberately deceived me?

LULU. (with animation) In what way have you been deceived? Your bodily charms have found so enthusiastic an admirer here that I ask myself whether I won't have to give piano lessons again to earn my daily bread. No seventeen-year-old child could make a man as mad for love as you, pervert that you are, have made this poor fellow with your capriciousness.

GESCHWITZ. Of whom do you speak? I do not understand a word.

LULU. (as above) I'm speaking of that acrobat of yours, Rodrigo Quast. He is a strong man. He can balance two saddled cavalry horses on his chest. Can a woman ask for anything more splendid? He's just told me that he will drown himself this very night if you don't take pity on him.

GESCHWITZ. I cannot envy the skill you show in tormenting the helpless victims which inscrutable destiny has delivered into your power. I do not envy you in any way. My own misery cannot arouse in me such a depth of pity as I feel for you. I feel as free as a god when I think of the sort of creatures whose slave *you* are!

LULU. Who are you talking about?

GESCHWITZ. I'm talking about Casti-Piani, whose vicious depravity is stamped in living characters upon his brow.

LULU. Shut up! I'll kick you in the stomach if you speak ill of the boy. He loves me with a sincerity which makes your spectacular sacrifices look pathetic. He gives me proofs of self-denial which make me realise for the first time how loathsome you are. You were uncompleted in your mother's womb, either as a man or a woman. You're not a human being like the rest of us. There wasn't enough material to make a man of you and for a woman you've got too much brain. That's why you're so queer!

Apply to Miss Bianetta. She's to be had for anything so long as she's paid for it. Press a gold piece into her hand and she's yours.

(BIANETTA, MAGELONE, LUDMILLA STEINHERZ, RODRIGO, CASTI-PIANI, PUNTSCHU, HEILMANN and ALWA enter the drawing-room from the gaming-room)

For heaven's sake, what has happened?

PUNTSCHU. Nothing at all! We're thirsty, that's all.

MAGELONE. Everyone has been winning; it's unbelievable!

BIANETTA. It seems to me I must have won a fortune.

LUDMILLA STEINHERZ. Don't boast about it, child, it's unlucky.

MAGELONE. But the bank won, too. How is that possible?

ALWA. It's simply prodigious where all the money comes from!

CASTI-PIANI. Let us not inquire into that! It's quite enough that we need not spare the champagne.

HEILMANN. At least I shall be able to buy my dinner at a decent restaurant after this.

ALWA. To supper, ladies, come in to supper!

(The whole company goes into the dining-room. RODRIGO detains LULU)

RODRIGO. One moment, my heart. Did you read my billet-doux?

LULU. Threaten me with the police as much as you like. I no longer dispose of money by the thousands.

RODRIGO. Don't lie to me, you bitch! You still have forty thousand in Jungfrau shares; your so-called husband was boasting of it just now himself.

LULU. Then apply your blackmail to him! I don't care what he does with his money.

RODRIGO. Thanks for the permission! With that blockhead it takes one twice twenty-four hours to make him understand what one is talking about. And then one gets his endless discussions which make one sick to death. Meanwhile my fiancée only has to write 'all is over!' and I can hang a barrel-organ round my neck.

LULU. Have you got yourself engaged?

RODRIGO. I suppose I ought to have asked your permission first? What reward have I received here for getting you out of prison at the cost of my own health? You have abandoned me! I might have had to become a porter if this girl hadn't taken me up. The very first evening that I appeared on the stage I had a plush armchair thrown at my head. This nation is too decadent to appreciate genuine feats of strength. If I were a boxing kangaroo I'd have been interviewed and had my picture in all the papers. Thank God I had already made my Celestine's acquaintance. She has the savings from twenty year's work deposited with the National Bank. And she loves me for my own sake. She isn't interested only in indecencies, as you are. She has three children by an American bishop and great things are expected of them. Day after tomorrow morning we are going to be married by the registrar.

LULU. You have my blessing.

RODRIGO. You can keep your blessings. But I told my fiancée I had twenty thousand in shares lying at the bank.

LULU. (amused) And the fellow can boast that the woman loves him for his own sake.

RODRIGO. My fiancée admires the man of feeling in me and not the man of strength like you and all the others. That's all over and done with. First they tear one's clothes off one and then they wallow about with the chambermaid. I'd rather be a skeleton than let myself in for such amusements again!

LULU. Then why the devil are you pestering the unfortunate Geschwitz with your proposals?

RODRIGO. Because the female is of the nobility. I'm a man of the world and I know more about elegant conversation than any of you do – but now I'm absolutely sick of all this talk. Are you going to let me have the money by tomorrow evening, or not?

LULU. I have no money.

RODRIGO. May I have fowl-droppings in my head if I'll let myself be fobbed off with that! He'll give you his last penny if you'll only do what's damned well no more than your duty by him. You enticed the poor boy here, and now he'll have a hard time finding a job suited to his abilities.

LULU. What business is it of yours whether he wastes his money on women or at the gaming-table?

RODRIGO. Are you both doing your utmost to throw every penny his father earned with his newspaper into the jaws of this pack? You'll make four people happy if you'll stop being so particular and sacrifice yourself for a useful purpose. Must it always be Casti-Piani and again Casti-Piani?

LULU. (lightly) Shall I ask him to light you down the stairs?

RODRIGO. As you please, milady. If I haven't had the twenty thousand marks by tomorrow night, I'll make a report to the police and that will be the end of this salon of yours. Goodbye.

(Enter JOURNALIST HEILMANN breathless backstage right)

LULU. Are you looking for Miss Magelone? – She isn't here.

HEILMANN. No, I'm looking for something else.

RODRIGO. (pointing to the doorway opposite) The second door on the left, if you please.

LULU. Did your fiancée teach you that?

HEILMANN. (in the doorway collides with BANKER PUNTSCHU) Excuse me, my angel!

PUNTSCHU. Oh, it's you! Miss Magelone is waiting for you in the lift.

HEILMANN. Please go up with her. I'm just coming. (Exit hurriedly through doorway. LULU goes into the dining-room, followed by RODRIGO)

PUNTSCHU. (alone) How hot it is! ... If I don't cut off your ears you'll cut off mine ... If I can't sell my John Thomas I'll have to fall back on my brain. It doesn't get wrinkles, my brain doesn't, it can't be indisposed, doesn't have to bathe in Eau de Cologne.

(BOB, a groom in a red jacket, tight leather breeches and glistening top-boots, fifteen years old, comes in with a telegram)

BOB. For Mr. Puntschu.

PUNTSCHU. (opens the telegram and murmurs) Shares of the Jungfrau cable railway fallen to ... well, well, that is the way of the world –! (To BOB) Wait a minute! (Gives him a tip) Tell me, what is your name?

BOB. My real name is Freddy, but they call me Bob because that's the fashion now.

PUNTSCHU. How old are you?

BOB. Fifteen.

KADIDJA. (enters uncertainly from the dining-room) Excuse me, but could you tell me if Mama is here?

PUNTSCHU. No, my child, no (Aside) What breeding!

KADIDJA. I've been looking everywhere for her; I simply can't find her.

PUNTSCHU. Your mama will turn up again all right, as sure as my name is Puntschu! – (Looking at BOB) And that pair of knee breeches! God of Justice! – One begins to feel uneasy. (Exit backstage right)

KADIDJA. (to BOB) Haven't *you* seen my Mama?

BOB. No. But just come with me.

KADIDJA. Where is she?

BOB. She went up in the lift. Come on!

KADIDJA. No, no, I'm not going up.

BOB. We can hide in the passage when we get up there.

KADIDJA. No, no, I'm not coming. I shall get a scolding.

(MAGELONE rushes through the doorway in great agitation and seizes KADIDJA)

MAGELONE. Ha, there you are at last, you little wretch!

KADIDJA. (weeping noisily) Oh Mama, Mama, I've been looking for you!

MAGELONE. You've been looking for me? Did I tell you to look for me? What have you been up to with this man?

(HEILMANN, ALWA, LUDMILLA STEINHERZ, PUNTSCHU, COUNTESS GESCHWITZ and LULU enter from dining-room. BOB has disappeared)

I won't have you crying in front of all these people, let me tell you!

(They all surround KADIDJA)

LULU. But you're crying, my little sweetheart! Why are you crying?

PUNTSCHU. God knows, she really has been crying! Who has done anything to hurt you, my little goddess?

LUDMILLA STEINHERZ. (kneels before her and puts her arms round her) Tell me, angel, what nasty thing happened? Would you like some cake? Some chocolate?

MAGELONE. It's her nerves. The child is developing them far too early. In any case the best thing is to take no notice.

PUNTSCHU. How like you to say that! You're an unnatural mother. The court will take the child away from you and appoint me her guardian! (Stroking KADIDJA's cheek) Won't they, little goddess?

GESCHWITZ. It will be a relief when we start playing baccarat again.

(The company move into the dining-room. LULU is detained at the door by BOB, who whispers something to her)

LULU. Of course! Tell him to come in!

(BOB opens the door into the passage and admits SCHIGOLCH. He is wearing a dress coat, white stock, down-at-heel patent leather boots and a shabby opera hat, which he keeps on his head)

SCHIGOLCH. (with a glance at BOB) Where did you get him?

LULU. From the circus.

SCHIGOLCH. What wages does he get?

LULU. Ask him, if it interests you. (To BOB) Close the doors.

(BOB goes into the dining-room and closes the door behind him)

SCHIGOLCH. (sitting down) I'm in urgent need of money. I've taken an apartment for my lady friend.

LULU. Oh, so you've got a lady friend here too?

SCHIGOLCH. She's from Frankfurt. In her youth she was the wife of the King of Naples. She tells me every day that once upon a time she was quite captivating.

LULU. (with apparent composure) Does she need the money very badly?

SCHIGOLCH. She wants to set up house for herself. Such sums of money are mere trifles to you.

LULU. (suddenly overpowered by a fit of weeping, falls at SCHIGOLCH's feet) Oh, God Almighty.

SCHIGOLCH. (patting her) There, there. What's the matter now?

LULU. (swallows convulsively) It's too terrible!

SCHIGOLCH. (pulls her onto his lap and holds her in his arms like a child) Hm – you're overdoing things, my child. You ought to go to bed early with a novel just for once. – That's right, have a good cry, a really good cry. – It took you like this once before, fifteen years ago. No one has ever screamed since the way you managed to scream then. In those days you didn't wear a plume of white feathers on your head, nor did you wear transparent stockings. You had neither boots nor stockings on your legs.

LULU. (howling) Take me home with you, take me home with you tonight! Please, please! There are plenty of carriages below!

SCHIGOLCH. I'll take you with me, I'll take you with me. But what's the matter?

LULU. A matter of life and death! They're going to hand me over to the police.

SCHIGOLCH. Who? Who's going to hand you over to the police?

LULU. The acrobat.

SCHIGOLCH. (with complete calm) I'll take care of him!

LULU. (imploringly) Do take care of him! Please take care of him! Then you can do what you like with me.

SCHIGOLCH. If he comes to me that's the end of him. My window opens onto the river. But (Shaking his head) he won't come, he won't come.

LULU. What number do you live at?

SCHIGOLCH. 376. The last house before the Hippodrome.

LULU. I'll send him there. He'll come with that daft creature who crawls round my feet. He'll come this very evening. Go home now, so they'll find it cosy when they get there.

SCHIGOlCH. Just send them along.

LULU. Tomorrow you can bring me the gold rings he wears in his ears.

SCHIGOLCH. Does he wear rings in his ears?

LULU. You can remove them before you tip him out. He doesn't notice a thing when he's drunk.

SCHIGOLCH. And then, child, what then?

LULU. I'll give you the money for your lady friend.

SCHIGOLCH. I call that mean.

LULU. Anything else you like! Whatever I have!

SCHIGOLCH. We haven't been together for almost ten years.

LULU. Is that all you want? But you have a mistress.

SCHIGOLCH. My lady-love from Frankfurt is no longer in her first youth.

LULU. You must swear, then.

SCHIGOLCH. Have I ever broken my word to you?

LULU. Swear that you'll take care of him!

SCHIGOLCH. I'll take care of him all right.

LULU. But swear! Swear!

SCHIGOLCH. (lays his hand on her ankle) By all that's holy. This evening, if he comes ...

LULU. By all that is holy! – How cool that feels!

SCHIGOLCH. It has the opposite effect on me!

LULU. Just you be off home. They'll be there in half an hour. Take a cab.

SCHIGOLCH. All right, I'm going.

LULU. Quickly, please ... Oh God! ...

SCHIGOLCH. *Now* what are you looking at me like that for?

LULU. Nothing ...

SCHIGOLCH. Well – lost your tongue?

LULU. My garter has broken.

SCHIGOLCH. What of it? Anything else?

LULU. What does it mean?

SCHIGOLCH. What does it mean? I'll fasten it for you if you'll stand still.

LULU. It means bad luck.

SCHIGOLCH. (with a yawn) Not for you, my child. Don't worry. I'll take care of him. (Exit)

(LULU puts her left foot up on a stool, fastens her garter and goes into the gaming-room. RODRIGO is propelled roughly from the dining-room into the salon by CASTI-PIANI)

RODRIGO. You might at least treat me with civility.

CASTI-PIANI. (quite impassive) I can see no reason why I should. I want to know what you said to the woman just now in this room.

RODRIGO. Go and boil your head!

CASTI-PIANI. Answer me, you dog! You asked her to go up in the lift with you!

RODRIGO. That's a miserable bare-faced lie!

CASTI-PIANI. She told me so herself! You threatened to denounce her if she didn't go up with you! Do you want me to shoot you?

RODRIGO. The shameless creature! – As if I would think of such a thing! If I want to have her, God knows I don't have to threaten her with prison first!

CASTI-PIANI. Thank you, that's all I need to know. (Exit through centre door)

RODRIGO. The dog? – A fellow whom I could chuck up to the ceiling so that he'd stick there like a Limburger cheese. – Come here, if you want me to twist your guts around your neck! ... The very idea! ...

LULU. (comes out of the dining-room. Playfully) Where have you been? It's like looking for a needle in a haystack.

RODRIGO. That'll teach him not to try things on with me!

LULU. Who?

RODRIGO. Your Casti-Piani. What made you tell the fellow I wanted to seduce you, you bitch?!

LULU. Well, didn't you ask me to give myself to my dead husband's son for twenty thousand in Jungfrau shares?

RODRIGO. Because it's your duty to have pity on the poor boy. You shot his father away from under his nose in the prime of life! But your Casti-Piani will think twice before he crosses my path again. I'll give him one in the stomach that'll send his guts flying up to heaven like fire-crackers. If you can't find anyone better to take my place then I'm sorry I ever enjoyed your favours!

LULU. Geschwitz is in a terrible state. She's writhing with pain. She's capable of jumping into the river if you keep her waiting any longer.

RODRIGO. What's the old cow waiting for?

LULU. For you to take her with you.

RODRIGO. Then give her my regards and tell her she'd better jump in the river.

LULU. She'll lend me twenty thousand marks to save me from ruin if you'll save her from it. If you take her away with you I'll deposit twenty thousand marks in your name tomorrow at any bank you choose.

RODRIGO. And if I don't take her away with me?

LULU. Then you'll have to denounce me. Alwa and I are cleaned out.

RODRIGO. Good heavens!

LULU. You'll make four people happy if you'll stop being so particular and sacrifice yourself for a useful purpose.

RODRIGO. It won't work. I can tell you that straight away. I've tried it often enough. Who would think the old bag of bones would be so honourable. My only interest in the creature lies in her being of the nobility. I've been more gentlemanlike in my behaviour to her than other German artistes would have been. I wish I'd given her one good pinch in the calf!

LULU. (watchfully) She's still a virgin.

RODRIGO. (with a sigh) If there's a God in Heaven you'll pay for your jokes one of these days, let me tell you!

LULU. Geschwitz is waiting. What shall I tell her?

RODRIGO. My respects, but that I'm a pervert.

LULU. I'll give her the message.

RODRIGO. Wait! Are you certain I'll get twenty thousand out of her?

LULU. Ask her yourself.

RODRIGO. Then tell her I'm ready. I'll wait for her in the dining-room. I must dispose of another barrel of caviar first.

(RODRIGO goes into the dining-room. LULU opens the door to the gaming-room and calls in a loud voice 'Martha', whereupon

COUNTESS GESCHWITZ comes into the drawing-room and closes the door behind her)

LULU. (gaily) My love, today you have an opportunity to save my life.

GESCHWITZ. How can I do that?

LULU. By going to a brothel with our acrobat.

GESCHWITZ. What for, my love?

LULU. He says he must possess you tonight or tomorrow he denounces me to the police.

GESCHWITZ. You know I cannot belong to any man; my destiny prohibits it.

LULU. If he isn't pleased he'll have to settle it with himself. Why has he fallen in love with you?

GESCHWITZ. But he'll be as brutal as a hangman's apprentice. He'll avenge himself for his disappointment and break my head open. It's happened to me before. Couldn't you spare me this terrible ordeal?

LULU. What will you get out of it if I'm denounced?

GESCHWITZ. I've still got enough money left for the two of us to travel steerage to America. There you'd be safe from all your pursuers.

LULU. (lightly and cheerfully) I want to stay here. I wouldn't be happy in any other city. You must tell him you can't live without him. That will flatter him and he'll be as gentle as a lamb. You'll have to pay the cab-driver, too. Give him this piece of paper; it has the address on it. Number 376 is a hotel of the sixth rank, and they are expecting you both there this evening.

GESCHWITZ. How can such an outrage save your life? – I don't understand. – In order to torment me you have conjured up the most dreadful fate that could befall an outcast like me.

LULU. (craftily) Perhaps the encounter will cure you!

GESCHWITZ. (sighing) Oh, Lulu, if there is such a thing as eternal justice I should not wish to be answerable for you. I cannot reconcile myself to the idea of there being no God watching over us. And yet, perhaps you are right to say there is nothing in it. For why should an insignificant worm like me provoke Him so to anger that my life is all horror while the rest of living creation swoons for joy!

LULU. You have nothing to complain of. When you *are* happy you're a hundred thousand times happier than one of us ordinary mortals can be.

GESCHWITZ. I know that; I envy no one. But I am still waiting for the happy day. You have deceived me so often.

LULU. If you will keep the acrobat quiet till tomorrow morning, I am yours. All he needs is to have his vanity soothed; you must implore him to take pity on you.

GESCHWITZ. And tomorrow?

LULU. I shall wait for you, my darling. I shall not open my eyes till you come. I shall see no chambermaid, receive no hair-dresser, I shall not open my eyes till you come.

GESCHWITZ. Then let him come.

LULU. But you must throw yourself at his head, my love! Have you still got the address?

GESCHWITZ. Number 376. But let us be quick!

LULU. (calls into the dining-room) Ready, darling!

RODRIGO. The ladies will excuse my having my mouth full.

GESCHWITZ. (seizes his hand) I adore you! Take pity on my plight!

RODRIGO. A la bonne heure! Let us mount the scaffold! (He offers COUNTESS GESCHWITZ his arm and leaves the drawing-room with her)

LULU. Goodnight, children! (She accompanies the pair into the hall and returns immediately with BOB) Quick, quick, Bob! We must leave at once! You shall come with me. But we must exchange clothes.

BOB. (curtly and clearly) As Madame wishes!

LULU. You can drop the 'Madame'! Give me your clothes and put on mine instead. Come on!

(Exeunt LULU and BOB into the dining-room. A commotion arises in the gaming-room. The doors are flung open. PUNTSCHU, HEILMANN, ALWA, BIANETTA, MAGELONE, KADIDJA and LUDMILLA STEINHERZ enter the drawing-room)

HEILMANN. (clutches a share certificate in his hand on which a picture of an Alpine sunset is visible. To PUNTSCHU) Perhaps you will accept these Jungfrau shares, Sir.

PUNTSCHU. But the stock has no official quotation.

HEILMANN. You scoundrel, you don't want to give me a chance of getting my own back!

MAGELONE. (to BIANETTA) Do you understand what's going on here by any chance?

LUDMILLA STEINHERZ. Puntschu has taken all his money off him and is giving up the game.

HEILMANN. Now he's getting cold feet, the pig of a Jew!

PUNTSCHU. Who says I'm giving up? Who says I'm getting cold feet? But the gentleman must put down cash! I'm not in my banking-house now. Let him offer me that trash tomorrow morning!

HEILMANN. Trash you call it? The shares stand, to my knowledge, at 210.

PUNTSCHU. They stood at 210 yesterday, in so far you are right. Today they are no longer standing at all. By tomorrow you'll find nothing cheaper or more tasteful to paper your staircase with.

ALWA. How is that possible? If it's true we're on the rocks!

PUNTSCHU. And what am I to say, who have lost my entire fortune? Tomorrow morning I shall have the pleasure of resuming the struggle for a secure existence for the thirty-sixth time.

MAGELONE. (pushing forward) Am I dreaming, or did I mis-hear? Did someone say the Jungfrau shares have fallen?

PUNTSCHU. Fallen even further than you have! – You can use them as curl-papers!

MAGELONE. Almighty God! Ten years' work! (Falls in a faint)

KADIDJA. Wake up, Mama! Wake up!

BIANETTA. Tell me, Mr. Puntschu, where are you going to dine this evening now that you've lost your entire fortune?

PUNTSCHU. Wherever you like, Mademoiselle. Take me wherever you will, but be quick about it. It's getting rather unpleasant in here. (PUNTSCHU and BIANETTA leave the drawing-room)

HEILMANN. (crumples his shares together into a ball and hurls them on the ground) That's what one gets from associating with such people!

LUDMILLA STEINHERZ. Why do you bother to speculate on the Jungfrau? Why don't you send one or two little articles on the present company to the German police and perhaps you'll make something on it after all.

HEILMANN. I've never tried such a thing in my life, but if you'd care to help me ...?

LUDMILLA STEINHERZ. Let's go to a restaurant that's open all night. Do you know the 'Five-footed Sheep'?

HEILMANN. I'm afraid I ...

LUDMILLA STEINHERZ. Or the 'Sucking Calf'? Or the 'Smoking Dog'? They're all here in the neighbourhood. We should be quite undisturbed. We ought to have produced a small article by daybreak.

HEILMANN. Don't you ever sleep?

LUDMILLA STEINHERZ. Of course, but not at night, naturally.

(HEILMANN and LUDMILLA STEINHERZ leave the drawing-room by the centre door)

ALWA. (has for some time been bending over Magelone, trying to bring her round from her faint) Cold as ice her hands are! But what a magnificent woman. Someone ought to undo her bodice. Come here,

Kadidja, undo your mother's bodice! She's terribly tight-laced.

KADIDJA. (without moving) I'm frightened.

(LULU comes out of the dining-room in jockey-cap, red jacket, white knee-breeches, top boots, a cycling cape around her shoulders)

LULU. Have you any money in cash, Alwa?

ALWA. (looking up) Have you gone mad?

LULU. In two minutes the police will be here. We have been denounced. You can stay here if you like!

ALWA. (jumping up) Good God!

(Exeunt LULU and ALWA through centre door)

KADIDJA. (in tears, shaking her mother) Mama! Mama! Wake up! Everyone has run away!

MAGELONE. (coming round) One's youth past – one's best days – oh, this life!

KADIDJA. But I am young, Mama! Why shouldn't I earn money? I don't want to go back to the convent. Please, Mama, let me stay with you.

MAGELONE. God bless you, my sweetheart, you don't know what you're talking about. – No, I'll look about for an engagement in a variety theatre and sing to people about my misfortunes with the Jungfrau shares. That sort of thing always goes down well.

KADIDJA. But you have no voice, Mama.

MAGELONE. Yes, that's true.

KADIDJA. Take me with you to the variety theatre.

MAGELONE. No, it breaks my heart! But if it cannot be otherwise, if it is so ordained for you, then I can do nothing to change it! – We can got to the Olympia hall tomorrow.

KADIDJA. Oh, Mama! I'm so happy!

A POLICE OFFICER. (in plain-clothes, enters from the hall) I arrest you
   – in the name of the law!

CASTI-PIANI. (languidly following him) What on earth do you think
   you're doing? That's the wrong one!

ACT THREE

(An attic room without windows save for two large panes of glass opening outwards. Right and left downstage ill-fitting doors. In the proscenium left a torn grey mattress. Downstage right a rickety flower-stand, on which are a bottle and a smoking paraffin lamp. In the corner backstage right an old chaise longue. Next to the centre door a cane chair with a broken seat. One can hear the rain beating on the roof; underneath the skylight stands a bowl full of water. Downstage on the mattress SCHIGOLCH is lying, in a long grey overcoat. On the chaise longue in the corner lies ALWA SCHÖN, wrapped in a rug, the strap of which hangs above him on the wall)

SCHIGOLCH. The rain is beating a tattoo.

ALWA. Very appropriate weather for her debut! – I was just dreaming that we were dining together in the Olympia rooms. Bianetta was there too. The tablecloth was positively dripping with champagne.

SCHIGOLCH. Yes, yes – and I was dreaming of a Christmas pudding.

(LULU, barefoot, her hair falling loose about her shoulders, in a torn black dress, enters by the door downstage right)

Where have you been, my child? To have your hair curled, I suppose.

ALWA. She does it solely to refresh old memories.

LULU. If only one could at least warm oneself up a little on one of you!

ALWA. Do you intend to embark upon your pilgrimage barefooted?

SCHIGOLCH. The first step always causes a lot of moaning and groaning. It wasn't a bit better twenty years ago, and think what she's learnt since! The first has to be kindled first, that's all. Wait till she's been at it a week. Ten locomotives won't be enough to keep her in our miserable garret.

ALWA. The bowl is already overflowing.

LULU. What shall I do with the water?

ALWA. Pour it out of the window.

LULU. (climbs on a chair and empties the bowl out of the skylight) It looks as if the rain were letting up after all.

SCHIGOLCH. You're wasting the time when the clerks go home after dinner.

LULU. I wish to God I were where no footsteps could wake me!

ALWA. So do I. Why should we prolong this life? Let us rather starve together in peace and harmony this very night. It's what we all come to in the end, after all.

LULU. Why don't you go out and earn us something to eat? You've never earned a penny in your life.

ALWA. In weather like this, that one wouldn't expect a dog to go out in?

LULU. But you expect *me to*! I'm expected to fill your mouths, with the bit of blood I still have in my veins.

ALWA. I shall not touch a farthing of the money.

SCHIGOLCH. Let her go. I crave for a Christmas pudding; after that I'll be satisfied.

ALWA. And I crave for a beefsteak and a cigarette, and then – death! I've just been dreaming of a cigarette such as has never been smoked before.

SCHIGOLCH. She'd rather we perished before her eyes than give herself a little fun.

LULU. The people in the streets would leave their coats in my hands sooner than go with me for nothing. If you hadn't sold my clothes at least I wouldn't have to avoid the light of the street lamps. I'd like to see the woman who could earn money with the rags I have on my body.

ALWA. I've tried everything a man could try. As long as I had any money left I spent whole nights working out systems by which one couldn't help winning, even against the cleverest cheats in existence. I lost more than if I'd poured the cold-pieces away by the bucketful. Then I offered myself to the courtesans, but they take no one who isn't officially stamped, and they pick up the faintest whiff of the gallows immediately.

SCHIGOLCH. Yes, yes.

ALWA. I spared myself no disappointment; but if I made jokes they made fun of *me*; if I was my own decent self they boxed me on the ears; and if I attempted improprieties they turned so coy and maidenly that my hair stood on end for shame. They have no faith in anyone who hasn't got the upper hand of human society.

SCHIGOLCH. Aren't you ever going to put your boots on, child? – I have a feeling I shall not grow much older in these lodgings. I have had no sensation in my toes for months. Towards midnight I shall have a drink or two in the public-house downstairs. The landlady told me yesterday that I had good prospects of becoming her lover.

LULU. The devil take it! I'm going down! (Takes the bottle from the flower-stand and drinks)

SCHIGOLCH. So that people can smell you coming half an hour away!

LULU. I won't drink all of it.

ALWA. You are not going down, woman! You are not going down! I forbid it!

LULU. Who are you to forbid your wife, when you can't even feed yourself?

ALWA. And who is to blame for that? Who but my wife brought me to my bed of sickness?

LULU. Am I ill?

ALWA. Who dragged me in the mud? – Who made me the murderer of my father?

LULU. Did **you** shoot him? He didn't lose much, but when I see you lying there I feel like cutting off both my hands for having committed such a crime against reason. (Exit into her room, right)

ALWA. It's a bequest from that Casti-Piani of hers. She's long since ceased to be susceptible to it herself.

SCHIGOLCH. It's never too early for devil's children like her to get acquainted with suffering, if they're to be angels in the end.

ALWA. She ought to have been Empress of Russia. A second Catherine the Second. That would be just where she belongs.

(LULU comes out of her room carrying a pair of shabby laced-boots and sits down on the floor to put them on)

LULU. If only I don't go headlong downstairs. Ugh! How cold. Is there a sadder sight in the world than a *fille de joie*!

SCHIGOLCH. Patience, patience! Wait till the business gets into its stride.

LULU. It's all the same to me; it doesn't matter about me any more. (She puts the bottle to her lips) That warms one up a bit! – To hell with it! (Exit through centre door)

SCHIGOLCH. When we hear her coming we must creep into my cubbyhole.

ALWA. It's a pity about her! – When I think back – in a way I grew up with her, you know.

SCHIGOLCH. I daresay she'll outlive me, at least.

ALWA. In the beginning we were like brother and sister to each other. Mama was alive then. One morning I chanced upon her while she was dressing. Dr. Goll had been called to a consultation. Her hairdresser had read the first poem of mine to be printed in *Society*, 'Drive your pack far over the hills, it will return, covered in dust and sweat ...'

SCHIGOLCH. Oh, yes!

ALWA. And then she came to the Spanish Ambassador's ball in pink tulle. She wore nothing underneath but a bodice of white satin. Dr. Goll seemed to have a foreboding of his imminent death. He begged me to dance with her, to prevent possible indiscretions on her part. Papa did not take his eyes off us the whole time, and during the waltz she looked away over my shoulder at no one but him. Later she shot him. It is incredible.

SCHIGOLCH. I very much doubt if anyone will bite.

ALWA. I shouldn't recommend them to, either!

SCHIGOLCH. What a fool!

ALWA. In those days, though she was already fully developed as a woman she had the expression of a bright, healthy, five-year-old child; even then she was only three years younger than me. But how long ago it all is! In spite of her amazing superiority in the practical questions of life, she let me explain the theme of 'Tristan and Isolde' to her. And how charmingly she understood the art of listening. Then from the little sister who still felt like a schoolgirl even after marriage she turned into an unhappy, hysterical artist's wife. The artist's wife became the wife of my lamented father. My father's wife became my mistress. That is the way of the world – who can hope to get round it?

SCHIGOLCH. Let's hope she doesn't run away from the gentlemen with honourable intentions and bring some tramp up here instead after exchanging bosom confidences with him.

ALWA. I first kissed her in her rustling bridal gown but she had no recollection of it later. All the same, I believe that in my father's arms her thoughts had already turned to me. It cannot have happened so very often. He had already seen his best days, and she betrayed him with coachman and bootblack. But when she gave herself to him I was in her heart. And so, almost before I was aware of it, she acquired this terrible power over me.

SCHIGOLCH. Here they come!

(Heavy footsteps are heard ascending the stairs)

ALWA. I won't stand for it! I'll throw the fellow out!

SCHIGOLCH. (rises with an effort, takes ALWA by the collar and shoves him across the stage, left) Come on! Come on! How can the lad pour out his troubles to her with us two lying about here?

ALWA. But what if he demands something foul of her?

SCHIGOLCH. Suppose he does, suppose he does. What else can he ask of her? He's only a human being like the rest of us.

ALWA. We must leave the door open.

SCHIGOLCH. (pushing ALWA into the cubby-hole) Nonsense! Shut up!

ALWA. (from within) I shall hear it all right! May Heaven have mercy on him!

SCHIGOLCH. (shuts the door. From within) Hold your tongue!

ALWA. (from within) He'd better look out.

(LULU opens the centre door and admits MR. HUNIDEI. MR. HUNIDEI is a man of gigantic stature with a clean-shaven rosy face, shy blue eyes and a friendly smile. He is wearing a cape and a top hat and carries a dripping umbrella in his hand)

LULU. This is where I live.

(MR. HUNIDEI puts his forefinger up to his mouth and looks meaningly at LULU. Then he opens his umbrella and sets it on the floor in the background to dry)

It isn't very cosy here, I must admit.

(MR HUNIDEI comes downstage and puts his hand over her mouth)

What do you wish me to understand by that?

(MR. HUNIDEI puts his hand over her mouth and puts his forefinger to his own lips)

I don't know what that means.

(MR. HUNIDEI hastily closes her mouth)

(Freeing herself) We're quite alone here, no one can hear us.

(MR. HUNIDEI puts his forefinger to his lips, shakes his head, points to LULU, opens his mouth as if to speak, points to himself and then to the doors)

(Aside) Good God – he's a monster.

(MR. HUNIDEI closes her mouth. Then he goes backstage, folds up his cape and lays it on the chair by the door. Then he comes downstage with a grinning smile, takes LULU's head between his two hands and kisses her on the forehead)

SCHIGOLCH. (behind the half-open door downstage left) That fellow has a screw loose somewhere.

ALWA. He had better look out!

SCHIGOLCH. She couldn't have brought up anything more dismal.

LULU. (stepping back) I hope you're going to give me something.

(MR. HUNIDEI holds her mouth shut and presses a gold piece into her hand.

LULU inspects the gold piece and tosses it from one hand to the other.

MR. HUNIDEI gives her an uncertain, questioning look)

Oh well, it's all right. (Puts the money in her pocket)

(MR. HUNIDEI holds her mouth shut, gives her a few pieces of silver and looks at her imperiously)

Oh! That is good of you!

(MR. HUNIDEI leaps madly about the room, waves his arms in the air, gazes despairingly at the ceiling.

LULU approaches him cautiously, puts her arm round him and kisses him on the mouth.

MR. HUNIDEI, laughing soundlessly, frees himself from her and looks enquiringly about him.

LULU takes the lamp from the flower-stand and opens the door into her chamber.

MR. HUNIDEI goes in with a smile, raising his hat in the doorway.

The stage is in darkness save for a shaft of light which comes from under the door of the chamber. ALWA and SCHIGOLCH creep out of their cubby-hole on all fours)

ALWA. Have they gone?

SCHIGOLCH. (behind him) Wait a little!

ALWA. One can hear nothing from here.

SCHIGOLCH. One has heard that often enough!

ALWA. I shall kneel down by her door.

SCHIGOLCH. Mama's boy! (He pushes past ALWA, gropes across the stage, picks up MR. HUNIDEI's cape from the chair and goes through the pockets.

ALWA has crept up to LULU's door)

Nothing but a pair of gloves! (He turns the cape over, searches the inside pockets and pulls out a book, which he hands to ALWA) Look and see what it is!

ALWA. (holds the book in the shaft of light from under the door and laboriously deciphers the title page) 'Exhortations to pious pilgrims and those anxious to become such' – Most helpful! – Price, two shillings and sixpence.

SCHIGOLCH. He struck me as being utterly God-forsaken. (Puts the cape back over the chair and creeps back to the cubby-hole) There's nothing doing with these people. As a nation their best days are over.

ALWA. Life is never as bad as one imagines it to be. (He, too, creeps back to the cubby-hole)

SCHIGOLCH. The fellow hasn't even got a silk scarf. And we in Germany crawl on our bellies to these people.

ALWA. Come on, we'd better disappear again.

SCHIGOLCH. I suppose she only thinks of herself and takes the first man to cross her path. I hope the fellow remembers her for the rest of his life.

(SCHIGOLCH and ALWA crawl back into their cubby-hole and close the door after them. LULU then enters and places the lamp on the flower-stand)

LULU. Will you visit me again?

(MR. HUNIDEI holds her mouth shut.

LULU looks up at the ceiling in a sort of despair and shakes her head.

MR. HUNIDEI has thrown his cape over his shoulders and now approaches her, grinning. She throws her arms round his neck, whereat he gently disengages himself, kisses her hand and goes towards the door. She tries to accompany him but he gestures to her to remain, and noiselessly leaves the garret.

SCHIGOLCH and ALWA emerge from their closet)

(Tonelessly) How exciting he was!

ALWA. How much did he give you?

LULU. (as before) Here it is! Take it! I'm going down again.

SCHIGOLCH. We can live like princes up here.

ALWA. He's coming back.

SCHIGOLCH. Then let us retire again immediately.

ALWA. He's coming for his prayer-book; here it is. It must have fallen out of his coat.

LULU. (listening) No, it isn't he. It's someone else.

ALWA. Someone is coming upstairs. I can hear them quite plainly.

LULU. Now someone's knocking at the door. Who can it be?

SCHIGOLCH. Some good friend, I dare say, to whom he has recommended us. – Come in!

(Enter COUNTESS GESCHWITZ. She is poorly dressed and carries a rolled up canvas in her hand)

GESCHWITZ. If I've come at an inconvenient time I'll go away again. But for ten days I haven't spoken to a soul. I must tell you at once that I didn't get any money. My brother didn't reply at all.

SCHIGOLCH. And so now your ladyship would like to stretch her legs out under our table?

LULU. (tonelessly) I'm going down again!

GESCHWITZ. Where are you going in that costume? – I haven't come empty-handed, all the same. I've brought you something else. On my way here a dealer offered me twelve shillings for it but I couldn't bring myself to part with it.

SCHIGOLCH. What have you got there?

ALWA. Let's have a look. (He takes the roll of canvas from her and unrolls it with manifest pleasure) Why, my God, yes! It's Lulu's portrait.

LULU. (screams) And you've brought it here, you monster? – Take that picture out of my sight! Throw it out of the window!

ALWA. (as if suddenly rejuvenated, greatly pleased) But why on earth?! In face of that portrait I regain my self-respect. It makes my destiny comprehensible. Everything we have been through is made as plain as daylight. (Rather plaintively) Let him who can feel his position in bourgeois society to remain unassailed in face of these full, ripe lips, these great innocent child's eyes, this exuberant pink and white body, let him be the one to cast the first stone.

SCHIGOLCH. We must nail it up. It will make an excellent impression on our clientèle.

ALWA. (very businesslike) There is a nail for it already sticking in the wall.

SCHIGOLCH. How did you happen to acquire it?

GESCHWITZ. I cut it out of the wall after you had all left the house.

ALWA. A pity that the paint is flaking off at the edges! You didn't roll it up carefully enough. (He fastens the picture at the top with a nail that is sticking in the wall)

SCHIGOLCH. It needs one at the bottom too if it's going to hold. The whole flat has a more elegant appearance.

ALWA. Leave it to me, I know what I'm going to do. (He pulls several nails out of the wall, takes off his left boot and with the heel drives the nails through the edges of the picture into the wall)

SCHIGOLCH. It must hang a while before it appears to full advantage. Anyone seeing it can pretend he's in an Indian harem.

ALWA. (putting on his boot again and drawing himself up proudly) Her body was at the height of its flowering when that picture was painted. The lamp, dear child! It seems to me to have darkened to an unusual extent.

GESCHWITZ. It must have been an outstandingly gifted artist who painted that!

LULU. (quite composed once more, goes up to the picture with the lamp in her hand) Didn't you know him then?

GESCHWITZ. No; it must have been long before my time. I merely heard occasional critical references among you to the effect that persecution mania drove him to cut his own throat.

ALWA. (comparing the portrait with LULU) In spite of all that she's been through since, the childlike expression in the eyes is still quite the same. (Pleasurably excited) But the dewy-freshness which was on the skin, the fragrant breath about the lips, the radiant whiteness of the brow, the bold splendour of the flesh on neck and arms –

SCHIGOLCH. All that has gone into the dustbin. But she can confidently say 'That's what I once was'. No one into whose hands she falls today can form any conception of the glories of our youth.

ALWA. (cheerfully) Thank God, one doesn't notice the advance of decay when one is constantly together. (Lightly) A woman blossoms for us precisely at the right moment to plunge a man into everlasting ruin; such is her natural destiny.

SCHIGOLCH. Down below in the glimmer of the street lamps she can compete with a dozen other phantoms of the streets. Anyone still anxious to make an acquaintance at this time of night looks more to qualities of the heart than to physical charms. He decides on the pair of eyes with the least thievish glint in them.

LULU. (as pleased as ALWA) I'll see whether you're right. Farewell!

ALWA. (in sudden rage) You shall not go down again, as true as I live!

GESCHWITZ. Where are you going?

ALWA. She wants to pick up a man and bring him up here.

GESCHWITZ. Lulu!

ALWA. She's done it once today already.

GESCHWITZ. Lulu, Lulu, I shall go with you wherever you go.

SCHIGOLCH. If you want to put your collection of bones up for hire, kindly find yourself your own beat.

GESCHWITZ. Lulu, I shall not leave your side. I am armed.

SCHIGOLCH. The devil you are! Your ladyship is scheming to fish with our bait!

LULU. You'll all be the end of me! I can't bear it any longer!

GESCHWITZ. Don't be afraid, I am with you!

(Exeunt LULU and COUNTESS GESCHWITZ through centre)

SCHIGOLCH. For God's sake, for God's sake!

ALWA. (throws himself whimpering onto his chaise longue) I fear I cannot expect much further good from this world.

SCHIGOLCH. We ought to have held that woman back by the throat.

She'll scare off any living breathing creature with that aristocratic death's head of hers.

ALWA. She cast me onto my bed of sickness and has beset me with thorns within and without.

SCHIGOLCH. On the other hand she has guts enough for ten men.

ALWA. No wounded man will ever receive the coup de grâce more thankfully than I.

SCHIGOLCH. If she hadn't enticed that jumping-jack to my apartment that time we'd still have him round our necks today.

ALWA. I can see him hovering above my head as Tantalus saw the bough with the golden apples.

SCHIGOLCH. (from his mattress) Would you mind turning the lamp up a little?

ALWA. I wonder if a simple child of nature in the wilds can suffer so unspeakably. My God, my God, what a mess I've made of my life!

SCHIGOLCH. And what a mess this filthy weather has made of my cape! – When I was twenty-five I knew how to look after myself.

ALWA. Not everyone enjoyed such a glorious sunny youth as mine!

SCHIGOLCH. I think it's going out. By the time they get back it'll be as dark in here as in one's mother's womb.

ALWA. With the utmost deliberation I sought the company of people who had never read a book in their lives. In complete self-abandonment and conviction I clung to these characters in order thereby to be born aloft to the pinnacle of fame as a poet. But it was a miscalculation. I am a martyr to my profession. Since my father's death I haven't written a single verse.

SCHIGOLCH. I only hope they haven't stayed together. Nobody but a fool goes with a pair anyhow.

ALWA. They won't have stayed together!

SCHIGOLCH. Let's hope not, anyhow. If the worst comes to the worse she'll fend the creature off with her feet.

ALWA. One man can rise from the dregs of society to become the most celebrated man in the country, while another, born to the purple, dies in the gutter and cannot die.

SCHIGOLCH. They're coming now!

ALWA. And what happy hours of joyful creation they have spent together.

SCHIGOLCH. They can do that even better now. – We must conceal ourselves again.

ALWA. I shall stay here.

SCHIGOLCH. Why are you sorry for her? – A man who spends his money has his reasons for it!

ALWA. I no longer have the moral courage to let my comfort be disturbed for the sake of a miserable sum of money. (He creeps back under his rug)

SCHIGOLCH. *Noblesse oblige*! A decent man acts as becomes his station in life. (Hides in his cubby-hole)

LULU. (opening the door) Come right in, darling!

(KUNGU POTI, Crown Prince of Uahubee, enters in a light-coloured overcoat, light trousers, white spats, yellow buttoned boots, and a grey top hat. The characteristic African sibilants are noticeable in his speech, which is interrupted by frequent belching)

KUNGU POTI. God damn! – Is very dark on stairs!

LULU. It's lighter here, sweetheart! (Taking him by the hand and leading him downstage) Come, come!

KUNGU POTI. But is cold here, very cold.

LULU. Will you have some brandy?

KUNGU POTI. Brandy? – Always I drink brandy! Brandy is good!

LULU. (gives him the bottle) I don't know where the glass has got to.

KUNGU POTI. No matter. (Puts the bottle to his lips and drinks) Brandy! – Plenty brandy!

LULU. You're a pretty young fellow.

KUNGU POTI. My father is Emperor of Uahabee. I have six wives here, two Spanish, two English, two French. Well – I don't like my wives. Always I must take bath, take bath, take bath ...

LULU. How much are you going to give me?

KUNGU POTI. Gold piece! You can be sure you will have gold piece! – Gold piece! – Always give gold piece!

LULU. You can give it to me later; but show it to me.

KUNGU POTI. Me never pay first.

LULU. But you can at least show it to me!

KUNGU POTI. Not understand! Not understand! Come, Ragaprischimulara! (Seizing LULU round the waist) Come!

LULU. (resists with all her strength) Let me go! Let me go!

(ALWA has struggled up from his bed, creeps up to KUNGU POTI from behind and pulls him back by the coat collar)

KUNGU POTI. (turning rapidly on ALWA) Oh, oh, here is den of murderers. Come my friend – will give you sleep-medicine. (He strikes him with a life-preserver, whereupon ALWA collapses with a groan) Here is opium! Nice dreams coming, nice dreams. (He gives LULU a kiss. Pointing to ALWA) Dreaming of you, Ragaprischimulara! Nice dreams! (Hastening to the door) Here is door! (Exit)

LULU. But I can't stay here! Who could bear it any longer! Better to go back onto the streets. (Exit)

(SCHIGOLCH emerges from his cubby-hole)

SCHIGOLCH. (bending over ALWA) – Blood! – Alwa! He'll have to be got out of the way. Look alive there! – Otherwise our friends might be put off by him. Alwa! Alwa! – No good wavering about it –! – One way or the other, or it might easily be too late. I'll soon get him on his legs. (He lights a match and thrusts it into his collar. As ALWA doesn't stir) He wants to be left in peace. But this isn't the place to sleep. (He drags him by the scruff of the neck into LULU's chamber. Then he tries to turn up the lamp) It's almost time for me, too, or there won't be any Christmas pudding left at the public house downstairs. God knows when those two will be back from their pleasure trip. (His eyes falls on LULU's portrait) She doesn't understand the thing. She can't make a living out of love because love is her life. Here she comes! I'll appeal to her conscience.

(The door opens and COUNTESS GESCHWITZ enter)

If you mean to make these your quarters for the night perhaps you'll keep a look-out that nothing gets stolen.

GESCHWITZ. How dark it is in here!

SCHIGOLCH. It's going to be darker still. The Doctor has already retired for the night.

GESCHWITZ. She sent me on ahead.

SCHIGOLCH. Very sensible of her. – If anyone asks after me, I'm downstairs in the public house. (Exit)

GESCHWITZ. (alone) I'll sit by the door. I'll watch it all without flinching. (She sits down on the cane chair by the door) – There people don't know themselves, don't know what they are like. Only someone who is not human himself can really know them. Every word they utter is false, a lie. But they don't know it, for today they are like this, tomorrow like that, according to whether they have eaten, drunk and made love, or not. The body alone remains for a time what it is, and only the children are rational. The adults are like animals. Not one of them knows what he is doing. In their happiest moments they groan and moan and in the depths of misery they are delighted by the tiniest trifle. It is strange how hunger deprives men of the strength to be unhappy. But when they have gorged themselves they turn the world into a chamber of horrors, throw their lives away for the satisfaction of a whim. I wonder if there have ever been people who were made happy by love. Their happiness after all consists of nothing more than being able to sleep better and forget everything. Lord God, I thank thee that I am not as other men are. I am not a human being at all – my body has nothing in common with other human bodies. But I have a human soul! The tormented have narrow shrivelled souls within them; but I know it is no merit on my part if I give up everything, sacrifice everything ...

(LULU opens the door and admits DR. HILTI. GESCHWITZ remains seated motionless by the door, unnoticed by either of them)

LULU. (gaily) Come in, come in! You'll stay the night with me?

DR. HILTI. But I have no more than five shillings on me. I never take more with me when I go out.

LULU. That's enough, because it's you. You have such honest eyes! – Come, give me a kiss.

DR. HILTI. Jesus, Mary, Joseph ...

LULU. Please, please, be quiet!

DR. HILTI. But devil take it, it's the first time I've ever been with a woman. That's really true. By God, I'd imagined it to be quite different!

LULU. Are you married?

DR. HILTI. For God's sake! What makes you think I'm married? – No, I'm a lecturer; I teach philosophy at the University. By God, I come of one of the best families in Basel; as a student I used to get only two francs' pocket money and I had better uses for it than women.

LULU. So that's why you've never been with a woman before?

DR. HILTI. Of course! Of course! But now I need it. I got engaged this evening to a girl from one of Basel's oldest families. She's here as a children's nurse.

LULU. Is your fiancée pretty?

DR. HILTI. Yes, she has two million. – I tell you, I can hardly wait to see what it's like.

LULU. (throwing back her hair) What luck I have! (She rises and takes

the lamp) Well, if you're ready then, Professor? (She conducts DR.
HILTI into her chamber)

GESCHWITZ. (pulls a small black revolver out of her pocket and holds it
to her forehead) Come, come ... beloved!

DR. HILTI. (snatches the door open from within and rushes out) What
sort of a dirty business is this! – There's a body in there!

LULU. (the lamp in her hand, holds him by the sleeve) Stay with me!

DR. HILTI. A dead body! A corpse?!

LULU. Stay with me, stay with me!

DR. HILTI. (freeing himself) There's a corpse lying in there in – A dirty
business, by God!

LULU. Stay with me!

DR. HILTI. How does one get out of here? (Catching sight of
GESCHWITZ) And there is the devil!

LULU. Please, please stay!

DR. HILTI. Dirty business, dirty business – My God! (Exit by centre
door)

LULU. Stop! – Stop! (Rushes after him)

GESCHWITZ. Better to hang! If she sees me lying in my own blood she
won't shed a single tear for me. I was never more to her than a
willing tool which didn't mind lending itself to the most difficult
tasks. From the very first she loathed me from the bottom of her
heart. Wouldn't it be better to jump off the bridge? Which is colder,
the water, or her heart? – I would dream till I drowned ... Better to
hang! ... Stab myself? – Hm, nothing to be gained by that ... How
often have I dreamed that she was kissing me! One minute more,
then an owl beats against the window and I wake ... Better to hang!
Not into the river; water is too pure for me. (Suddenly starting up)
There! – There! – There it is! – Quickly now, before she comes! (She
takes the rugstrap from the wall, climbs on a chair, fastens the strap
to a hook sticking into the doorpost, puts the strap round her neck,
kicks the chair away with her feet, and falls to the ground) Accursed

life! – Accursed life! ... could it still be in store for me? ... Let me
appeal once more to your heart, my angel! But you are cold! – I need
not go yet! Perhaps I am to have my taste of happiness. Listen to
him, Lulu; I need not go yet! (She drags herself over to LULU's
picture, sinks onto her knees and clasps her hands) My adored angel!
My beloved! My star! Have pity on me, have pity on me, have pity
on me!

(LULU opens the door to admit JACK. He is a square-built man,
elastic in his movements, with a pale face, inflamed eyes, thick
arched eyebrows, drooping moustache, sparse beard, matted
sidewhiskers and fiery red hands with gnawed finger nails. His eyes
are fixed on the ground. He is wearing a dark overcoat and a small
round felt hat)

JACK. (noticing GESCHWITZ) Who is that?

LULU. It's my sister, Sir. She's mad. I don't know how to get rid of her.

JACK. You seem to have a pretty mouth.

LULU. I get it from my mother.

JACK. It looks it. – How much do you want? – I haven't much money
left.

LULU. Don't you want to stay all night, then?

JACK. No, I haven't time. I must go home.

LULU. You can tell them at home tomorrow morning that you missed
the last omnibus and spent the night with a friend.

JACK. How much do you want?

LULU. I'm not asking for any gold nuggets, but – just a little something.

JACK. (turns towards the door) Good evening! Good evening!

LULU. (holds him back) No, no! Stay, for God's sake!

JACK. (walks past GESCHWITZ and opens the closet) Why should I stay
till morning! – It sounds suspicious! – While I'm asleep my pockets
will be turned out.

LULU. No, I shan't do that. No one will do it! Don't go because of that! Please!

JACK. How much do you want?

LULU. Give me half of what I asked before.

JACK. No, that's too much. – You don't seem to have been at this game long.

LULU. Today is the first time. (She pulls GESCHWITZ who, still on her knees, has half risen towards JACK, back by the strap round her neck) Lie down, will you!

JACK. Let her be. She's not your sister. She's in love with you. (He strokes GESCHWITZ's hair as if she were a dog) Poor creature!

LULU. Why are you staring at me like that?!

JACK. I sized you up by the way you walk. I said to myself you must have a well-made body.

LULU. How can anyone see such things?

JACK. I even saw that you had a pretty mouth. – I've only a silver piece on me.

LULU. Oh, well, what does it matter! Give it to me!

JACK. But you must give half of it back to me in change, so I can take the omnibus tomorrow morning.

LULU. I have nothing in my pocket.

JACK. Have a good look! Go through your pockets! There, what's that? Let me see it!

LULU. (holds her hand out to him) That's all I have.

JACK. Give me the money!

LULU. I'll change it tomorrow morning; then I'll give you half of it.

JACK. No, give me the whole thing.

LULU. (gives it to him) For God's sake! – But now, come. (She takes up the lamp)

JACK. We don't need any light. The moon's shining.

LULU. (puts down the lamp) Just as you like. (Throws her arms round JACK's neck) I won't do you any harm! I like you so much. Don't let me beg any longer!

JACK. I'm quite ready. (He follows her into SCHIGOLCH's cubby-hole)

(The lamp goes out. On the boards under both windows appear two harsh squares of light. Everything in the room is clearly visible)

GESCHWITZ. (alone, speaks as if in a dream) This is the last evening I shall spend with these people. – I shall go back to Germany. My mother will send me money for the fare. I shall take my matriculation. I must fight for women's rights, study jurisprudence.

LULU. (barefoot, in chemise and petticoat, tears the door open, screaming, and holds it shut from the outside) Help! – Help!

GESCHWITZ. (rushes to the door, pulls out her revolver and pushing LULU behind her, aims it at the door. To LULU) Let go!

(JACK, bent double, pulls the door open from inside and plunges a knife into GESCHWITZ's stomach.

GESCHWITZ fires a shot at the ceiling and collapses, whimpering)

JACK. (snatches the revolver from her and hurls himself against the outside door) God damn! I've never seen a prettier mouth. (Sweat is dripping from his hair, his hands are bloody. He pants as if to burst his lungs and stares at the ground with bulging eyes)

LULU. (trembling in every limb, looks wildly round her. Suddenly she seizes the bottle, dashes it against the table and rushes at JACK with the broken-off neck in her hand)

(JACK raises his right foot and sends her hurtling to the floor. Then he picks her up)

No, no! Have mercy! – Murder! – Police! – Police!

JACK. Shut up! You're not going to get away from me again! (He carries her into the closet)

LULU. (from within) No, no! — Oh! Oh ...

JACK. (returns after a while, and sets the bowl on the table) That was a good piece of work! (Washing his hands) What a damned lucky fellow I am! (Looks round for a towel) They haven't even got a towel! A miserable hole! (He dries his hands on GESCHWITZ's petticoat) This monster has nothing to fear from me! – (To GESCHWITZ) You're not long for this world, either. (Exit through the centre)

GESCHWITZ. (alone) Lulu! – My angel! – Let me see you once more! – I am near you – will stay near you – in eternity! (Her arms give way) Oh, God! – (She dies)

DEATH AND DEVIL

A Death Dance in Three Scenes

Jesus saith unto them,
Verily I say unto you,
That the publicans and
The harlots go into the
Kingdom of God before you.

(Matthew 21, 31)

CHARACTERS

MARQUIS CASTI-PIANI
MISS ELFRIEDE VON MALCHUS
MR. KÖNIG
LISISKA
THREE GIRLS

(A room with curtained windows. Two red easy chairs facing each other. In the proscenium right and left a small screen of ivy, behind which it is possible to hide without being hidden from the audience or visible from the stage. Behind the screens of ivy stand two stools upholstered in red. Central door and side doors.

ELFRIEDE VON MALCHUS sits in one of the armchairs. One can see that she feels ill at ease. She wears a simple dress cut in the 'reformed' style, hat, coat, and gloves)

ELFRIEDE. How much longer are they going to keep me waiting! (Long pause, during which she sits motionless) How much longer are they going to keep me waiting! (After a pause she rises, takes off her coat and lays it over one of the easy chairs, removes her hat and puts it on top of the coat. After which she walks back and forth twice, in manifest agitation. – Comes to a standstill) How much longer are they going to keep me waiting!

(As she finishes speaking MARQUIS CASTI-PIANI enters through the centre door. He is a tall man with a bald head, high forehead, large melancholy black eyes, powerful aquiline nose and a thick drooping black moustache. He wears a black morning coat, a fancy waistcoat, dark in colour, dark grey trousers, patent leather boots, black tie with a diamond pin)

CASTI-PIANI. (bowing) What can I do for you, Madame?

ELFRIEDE. (excitedly) I have already explained to the – lady, as clearly as anyone could, why I am here.

CASTI-PIANI. The – lady told me why you are here. The lady also told me that you are a member of the International Society for the Suppression of the White Slave Traffic.

ELFRIEDE. And so I am! I *am* a member of the International Society for the Suppression of the White Slave Traffic. But even if I were not, I would not have spared myself this journey for anything in the world. For nine months I have been on the track of this unfortunate creature. Everywhere where I have so far been the girl has always just been moved to another city. But she is here in this house! She is still here! The – lady made no bones about that. The lady gave me an assurance that she would send the girl to this very room, so that I may speak to her without being disturbed. I am here only to wait for the girl. I have no wish to submit to further inquisition, nor is there any occasion for me to do so.

CASTI-PIANI. Madame, I beg you not to excite yourself still further. The girl wishes to appear before you – decently clad. The lady asked me to tell you this, fearing that in your agitation you might needlessly be goaded into taking violent measures, and also as far as possible to alleviate the uneasiness which your having to wait in this room must cause you.

ELFRIEDE. (walking up and down excitedly) Please don't trouble yourself to make these polite remarks. The atmosphere which prevails here is nothing new to me. When I entered such a house for the first time I had to fight down nausea. That day for the first time I became aware of the extravagant exercise of self-control which my membership of the Society for the Suppression of White Slave Traffic would entail. Till then our efforts had been no more to me than a futile pastime in which I took part simply in order not to grow old and grey without ever having done anything useful.

CASTI-PIANI. Your remarks awake so much sympathy in me that I feel tempted to ask you to do me the honour of establishing your credentials as a member of the International Society for the Suppression of White Slave Traffic. It is a matter of experience that a number of persons push their way into this work whose object is something quite clear other than the rescue of fallen women. If you are serious in the pursuit of your lofty purpose, then the rigid control which we are forced to exercise should be in the highest degree welcome to you.

ELFRIEDE. I have been a member of our society for almost three years. My name is – Miss von Malchus.

CASTI-PIANI. Elfriede von Malchus?

ELFRIEDE. Yes. Elfriede von Malchus. How do you come to know my christian name?

CASTI-PIANI. We read the Society's annual report. If I remember rightly, you attracted notice as a speaker at the annual conference in Cologne last year.

ELFRIEDE. To my shame, for two long years I did nothing but write and speak, and speak and write, without finding the courage to get to grips with the traffic itself, till finally the traffic found its victim under my own roof, in my own family!

CASTI-PIANI. But if my information is correct your own papers, books and journals were solely responsible for this misfortune, in that you were not careful enough to keep them from the young creature whom you have come here to rescue.

ELFRIEDE. You are entirely right! Unfortunately I cannot contradict you! Night after night, when I had stretched out under the bedclothes, well satisfied with myself and the world in general, to enjoy ten hours of sleep which no power on earth could disturb, this seventeen-year-old creature, without my ever dreaming of it, crept into my study and from my piles of literature on the campaign against the white slave traffic allowed her love-starved imagination to conceive the most seductive pictures of sensual pleasure and appalling vice. And I, poor fool that I was, and for all my twenty-eight years, never even noticed next morning that the girl had been up all night. I had never had a sleepless night in all my life. When I went to my work the next morning I never once wondered how the hair-raising confusion among my papers had come about.

CASTI-PIANI. I am right in thinking, am I not, Miss von Malchus, that the girl was engaged by your parents to do light house-work?

ELFRIEDE. And it was the ruin of her! Yes! Mama and Papa were both enchanted by her modest propriety of manner. Papa, who is a civil servant and bureaucrat of the first water, felt her presence in the house to be a ray of light. After her sudden disappearance Mama and Papa no longer referred to my activities in the Society as spinsterish hysteria, but roundly called them a crime.

CASTI-PIANI. The girl is the illegitimate child of a washerwoman, is she not? Do you by any chance know who her father was?

ELFRIEDE. No, I never asked her. But who are you? How do you know all this?

CASTI-PIANI. Hm – The girl had read in one of your Society's reports that certain advertisements appear in the daily papers whereby, after making various misleading representations, the white slavers succeed in enticing young women and introduce them into the trade. Whereupon the young woman searched the next paper that came to hand for an advertisement of this kind and when she had found one, wrote a very correct letter proposing herself for the situation which had been falsely represented in the advertisement. It was in this way that I made her acquaintance.

ELFRIEDE. And you dare to speak to me of it so cynically?!

CASTI-PIANI. So realistically, my dear Miss von Malchus.

ELFRIEDE. (greatly agitated, clenching her fists) So you are the monster who consigned this girl to disgrace!!

CASTI-PIANI. (with a melancholy smile) My dear young lady, if you had any idea of the real cause of your burning agitation, I imagine you might be clever enough to keep quiet in the presence of a monster such as I appear to be.

ELFRIEDE. I don't understand. I don't know what you are trying to say!

CASTI-PIANI. You – are still – a virgin?

ELFRIEDE. (with a gasp) What right have you to ask such a question?

CASTI-PIANI. What in all the world is there to stop me?! – But be that as it may – at all events you are not married. You are, as you yourself just informed me, twenty-eight years old. These facts are proof enough that in comparison with other women, not to mention the person you have come here to rescue, you have only a meagre degree of sensual awareness.

ELFRIEDE. You may be right.

CASTI-PIANI. Of course I am only telling you this on the understanding that I do not annoy you with my disquisitions. I am far from regarding you as being in any way pathological or abnormal. But are you aware, my dear young lady, how you have satisfied your sensuality, feeble though it admittedly is?

ELFRIEDE. Well?

CASTI-PIANI. By joining the Society for the Suppression of the White Slave Traffic.

ELFRIEDE. (controlling her anger) Who do you think you are, Sir? I have come here to rescue an unhappy creature from the claws of vice! I have not come here to listen to your unsavoury observations.

CASTI-PIANI. Nor did I expect you to. But you see, in this respect we are closer to each other than your middle-class self-righteousness would ever let you suppose. To *you* nature has vouchsafed an extremely limited sensuality. And the storms of life have long since made a barren wilderness of *me*. And the fight against white slavery is to *your* sensuality what white slavery itself is to *mine*, assuming you feel inclined to concede me the possession of any such thing.

ELFRIEDE. What shameless hypocrisy! You worthless creature! Do you think you can fob me off with this sensational sort of hocus-pocus about the emotions, when like a weary hound I have been chasing the girl from one den of vice to the next? I stand here no longer as a member of the Society for the Suppression of the White Slave Traffic. I stand here as a wretched criminal, as one who without realising it has brought a fresh young life to misery and despair! I shall never permit myself to enjoy another mouthful as long as I live if I cannot snatch the child from ruin. You try to make me believe that sordid curiosity drove me to this house! You are a liar! You do not believe your own words! You have put the girl on the market not from unsatisfied sensuality but from a greed for money. You have put her on the market to make a good bargain out of her!

CASTI-PIANI. A good bargain! Exactly! But good bargains involve the satisfaction of both parties. I never make any bargains but good ones. Any other kind would be immoral! – Or are you perhaps of the opinion that for the woman the love market is a *bad* bargain?

ELFRIEDE. What do you mean by that?

CASTI-PIANI. I mean simply this: – But I'm not sure you are in the right frame of mind at the moment to listen to me with any attention.

ELFRIEDE. In heaven's name, spare us the introductory remarks!

CASTI-PIANI. Well, this is what I mean. When a man finds himself in want he often has no choice but to steal or starve. On the other hand, when a woman is in want there is beside this choice the possibility of selling her favours. This course is open to her only because in bestowing her favours a woman need herself feel nothing. Women have been exploiting this advantage since the world began. Quite apart from anything else man is by nature infinitely superior to woman if only because a woman suffers in bearing children ...

ELFRIEDE. Yes, that is just it, a contradiction which cries to heaven! That is what I am always saying! To bear children is anguish and tribulation; to beget them is regarded as a pleasant way of passing the time. And yet beneficent Providence, which has many other pieces of folly to its credit, has imposed this agony and tribulation upon the weaker sex!

CASTI-PIANI. My dear young lady, in this we are entirely of one mind! – And now you're trying to deprive your unfortunate sisters of the one small advantage which a – misguided creation has given them over men, the advantage of being able, in extreme necessity, to sell their favours, by representing such transactions as an indelible disgrace! A fine feminist you are, I must say!

ELFRIEDE. (almost in tears) It is an unspeakable misfortune, an everlasting curse upon our down-trodden sex, this ability to sell ourselves.

CASTI-PIANI. But God knows, it's not our fault that the love market is regarded as a curse upon the female sex! We traders have no higher ideal than that the trade should be conducted as openly, as freely as any other respectable trade. We traders have no higher ideal than that prices in the love market should be as high as possible. If you want to combat the oppression of your unhappy sex hurl your accusations in the face of bourgeois society. If you wish to protect the natural rights of your sisters then begin by suppressing the Society for the Suppression of the White Slave Traffic!

ELFRIEDE. (flaring up) I'm not staying here to listen to any more of your humbug! I am convinced that you have no serious intention of letting the girl go! While like a fool I have been listening to your sociological theorising I expect the poor wretch has been bundled into a cab, taken to the station and sent somewhere where she will be safe from members of the Society for the Suppression of the White Slave Traffic for good! Very well, then; I know what I have to do! (Picks up her hat and coat)

CASTI-PIANI. If you had any idea, my dear young lady, how much your outburst of rage has improved your humdrum appearance, you would not be in such a hurry to leave!

ELFRIEDE. Let me go! It is high time!

CASTI-PIANI. Where were you thinking of going?

ELFRIEDE. You know as well as I do where I am going!

CASTI-PIANI. (seizes ELFRIEDE by the throat, compresses her windpipe and forces her into one of the armchairs) You will stay here! I have something else to say to you. Do try to scream if you feel like it! We are used to every conceivable noise a human being can make. Scream as loud as you can! (Releasing her) I shouldn't be surprised if I didn't manage to make you see reason before you leave the house and run straight to the police!

ELFRIEDE. (with a gasp, tonelessly) It is the first time in my life that I have been subjected to violence in this way.

CASTI-PIANI. You have wasted so much of your life needlessly trying to redeem *filles de joie*! Why don't you do something to promote joy itself for once! Then you wouldn't have to worry about the poor creatures any more. Because the love market has been branded as the lowest, most disgraceful profession of all, girls and women of good family would rather give themselves to a man for nothing than receive payment for their favours! Whereby these women and girls degrade their sex as a tailor degrades his trade if he makes his customers' clothes for nothing!

ELFRIEDE. (still as if dazed) I don't understand a mortal word of what you say – I went to school when I was six and stayed there till I was fifteen. Later I spent a further three years on the schoolbench to take my examinations as a teacher. When I was a girl men from the best families were guests in my parents' house. I received a proposal from a man who had inherited an estate of twenty square miles, and who would have followed me to the ends of the earth if I had asked him to. But I felt I could not love him. Perhaps I was wrong. Perhaps I lacked that trace of ardour, however small, which is essential to marriage in any circumstances.

CASTI-PIANI. Are you tame at last?

ELFRIEDE. Tell me just one thing: if as a result of the life she leads here the girl should have a child, who is to look after it?

CASTI-PIANI. Look after it yourself, unless as a feminist you have something more important to do in the world. As long as one woman on God's earth still has to fear that she may become a mother, the emancipation of women will remain idle talk. To a woman maternity is a necessity of nature, like breathing or sleeping. Bourgeois society has curtailed this inborn right in a barbaric way. An illegitimate child is almost as great a disgrace as the love market. You're as much a whore with the one as with the other. The mother of an illegitimate child is no more spared the name of 'whore' than a girl in this house. If there is anything about this feminist movement of yours which has always sickened me it is the morality that you have instilled into your disciples for their way through life! Do you believe that the love market would ever in the world have been denounced as a disgrace if men could compete in this market with women? Professional jealousy, pure professional jealousy! Nature affords woman the advantage of being able to traffic with her love, for which reason bourgeois society, being dominated by men, is forever representing this traffic as the most shameful of all crimes!

ELFRIEDE. (stands up and takes off her coat, which she lays over the chair; walks up and down) At the moment I must confess I am in no condition to examine the validity of your assertions. – But how in the world is it possible for a man of your education, with your outlook on society, of your intellectual ascendancy, to pass his life among the most worthless elements of society! – God knows, perhaps it was your bestial violence which forced me to take your theories seriously! At all events I am acutely aware that you have given me enough to think about for a long time to come, ideas which I would never in all my life have hit upon of my own accord. For years, winter after winter, I have listened to from twelve to twenty lectures given by every conceivable male and female authority on feminism. I cannot remember having heard one word that went to the heart of the matter as your statements have.

CASTI-PIANI. (in a lecturing tone) We should all understand clearly, my dear young lady, that this life is like walking in our sleep along the ridge-pole of a roof and that any sudden flash of light may break our necks for us.

ELFRIEDE. (staring at him) Now what do you mean by that? – Something outrageous, I suppose.

CASTI-PIANI. (very quietly) I said it only in reference to your own views about which you have hitherto felt so confident that you could freely pass judgments such as 'decent' or 'worthless' as if you had been specially and exclusively appointed by God to sit in judgment on your fellow men.

ELFRIEDE. (staring at him) You are a great man! – You are a noble man!

CASTI-PIANI. Your words touch upon the mortal wound which I brought with me into the world and of which I suppose one day I shall die. (Throws himself into a chair) – I am – – a moralist!

ELFRIEDE. And you bemoan the fact? – The fact that fate has given you the power to make other people happy? (After a brief inner struggle casts herself at his feet) In the name of Divine Mercy, marry me! Until I met you I could never imagine the possibility of giving myself to a man! I am utterly without experience; I swear it by all that is sacred. Till this hour I had no idea of what the word 'love' could mean. And here, with you, I feel it for the first time! Love lifts man above his wretched self. I am an ordinary, everyday woman, but my love for you makes me so free and bold that nothing is impossible to me. You may go from crime to crime, but I shall go before you! Go to prison, I go before you! From prison to the gallows, I go before you. Do not let this opportunity slip, I implore you! Marry me! Marry me! Marry me! It is the solution for us both, poor creatures that we are!

CASTI-PIANI. (strokes her head without looking at her) You are a good soul, but I am utterly indifferent as to whether you love me or not. – Of course, you cannot possibly know how many times I have had to submit to similar outpourings. Not that I under-estimate the value of love. But unfortunately love is made to provide the justification for all the countless women who are merely satisfying their sensuality without demanding remuneration for it, and who ruin the market for us by their undignified surrender.

ELFRIEDE. Marry me! There is still time for you to begin a new life! Marriage will make an orderly being of you. You could be the editor of a socialist paper, you could become a member of the Reichstag! Marry me, and for once in your life you will experience the superhuman sacrifice of which in her limitless love a woman is capable!

CASTI-PIANI. (stroking her hair without looking at her) At best your superhuman sacrifices would turn my stomach. All my life I've loved tigresses. For bitches I'm simply a piece of wood. My only consolation is that marriage, which you extol so enthusiastically and for which bitches are bred, is a cultural institution. Cultural institutions exist to be outgrown. Humanity will outgrow marriage just as it has conquered slavery. The free love market in which the tigress is triumphant is founded on an eternal natural law of immutable creation. And how proudly a woman will face the world when she has won the right to sell herself to the highest bidder without being stigmatised for it! Illegitimate children will be better off with their mothers than legitimate ones with their fathers. Woman's pride will no longer relate to the man who assigns her her position in life but to the world in which she wins the highest place to which her worth entitles her. What a glorious fresh sound the expression 'fille de joie' will acquire! The story of Paradise relates that woman was given the power to seduce. Woman seduces whom she will and when she will. She does not wait for love. Bourgeois society meets this fearful menace to our sacred culture by bringing up its women in an artificially induced intellectual darkness. Woman, as she develops, must not know what it really means to be a woman. Political constitutions might come to grief over it. No trick is too cruel or underhand for bourgeois society in its own defence. With every cultural advance we make, the love market extends itself. The cleverer the world becomes, the larger the love market. And our much praised culture in the name of morality condemns these millions of women to death by starvation or in the name of morality robs them of their honour and the right to live, in the name of morality thrusts them down into the realm of the beasts! How much longer shall an immorality which cries to heaven devastate the world with the executioner's axe of morality?

ELFRIEDE. (whimpering tonelessly) Marry me! You are above humanity. Today for the first time I am offering a man my hand.

CASTI-PIANI. (stroking her hair without looking at her) Bread and butter culture! Bread and butter culture! What would the world hear of this stuff and nonsense about morality if man could control love as he can politics?

ELFRIEDE. I ask no greater happiness of our marriage than to spend my life at your feet, listening to your words!

CASTI-PIANI. (not looking at her) Have you ever stopped to ask yourself what marriage is?

ELFRIEDE. Till now I have had no reason to do so. (Rising) Tell me! I will do everything to meet your requirements.

CASTI-PIANI. (drawing her onto his knee) Come then, child, I'll tell you. (As ELFRIEDE momentarily resists him) Keep still, please.

ELFRIEDE. I've never sat on a man's knee before.

CASTI-PIANI. Give me a kiss!

(ELFRIEDE kisses him)

Thank you. (Pushing her away) So you want to know what marriage is? – Tell me, which is the stronger, a man who *has* a dog or a man who has no dog?

ELFRIEDE. The man who *has* a dog is the stronger.

CASTI-PIANI. And now tell me which is stronger, a man who has *one* dog or a man who has two dogs?

ELFRIEDE. I think the man with *one* dog is stronger because two dogs couldn't help being jealous of one another.

CASTI-PIANI. To say the least. But then he'd also have to feed *two* dogs, otherwise they would run away, while one dog can look after itself and if need be protect its master from robbery.

ELFRIEDE. And you choose this repellent simile in order to explain the selfless, indissoluble union between man and woman? Merciful heavens, what experiences you must have had!

CASTI-PIANI. The man who has a wife is economically stronger than if he had none. But he is also stronger than if he had two or more wives to look after. There you have the foundation stone of marriage. A woman would never in her dreams have hit upon this ingenious invention!

ELFRIEDE. Poor pitiable creature! Have you known life under the paternal roof? Did you have a mother who tended you when you were ill, read fairy tales to you during your convalescence, in whom you could confide when something lay heavy on your heart, and who always, always helped you, even when you had given up hope of there being any help left for you in the world?

CASTI-PIANI. No one can experience what I experienced as a child without it destroying his energy for ever. Can you imagine yourself inside the skin of a young man of sixteen who is beaten because he can't get logarithms into his head? And the person who beat me was my father! And I beat him back! I beat my own father to death! He died after I had beaten him for the first time. – But these are trifles. You see the sort of creatures among whom I live here. Never have I had to hear from these creatures the insults which in my childhood were my mother's daily lot and which she daily challenged with abuse of her own. But these are trifles. The slaps, blows and kicks which father, mother and a dozen tutors competed with each other to inflict on my defenceless body were nothing to the slaps, blows and kicks with which the vicissitudes of my life have sought to degrade my defenceless soul.

ELFRIEDE. (kisses him) If you had any idea how deeply I love you because of these terrible experiences!

CASTI-PIANI. Human life is tenfold death in life! I do not mean for me. For you! For everyone who draws breath! For the simple man life consists of pain, suffering and torment which have to be endured by his body. And should he succeed in struggling up to a higher level of existence in the hope of escaping from the bodily torment then his life consists of pain, suffering and torment which must be endured by his *soul*, and in comparison to which the torments of the body were a pleasure. The cruelty of this life is sufficiently demonstrated by the fact that men had to imagine for themselves a being who was nothing but goodness, love and kindness and that all humanity, simply in order to be able to endure life at all, must pray to this being daily, even hourly!

ELFRIEDE. (fondling him) If you marry me your torments of soul and body will be at an end! You will no longer need to concern yourself with these dreadful problems. My mamma has a private fortune of sixty thousand marks of whose existence Papa is unaware, in spite of twenty-five years of happy marriage. Doesn't the prospect tempt you at all, if you marry me, of having sixty thousand marks in cash suddenly at your disposal?

CASTI-PIANI. (pushing her away, nervously) You do not know much about love-making, my dear lady. You are like the donkey who wanted to be a lap-dog. Your hands hurt me! That is by no means due to your having had no experience. It is due to your having your origins in the inhibited love-life of bourgeois society. There is no breeding in your body. It lacks the necessary sense of delicacy. Sense of delicacy and sense of shame! You lack any appreciation of the effect of your caresses; an instinct which all creatures of breeding are born with.

ELFRIEDE. (jumps up, outraged) And you dare tell me that in this house?

CASTI-PIANI. (who has also risen) I dare tell you that in this house!

ELFRIEDE. In this house?! That I have no sense of delicacy, no *sense of shame*?!

CASTI-PIANI. That you have no sense of delicacy, no sense of shame! In this house of ill-repute I dare tell you that! Satisfy yourself of the tact and delicacy with which these creatures apply themselves to their disreputable profession. There isn't a girl in this house who doesn't know more about the human soul than the most famous psychologist at the most famous university. Of course, my dear young lady, you would experience here that disillusionment which your past has stored up for you. I can recognise a woman who is made for the love-market at first glance by the innocent happiness and happy innocence which radiate from her frank, harmonious features. (Examining ELFRIEDE) In your features, my dear young lady, there is no trace either of happiness or of innocence.

ELFRIEDE. (hesitantly) But I am industrious and energetic and I have an invincible enthusiasm for the beautiful – don't you think I might acquire the sense of delicacy and tact of which you speak?

CASTI-PIANI. No, no! Dismiss any such idea from your mind at once!

ELFRIEDE. I am so convinced of the moral validity of all you say that no sacrifice would be too great if it would help me to overcome my middle-class inadequacy.

CASTI-PIANI. No, no, none of that for me! That would be dreadful. Life is dreadful enough as it is. No, my lady! Keep your dread hand off the *only ray of light* to penetrate the awful darkness of our earthly existence! What am I living for? Why do I play my part in this civilisation of ours! No, no! The *only pure, celestial flower* in the sweat-and-blood-stained thicket of life must not be trampled by clumsy feet! Believe me when I tell you that I would have put a bullet through my head fifty years ago if there had not been this one *bright star* shining above this howl of anguish evoked by the pangs of birth, life and death!

ELFRIEDE. Strain my mind as I may, I cannot guess the meaning of your words! What is this *one ray* of light which penetrates the night of our existence? What is this *one celestial flower* which must not be trampled in the mud?

CASTI-PIANI. (taking ELFRIEDE by the hand, in a whisper) The pleasures of the senses, my dear young lady, the *smiling, sunlit pleasures of the senses! Sensual enjoyment* is the *ray of light*, the *celestial flower*, because it is the one *unqualified delight*, the *one pure unalloyed pleasure* which earthly existence affords us. Believe me, for fifty years the one thing that has kept me in the world has been the selfless worship of this unique joy with its full-throated laughter which recompenses us through the senses for all the torments of existence!

ELFRIEDE. I think someone is coming.

CASTI-PIANI. That will be Lisiska.

ELFRIEDE. Lisiska? – Who is Lisiska?

CASTI-PIANI. The girl who reads the books on the International Campaign against the White Slave Traffic in your house! Now you will be able to see for yourself whether I have been boasting or not! We are well equipped for such occasions here, thank God. (He conducts her to the right hand corner of the proscenium) Please be so good as to sit down behind this screen of ivy! From here you will be able to observe the unalloyed, unmitigated happiness of two creatures brought together by the pleasures of the senses!

(ELFRIEDE sits down on the stool behind the ivy screen on the right. CASTI-PIANI goes to the centre, glances outside, and then sits down behind the ivy screen on the left.

MR. KÖNIG and LISISKA enter by the centre door. MR. KÖNIG, 25 years old, wears a light-coloured knickerbocker suit. LISISKA wears a simple white garment reaching to her calves, black stockings, black patent leather shoes, a white bow in her loose black hair)

MR. KÖNIG.
I do not come to waste my time with you

A libertine who's captured by your charms.
I shall be grateful and remain your friend
If, being destroyed to sanity, I leave here soon.

LISISKA.
Don't speak to me so kindly, please.
Here you are master and you give commands.
Don't hesitate to paint my bloodless face
With striking me across the cheeks.
For a whore, such as I am,
That is unprecedented gain.
Helpless complaints and whimpering and sobbing
Needn't in the very least disturb you.
Such pleasing scolding is already stale.
Heap torment onto torment without pity!
And if you smashed my face in with your fist
Even that would not satisfy my longing.

MR. KÖNIG.
I wasn't ready quite for words like this.
Is this a cheerful welcome for your guest?
You speak as though this place were purgatory
Where you atoned here for your past debauches.

LISISKA.
Not so at all! Desire, the monstrous beast,
Still rages unassuaged within this breast.
Do you think this devil's child I am
Had ever come into this house,
Could happiness have liberated me
From the beating horror of my heart?
Joy evaporates, a water-drop
On a hot stone!
And lust, which is unappeased,
Is a ravening despair
Which plunges downwards, seeking death,
In the bottomless abyss!
Are you not cruel then, my honoured sir?
How much then, I regret it.
What interest is my chatter to you,
When you strike out at me?

MR. KÖNIG.

If it is really then your fate that you are driven
Out of the deepest depths to plunge still lower,
Then I could weep that out of all the bevy
Of amorous girls, you are the one I chose.
Out of your eyes there struck upon my senses
A shaft of innocent well-being happiness.

LISISKA.

Are you willing that our time
Should slip away unused by us?
Down below there, watch in hand,
Mother Adele is sitting;
She counts and reckons without pause
The minutes of my happiness.

MR. KÖNIG.

You are quite surfeited with supreme pleasure
And hope that pain and tears will so fatigue you
That deep repose will finally overwhelm you,
For which in vain you yearn all day and night.

LISISKA.

If I should sleep, I beg you, with a mighty
Dig in the ribs, to make me wake.

MR. KÖNIG.

That rang false! The glass has a crack
How is a man supposed to understand it!
You might not care for joy, for life itself!
And yet for sleep? No, that was blasphemy!

LISISKA.

I am not your property,
You are not my keeper,
Do not then be sparing of
Using my life's properties.
Don't try, with your humanity,
To comfort my heart.
Who thrashes me unmercifully
Him I most respect.
     You ask
     If I still
     Am able to blush?

> Then hit me, and so
> You will see
> How it's done!

MR. KÖNIG.
> Cold shudders run across my back and chest.
> Let me out! I hoped, half in ecstasy,
> To pluck love's sweet fruit from the tree.
> You offer thorns to me instead.
> How could it be, your young wild life could stray
> From paths of flowers, to be caught in the thicket?

LISISKA.
> Do not let my lustful longing
> Go unappeased!
> Turn not heartlessly away!
> Before me lies my grave,
> And my one hope is from this world
> As much as possible to take down with me.
> Do you imagine that these longings come
> Through this house holding us as prisoners?
> No! Only our own senses' torturing greed
> Has put us here!
> But even this way of reckoning was
> Unreasonably made.
> Night on night
> I see it revealed sunlight-clear
> That even in this house there is no peace
> Afforded to the senses.

ELFRIEDE. (still in her hiding place, a look of astonishment on her face)
> Almighty God! That is *diametrically opposite* to what I've believed these
> past ten years ...

CASTI-PIANI. (still hidden, with an expression of horror on his face)
> The devil! That is *diametrically opposite* to what I've believed these past
> fifty years!

LISISKA.
> Don't go away! But stay and listen to me!
> I was an innocent child and I began
> My life so seriously, with zeal and duty!
> To wear a carefree smile was not my way.
> I heard my teachers, even my brothers and sisters,

Whisper about me in an awestruck way,
And both my parents said to me:
You'll live to be the joy of our old age!
And suddenly as the cock's cry
All that was past!
And my once-awakened longings
Grew beyond all bounds
Beyond all my thoughts,
Beyond all the tree feelings in my heart
Until I was amazed at what had happened,
At this which so befooled and lorded me
So that the lightning was unnoticed by me
Unheard the thunder falling from the sky.
I thought and I hoped life was given to us
To satisfy inexhaustible joy.

MR. KÖNIG.

Didn't you find this high hope fulfilled?
I'm speaking of course as the blind might of colours.

LISISKA.

No, there was only the devilish urging
In which there was left no place for joy.

MR. KÖNIG.

Of so many girls who died for love
Did all their desires go unappeased?
How is it then that so many women
Press in their thousands along this, your chosen path?

LISISKA.

Would you not like to boast
Of the weals on my body?
Why else was it made so soft,
Why else so delicate?
Men gaze speechless
at the marks, stroke on stroke.
And I to kindle fresh desire
Boast of whence they came.

MR. KÖNIG.

Be quiet, I say! Another word about it,
And I shall have been here for far too long!
There's written on the lines of your pale features

How swift as the storm-wind your youth has fled.
And the first time you lost your innocence
Did he who took you, leave you then in need?

LISISKA.
    No, but another came,
    Found joy, then grief.
    For I have always sworn eternal faith
    To every one of the young fools.
    Always I lived hoping that my torture
    Surely with the next would disappear.
    Every time it was but bitterness
    Every time I found no peace,
    And always there was this demonic urging
    In which there was not any place for joy.

MR. KÖNIG.
    And so you finally came into this house
    And here you lead your life of dissipation!
    Blaring music, and champagne on the tables,
    And boisterous laughter, attend each break of day.
    The long working day knows of no noise
    But of tongues whispering hotly of love.
    What a wretched beggar am I then
    In front of you, O you proud queen of love!
    I came with that, which is mine, so that I
    Might buy from you a plain exchange of joy.
    I could tear out my hair with fury now!
    Your life is but a grim pursuit of pleasure.
    The libertine's your friend who knows no bounds
    Of human restraint, set against his pleasure!
    Hurry then, go and embrace his limbs.
    A purer element sustains and feeds me.
    I sought refreshment and I have no longing
    To be embroiled in the world's filthiest depths.

LISISKA. (beseechingly)
    O but please stay! For if you leave me now
    Night will descend on me again. Don't go!
    Already each word falling from your lips
    Is like a whip-stroke goading my desire.
    May you but hate me with such fervour
    Instead of lips, that it may be your fists
    Which blow on blow upon my body smart.

Having once embraced you,
Then go back whence you came,
And then inscribe my name
Laughingly in your note-book ...
And I – for me the hateful curse
Remains, that it was the demonic urging
Again, which left no place for joy.

MR. KÖNIG. (very earnestly)
Now I don't trust my senses. Now it seems
You are in love with me? O what a torment!
How many nights of weeping I have spent
Having been cruelly repulsed by women.
Now shall a whore, for the first time in my life,
Whisper to me of love? Is it not your custom
To give yourself without discrimination?
And yet you seek from me your hoped-for comfort?
And sedulously bare your soul to me
So that its sombre charm enmeshes me?
Were I placed so closely at your side
I would be seized with horror at my fate!

LISISKA.
For God's sake, do not trust my love!
My duty here is to pretend I love.
Imagine for a moment what it's like
When someone suddenly throws wide the door;
And then one has to scrape one's love together.
There is a man, God made him as he is.
Do you wish then that I should start to play
This desperate game with you?
That I should at your feeling's culmination
Disgust only feel?
But if you should chastise my body
With your doughty peasant's fists,
That could, if you take your pleasure in it,
Bind us together, till death tear apart.

MR. KÖNIG.
You wear white robes of innocence. Even
This house has not defiled your soul.
My sight is blinded by your purity,
My heart cannot be sated with your image.
Weltering in suicide which never ceases;

With never-ending agony of soul
You struggle, in your face death, and hot hatred
In your heart at vain human happiness.

(He kneels before her)

Let me become your friend, a brother to you.
Whether you give your body to me will be
A deep secret between us. So you have raised me up!
Though I give praise here to these slender knees
You are mine only as the soul submits
To another soul. So only am I yours.
From hells or torment heavenwards you'll climb
And will no more be tortured by desires.
You will give up your breath on heavenly heights.
Through me humanity will learn of this.
In my chaste verse, will the world
Measure the anguish of commercial love.
I swear it by the heaven's eternal stars
Brightest illumination of our night.
Give me a pledge, now tell me honestly,
Have you ever found happiness in love?

LISISKA. (raising him up)
Whether you kill me on the spot,
Could I not answer otherwise.
Anyways it was demoniac urging
From which remained no place for joy.
So is it now within this house.
Here congregate all those
To whom love is unending torment
Insatiable greed.
Any other visitors who come
They are not taken seriously by us.
People like you are rare,
Because they do not matter,
Like us
Who with the unreasoning brutes
Are compared.
But is it possible that now at last
You are the one who may appease
My savage longing?

MR. KÖNIG.
  Whatever wandering paths you lead me through,
  Yet shines a star on us to keep us company.

LISISKA. (embraces and kisses him)
  Then come, my sweetheart! Now finally you're amenable.
  My dream of supreme pleasure long has been
  A land of undisturbed eternal rest.
  Oh, if I could but die beneath your fists!
  (Exeunt right)

CASTI-PIANI. (bursting out of his hiding place as if he had seen a ghost)
  What were they saying?!

ELFRIEDE. (bursting out of her hiding place, vehemently) What were
  they saying?! Worthless parasite that I am, what sort of a picture of
  sensual pleasure has this dried-up brain of mine conceived! Life in
  this house is self-sacrifice, blazing martyrdom. In my false conceit
  and threadbare self-righteousness I had held this house to be a
  hotbed of depravity!

CASTI-PIANI. I AM *shattered*!

ELFRIEDE. My youth, prodigally endowed by heaven with the need to
  be loved and the power of loving, all this I have wantonly dragged
  through the clogging grey filth of the gutter. Coward that I am, I saw
  the sanctity of sensual passion as the basest indecency.

CASTI-PIANI. (still as one who has seen a ghost) There we have our
  sudden blinding flash which came when one was sleepwalking along
  the roof and made one fall and break one's neck!

ELFRIEDE. (passionately) It was a blinding flash.

CASTI-PIANI. What is there left for me to do in the world when even
  sensual pleasure is nothing but diabolical slaughter, nothing but
  satanic slaughter, like the rest of existence? So this is how it really
  looks, this one divine ray of light to penetrate the dreadful midnight
  martyrdom of human existence. If I had only put a bullet through my
  head fifty years ago! Then I would not have been forced to
  acknowledge my spiritual bankruptcy, all the capital I've swindled
  together, worthless!

ELFRIEDE. What is there left for you to do in the world? I can tell you that! You traffic in women. You boast of doing so. At least you have influential connections with all the places that count where the traffic in women is concerned. Sell me! I implore you, sell me into a house like this one! You could make quite an advantageous deal with me. I have never loved, but at least that does not detract from my value. You shall have no cause to be ashamed of me, in fact your reputation among your customers will be enhanced. I'll vouch for it with any oath you care to ask of me!

CASTI-PIANI. (almost demented) What shall save me from the headlong plunge? What can help me to overcome the icy fear of death?!

ELFRIEDE. I will help you to overcome it. I will! Sell me! Then you will be saved!

CASTI-PIANI. Who are you?

ELFRIEDE. I long to find death in sensual pleasure, to be slaughtered on the sacrificial altar of sensual love!

CASTI-PIANI. You want me to sell *you*? You!

ELFRIEDE. I want to die the martyr's death which that girl who was just here is dying! Have I not then the same rights as other people?!

CASTI-PIANI. May heaven preserve me from this!! (With mounting passion) This – this – this is the mocking laughter of the fiend ringing out over my plunge to death!

ELFRIEDE. (falls at his feet) Sell me! Sell me!

CASTI-PIANI. The most ghastly occasions of my life are rising up again before me. Once before I consigned a girl to the love-market who was not by nature adapted to it and for that crime against nature I spent six whole years *behind bars*. Naturally she was one of those insipid creatures whose *big feet one can see written in their faces*!

ELFRIEDE. (clasping his knees) By the heart that beats within me I implore you to sell me! You were right. My activities in the Society for the Suppression of the White Slave Traffic were nothing but unsatisfied sensuality. But my sensuality is not feeble! Why do you not ask me to prove it? Shall I madly cover you with kisses?

CASTI-PIANI. And this ear-splitting howl of misery at my feet?! What is it? This shrill cry of distress, the pangs of birth, life and death, I can bear it no longer! I cannot endure this shriek of mortal pain!

ELFRIEDE. (wringing her hands) If you wish it, I will even sacrifice my innocence to *you*. If you wish it I will offer *you* my first night of love!

CASTI-PIANI. (with a scream) The *coup de grâce*!

(A shot is heard. ELFRIEDE utters a piercing shriek. CASTI-PIANI, his right hand clutching the smoking revolver, his left hand pressed convulsively to his breast, staggers to one of the armchairs and collapses into it)

Excuse me, Baroness – I – I – have hurt myself – it – it was not – not polite of me –

ELFRIEDE. (jumps up and bends over him) In God's name! You have not hit yourself, have you?!

CASTI-PIANI. Do – not scream – at me – like that. Be – be kind – kind to me – if you – if you can –

ELFRIEDE. (recoiling horrified, tearing her hair, staring at CASTI-PIANI, with a scream) No! No! No! How can I be kind, at such a sight as this! How can I!

(At the sound of the shot three slim young GIRLS dressed exactly like LISISKA have looked out inquisitively, one from each of the three doors. They have approached CASTI-PIANI uncertainly and are now with the utmost restraint, exchanging mute gestures with one another, trying to ease his death struggle)

CASTI-PIANI. (noticing the GIRLS) – And these – and these – avenging spirits – avenging spirits?? – – No, no! – this is – is Maruschka! – I can see you quite plainly. – And this – Euphemia! – this Theophila! – Ma – Ma – Maruschka! Kiss me, Maruschka!

(The slenderest of the three GIRLS bends over CASTI-PIANI and kisses him on the mouth)

(Anxiously) – No, no, no! That was no good! – Kiss – Kiss me properly!

(The girls kisses him again)

– Ah! – That's right! That's right! – Well – well – I – I – I have
betrayed – you – (Pulling himself slowly upright against
MARUSCHKA) – betrayed – you all! – Sensual pleasure – torture –
slavery – at last – at last – release! (He stands stiffly erect as if seized
with a convulsion, his eyes staring) I suppose – we must – receive –
our lord and master – standing ————-

(He collapses and dies)

ELFRIEDE. (weeping, to the three GIRLS) Well? – Has not one of you
three girls the courage? After all, you have been more to this man
than I was allowed to be!

(The three GIRLS draw back coldly, shaking their heads, timid and
uncertain)

(Sobbing, turns to CASTI-PIANI's corpse) You must forgive me, then,
miserable creature that I am! In life you abhorred me from the
bottom of your heart. Forgive me if I approach you again! (She kisses
him passionately on the mouth. Breaks into a flood of tears) This
final disappointment is one you did not imagine even in your deepest
gloom – that a *virgin* should close your eyes in death! – (She closes
his eyes and falls at his feet weeping bitterly)

CASTLE WETTERSTEIN

A Play in Three Acts

CHARACTERS

RÜDIGER Freiherr von Wetterstein

LEONORE VON GYSTROW

EFFIE her daughter

MEINRAD LUCKNER

KARL SALZMANN

PROF. SCHARLACH

WALDEMAR UHLHORST

MATTHIAS TAUBERT

SCHIGABEK

HEIRI WIPF

CHAGNARAL TSCHAMPER OF ATAKAMA

VAN ZEETER a hotel manager

DUVOISIN a police inspector

A PARLOURMAID

A WAITER

TWO GENDARMES

The play *Castle Wetterstein* embodies my views on the interior compulsions which are at the basis of marriage and family life. The substance of it, the events, the progress of the plot, are purely secondary. The romantic element in it was dictated by my need for space and freedom of movement whereby to provide scope for my ideas. More important to me was that it should have tension and be dramatically effective. I ask the critics, with all respect, to defer the formation of an opinion till such can be based on an actual performance. I should not be surprised by a ban on the play, since it would be no more than a logically inevitable consequence of the notorious indifference and apathy which characterise the whole of our public life.

ACT ONE

Scene One

(LEONORE, 32 years old, lies asleep on the sofa. She wakes, yawns and rubs her eyes. Sits up)

LEONORE. What sort of a novel have I got hold of here? – *A Slave in Europe* – – (Sitting upright on the sofa) And I dreamed about *him* again. – – As soon as I have drunk my tea I will waste no more thoughts on him. – (She stands up and rings the bell) – Then I'll feel quite sure again what attitude to adopt to my dream life.

A PARLOURMAID. (enters) Madame rang?

LEONORE. The tea.

(Exit the PARLOURMAID)

God knows, it looks to me as if he could not get on without me even now.

EFFIE. (fifteen years old, enters) I hear you ordered the tea, Mother. Did you have a good sleep?

LEONORE. Who said I had been asleep?

EFFIE. I didn't mean to hurt your feelings. Most people sleep in the afternoons. – Tell me, Mother dear, would you let me go to the theatre next Sunday with Gertrud Rickenbach?

LEONORE. My child, you speak as if I were a complete stranger to you.

EFFIE. I daresay I do. As far as I'm concerned the main thing is that in the next few years I shouldn't be a stranger to myself.

LEONORE. I don't understand what you mean.

EFFIE. At all events there's nothing more important for me at present than that I should make a good marriage.

LEONORE. Of course, child. Nor should it be difficult for you, I hope.

EFFIE. You needn't be in the least concerned, Mother. I think of nothing else day and night. – Here is the tea.

(The PARLOURMAID brings the tea and goes out)

LEONORE. (pouring out) For a woman, everything depends on her not lowering herself by her marriage. A woman who is unhappy in her marriage has no one but herself to blame.

EFFIE. Then why won't you let me go to the theatre on Sunday?

LEONORE. Words fail me, Effie. Have you forgotten your father already?

EFFIE. My not going to the theatre on Sunday won't bring Father back to us.

LEONORE. In this absurd behaviour of yours it is not so much a question of your father as of you yourself. As you honour your father, so will people respect you. Can one say anything better of you than that you are your father's child?

EFFIE. Half of me is. The other half is the child of my mother.

LEONORE. That won't get you anywhere.

EFFIE. Frankly, I don't think I suffer from vanity or conceit. But if I am anything at all, I am at least one thing thanks to you, Mother dear, and that is a good match.

LEONORE. We women can only use that as a sort of advertisement. A wise woman would rather witness the squandering of her entire fortune in cold blood than exploit it as something personal to herself.

EFFIE. (gaily) Then, Mother dear, it is all the more important that we should perfect our feminine virtues and accomplishments as early as possible.

LEONORE. I entirely agree with you. We women cannot set too high a value on our feminine virtues.

EFFIE. Then why can't I go to the theatre next Sunday?

LEONORE. How can you even ask such a thing? – We are in mourning!

EFFIE. It will soon be eighteen months!

LEONORE. Quite apart from the possibility of your being seen by someone in the theatre – so long as you are my daughter I simply will not tolerate your making so light of your father's death!

EFFIE. (after a pause) Did you know, Mother, that Gertrud von Rickenbach is going on the stage herself?

LEONORE. I had heard as much. For her it is the best thing. Her father is completely thriftless and her mother's behaviour is in itself enough to preclude her marrying in her own station.

EFFIE. But supposing I too take it into my head to cast off with one good shove all considerations of rank and position, to give up the idea of a marriage among our own sort and simply go on the stage myself?

LEONORE. (simply and unemphatically) Then, Effie, however much I might regret it, you would no longer be my child.

EFFIE. Of course, you've already made up your mind that I haven't the slightest talent for acting?

LEONORE. But why should I have! What utter nonsense. In the first place women are actresses by nature, because no woman can keep a man happy by being sincere. And secondly, you're nobly-born. You have inherited in your own flesh and blood by far the larger part of what in these wretched worms who earn their livings on the stage is admired as histrionic artistry. But let me tell you one thing, Effie. Anyone who shows themselves off for money doesn't belong to good society. I don't dispute that there are women on the stage against whom nothing can be said. But those are the exceptions. My own acquaintance with men has taught me that. But for business reasons everything is always purposely arranged in the theatre as if all the spectators were as dishonourable and depraved as the show-folk themselves.

EFFIE. I've always thought that acting must be a far greater pleasure for the actors than for the audience.

LEONORE. That is just what makes it so undignified. Acting is a profession in which one gets paid for one's own enjoyment. That is something no decent person would do.

EFFIE. But doesn't a woman do that when she marries?

LEONORE. I don't understand what you mean.

EFFIE. I mean that she lets herself be paid for her own enjoyment.

LEONORE. By whom does she let herself be paid?

EFFIE. By her husband, of course. Who else?

LEONORE. Heaven forbid! What an idea. A woman no more lets herself be paid for her own enjoyment in marriage than a man does. They both do what they do for each other for nothing.

EFFIE. How strange! I'd always imagined it to be quite different.

LEONORE. You are obviously confusing two activities which have nothing to do with each other. Actors used to come to my parents' house in Hamburg, it's true. But they were allowed in on sufferance. In return for which they were expected to be entertaining. But one permitted them no greater intimacy than was socially unavoidable. – What play are they doing on Sunday?

EFFIE. *The Wild Duck*.

LEONORE. I don't know it. I've never heard of it.

EFFIE. By Ibsen.

LEONORE. But Good Heavens! Isn't he the scoundrel who has been dragging marriage and the family through the mud and declaring all respectable people to be mad?

EFFIE. You've no idea how uneducated you are, Mother! Ibsen is quite the fashion!

LEONORE. Really!?

EFFIE. The Court goes to the theatre when they're playing Ibsen. You don't like Ibsen simply and solely because Father always spoke so disparagingly of him. But I'm quite sure even Father would speak differently of him today.

LEONORE. Really? Are you sure?

EFFIE. Today Father would say. – Ibsen? Upon my soul! Splendid fellow!

LEONORE. Tell me, Effie, what sort of thing does he write about? Can you enlighten me in a few words?

EFFIE. Almost always he writes about the lives of people like us.

LEONORE. People like himself?

EFFIE. Like us! – Us! – You and I!

LEONORE. How does he know about that?

EFFIE. Lord knows! I certainly didn't tell him anything.

LEONORE. Then surely he can't drag family life through the mud after all?

EFFIE. (cautiously) Well, Father was unfaithful to you ...

LEONORE. (rising indignantly) How dare you say such a thing, child?

EFFIE. How dare I, Mother dear? I dare to answer your question, as decently as a young woman can.

LEONORE. Be quiet, I tell you! No young girl talks as you have just been talking!

EFFIE. (with a pleasant smile) I can't afford to have my young girlhood called in question if I am to marry a man in our own circle. Least of all by you, because everyone will say you are the one to know all there is to know about me. As a matter of fact, I am a young girl. Or has anyone ever said anything different about me?

LEONORE. No. As far as I know there is no gossip about you.

EFFIE. God knows, I'm not particularly proud of the fact. But at the moment I've no more important task in life than to be a young girl. That's why I think I have a certain right to stick up for myself.

LEONORE. At all events you have all the more reason to honour your father's memory and not to speak ill of him even in the grave.

EFFIE. Do you really think that was such a terrible thing to say of him, Mother?

LEONORE. You are inhuman, Effie. I beg you, never, never speak of this dreadful thing again! From the day we married, your father was a man of honour. – That was my pride – was everything to me! – or – or –

EFFIE. Or?

LEONORE. But this is something the human mind simply cannot take in! – or he must have deceived me from the day we first met! – No! No! No! I forgave him because I knew him through and through – And because I knew myself – I trusted him and I trusted myself, and no power on earth is going to rob me of this trust!

EFFIE. (rises, embraces and kisses LEONORE) You're so amazingly beautiful, Mother, when you are roused on Father's behalf. All the love I feel for you can't bring me to ask your forgiveness!

LEONORE. (her handkerchief to her eyes) You have hurt me unspeakably with this cruel heartlessness of yours!

EFFIE. Don't be cross with me, Mother. No one at Madame Duplan's finishing school in Lausanne thought of teaching us when to be as insensible as blocks of wood and when to be as sensitive as plants. Don't worry, Mother. I shall learn it soon enough.

LEONORE. Leave me alone, child. – I feel like a fish that has been cast up on the shore. – Emotions are crowding in on me from all sides.

EFFIE. May I kiss your hand, Mother?

LEONORE. Kiss me on the mouth!

(EFFIE gives her mother a fleeting kiss on the mouth)

(Recoiling) Child!

EFFIE. What's the matter, Mother?

LEONORE. You must get married as soon as possible.

EFFIE. (gaily) I shall manage that perfectly. Cheer up, Mother! I may
give you a big surprise even yet! (Exit)

LEONORE. (with a sigh of relief) Thank goodness! – I know I'm irritable
with her. – (She picks up the book which is lying open on the sofa) *A
Slave in Europe*. Who on earth is it by? (Looks at the title page)
Hackländer! – Who knows – I may be reading Ibsen next. I hope he
knows something about the interpretation of dreams! (She lies down
on the sofa and begins to read. There is a knock) Come in!

Scene Two

(The PARLOURMAID enters noiselessly and offers a card on a silver tray)

LEONORE. (reads from the card) 'Dr. Thilo von Chrysander, chaplain-
in-ordinary retired, ecclesiastical commissioner'. (To the
PARLOURMAID) Just a moment! (She sits down in front of the
mirror and carefully arranges her hair. Rises) Show him in. (Exit the
PARLOURMAID)

RÜDIGER. (27 years old, in elegant mourning dress, enters rapidly. As
LEONORE seems about to lose her composure) You may trust the
sight of your own eyes. I am not my own double! I am myself. Do
not faint now, will you? Confirm my unshakeable faith in your
unconquerable fortitude!

LEONORE. (fighting for self-control) Oh God – how can I survive it!

RÜDIGER. So you are not going to have me shown out?

LEONORE. The necessary words fail me.

RÜDIGER. One word would be enough! – – (As LEONORE makes no

reply) My gratitude is boundless – like your generosity. –
(Cautiously) Now I must ask you to listen to me for a moment.

LEONORE. (stammering) You are in distress – of some sort – I suppose.
You need my – help ...

RÜDIGER. I do indeed. Yes.

LEONORE. Speak.

RÜDIGER. Won't you sit down first?

LEONORE. That will not be necessary.

RÜDIGER. Very well. We shall sit down soon enough.

LEONORE. Please come to the point.

RÜDIGER. I have come straight from the fortress, just as you see me.
You know I was punished with six months' imprisonment. If court-
martials were anything but an empty formality I would have been
sent to prison for life.

LEONORE. Why are you telling this to me?! – To me!? You, my
husband's murderer, you are too presumptuous – I suppose you are
afraid that my despair has not been heart-rending enough?!

RÜDIGER. I am afraid of something more serious than that, I am afraid
you are wronging the deceased.

LEONORE. You, who murdered him, are afraid that I, his unfortunate
wife, am wronging him? Do not imagine I will tolerate your inhuman
insolence a moment longer!

RÜDIGER. If your husband's memory is precious to you, and your spon-
taneous indignation shows me that it is, you will thank me from the
bottom of your heart for my incredible boldness.

LEONORE. Thank you?! I?! Does not the crudest feeling tell you what a
– what a monster you appear in my eyes? I loved my husband! I
don't suppose you know what that means. I cannot possibly forget
how much lightheartedness, strength and patience I have sacrificed.
Not that I am complaining! God forbid! What was I, after all, till he
made a woman of me worthy of his love. In his happiness I found my

happiness. If he liked a thing I was fired with enthusiasm for it. If something pained him I would without reflection have wiped it off the face of the earth. I loved with such ardour, hated so implacably that I thought I must be the most heroic woman that had ever lived. And now the creature who murdered him is trying to tell me that I am wronging the deceased!

RÜDIGER. Of course you are wronging him if what you honour in him are no more than virtues which any woman must see in her husband if she is not going to have to look about her for another.

LEONORE. How dare you say such a thing of me? – You surely do not imagine that I could have been fond of an ordinary man?! God knows, there were enough men after me. But when I look back, what commonplace people they were in comparison with him. The limitless capacity of his heart was something I had never dreamed of, of which an ordinary man can have no conception. And his refinement! His inexhaustible generosity to me! And then, all his life he excelled in every field, the finest horseman, the most entertaining companion. If the talk was of military service or campaigns I do not think anyone ever got the better of him in argument.

RÜDIGER. In his wife's presence that would go without saying.

LEONORE. You attribute these virtues to me? – It only shows that you had no idea of the stature of the man you did to death!

RÜDIGER. Now you are giving me proof of the fact that you are wronging him.

LEONORE. (recovering from her astonishment) You are showing an unparalleled insolence.

RÜDIGER. Am I to reckon it a particular distinction on Major von Gystrow's part that his wife regarded him as the most splendid fellow that ever lived?

LEONORE. Your remarks strike me as those of a madman.

RÜDIGER. It seems to me no higher valuation than if he counted it a particular virtue on your part that no other woman loved him as devotedly as you did.

LEONORE. (paralysed with astonishment) But what finer thing can you say of a married woman than that she loved her husband above all else?

RÜDIGER. That is mere natural history. But I could for example say of her that she is the embodiment of youthful freshness. That she has a lucid mind, which if she is free to develop it, will hold nothing sacred but crystal-clear, remorseless reason. I could say of her that her powers of apprehension function with an agility which one only rarely encounters even in men. But above all I could say of her that there is passion chained up within her so tempestuous in its force that from her very childhood she has looked forward with shuddering awe to the moment when she should see her pathetic ego with its paltry tribulations sink away beneath her into the abyss.

LEONORE. And you would let this distorted creature draw you into her toils with all this mischievous rubbish? You, a man entitled to expect something of life?! – There is not a single quality which you admire in this paragon that you would not have ruthlessly to oppose if your life were not to be made a hell. Except for our birth and our death, marriage is the most inexorable condition to which we human beings are subject. If you regard yourself as an exception to this you will only have to put up with quite exceptional discord and degradation in your marriage.

RÜDIGER. (with a smile) You have no idea how amusing your apprehensions sound. If ever I feel myself degraded I need only turn my back. Then I will get as much respect as I could wish for. – And by the way, I entirely forgot to mention one of my chosen one's finest qualities.

LEONORE. Then mention it now! What are you waiting for?

RÜDIGER. The woman I admire would go to her death for the man she loves.

LEONORE. If you value your own life, beware of such a woman! A woman who will die for her husband would put a bullet through his chest if she felt herself injured by him!

RÜDIGER. Then why didn't you shoot the major?!

LEONORE. Why didn't I shoot my husband?! – You ask me that?!

RÜDIGER. But he certainly injured you!

LEONORE. Because I loved him. Who could do the slightest hurt to anyone they loved? But even if I had wanted to kill ten times over, he was stiff and cold by the time I learnt of his misdeeds. You had been too quick for me, in treacherously forcing him out to face your murderous weapon.

RÜDIGER. For the sake of the major's honour I must point out that a bullet fired by a regular soldier can be just as deadly as one fired by a reservist.

LEONORE. (flaring up) How dare you come here and joke about his fate! As the custodian of his memory, I cannot permit it! A man like you has no business to challenge anyone to a duel with pistols, a man of whom it is rumoured that he had earned his living by putting his proficiency with the pistol on public display!

RÜDIGER. I cannot use this moment, sacred as it is, as an opportunity to defend myself against newspaper insinuations. Had the rumour of which you speak been confirmed I should have been punished not with detention but with imprisonment, perhaps even in the penitentiary. Anyhow, you know as well as I do that I had no choice. Had I not called the major out I would today be a man without honour.

LEONORE. What do I care about your honour!

RÜDIGER. But I care about it! For example, it would have been quite out of the question for me to enter your house.

LEONORE. Out of the question – my house ... why you think you still have any such right is beyond me.

RÜDIGER. We are companions in misfortune. It was through your husband that I lost my own spouse.

LEONORE. You mean your wife?! – I felicitate you on your loss! Your wife threw herself at my husband's feet like some wild bird which no longer hopes for human mercy. On the evening of that winter's day on which my husband was buried I found a letter from your wife in which she signed herself 'Your slave'. – What is there to mourn in the loss of a woman who exposes her husband to ridicule and at the same time destroys the happiness of another woman who has never done her the slightest harm?

RÜDIGER. I was divorced from her four weeks ago. Both the children were of course committed to me. I have entrusted them to my wife's mother to be brought up.

LEONORE. And what is to become of her now?

RÜDIGER. Of whom?

LEONORE. Of the unhappiest creature on God's earth. What a scene of devastation there must be in her soul! Everything lost, her last pathetic happiness thrown away! But such Jezebels deserve no better fate than to perish. Life would be unalloyed happiness if it were not for these desperate mischief-makers spreading their poison from below.

RÜDIGER. My divorced wife was not as depraved as all that. She did not give herself away from senseless frivolity. She let herself be carried away by her fatal spite. She believed I had betrayed her, because someone had falsely cast suspicion on me.

LEONORE. Someone had cast suspicion on you? What do you mean?

RÜDIGER. Someone wrote her an anonymous letter informing her that while I was spending the evenings with my companions I was really with a dancer from the Olympia Theatre.

LEONORE. And as a result of this hocus-pocus my husband is supposed to have let himself be taken up by this person as a stop-gap? Yes, as a stop-gap! You dare to say such a thing in my presence?

RÜDIGER. It grieves me very much, Madame, but you are still wronging the major.

LEONORE. Are you trying to tell me that he would have had to wait upon your wife's despair if he had ever felt an inclination to amuse himself with other women?

RÜDIGER. At any time of his life the major could always have had any woman he fancied. Of course! But as your husband he could have had nothing from them but the most wretched disillusionment. What interested him in my wife was the similarity between his unhappiness and hers. He sought consolation.

LEONORE. Why consolation, if he was so happy with me?

RÜDIGER. Doubts concerning you had been sown in his mind.

LEONORE. Concerning me?

RÜDIGER. He had received letters, conclusively proving that you were deceiving him.

LEONORE. I! That I was ...?! – Good God! And he believed it?!

RÜDIGER. He was an honest man. He did not overestimate his own attractions.

LEONORE. (crying out) No, no! That is impossible. He cannot have doubted me for an instant!

RÜDIGER. He doubted to the point of despair.

LEONORE. He cannot have! It is against reason! No, no! Now that he is no longer able to speak for himself I am not going to listen to such a thing from any living person!

RÜDIGER. Reason is always the first comrade to desert us in an emergency. If he had cold-bloodedly believed these insinuations he would have been just as cold-blooded about investigating them. In which case he would have discovered in the simplest possible way that the suspicions were false. But his love for you made it quite impossible for him to credit the insinuations even for an instant. He could feel only the unutterable pain of seeing his life's happiness destroyed.

LEONORE. But I must be a block of wood! Those last few weeks before New Year's morning I spent in unsuspecting happiness at his side. How can I not have felt the faintest sign of his suspicion, his bewilderment, all his cruel torment?

RÜDIGER. He wasn't a soldier for nothing. He controlled himself. The faintest hint of suffering would have meant your having it out between you, and for that he had not the necessary courage. Meanwhile the agonising need for dissimulation in his own home drove him to the house of my former wife, at whose hands he received the sincerest possible understanding.

LEONORE. (wringing her hands) So it is true! It is true. It is the most dreadful thing I have ever heard of! He could have believed for a moment that I – that I would do him even the smallest injury! – And with this picture in his heart he went into the fight, stood face to face with death! One cannot bear to think of his despair – it must have cried to heaven! With a curse on his lips – against me – he took up arms, with a curse he sank to his knees. Then he was not even murdered! He was seeking death! And I am his murderess! What in the world can he have been told about me?

RÜDIGER. How should I know?

LEONORE. (screams) You do know! I see it in your face! Tell me!

RÜDIGER. You are in no state to hear it now.

LEONORE. Have I not already heard the worst? Do you want to keep me on the rack in my present state?

RÜDIGER. It is too silly for you to her at this solemn moment.

LEONORE. So you do know it?

RÜDIGER. Yes.

LEONORE. Where in heaven's name did you hear all these dreadful things?

RÜDIGER. At the court-martial, which took place *in camera*. Naturally particular care was taken to conceal these unedifying facts from you.

LEONORE. Then the court-martial was nothing but a dishonest sham! – Why was I not called?!

RÜDIGER. Your innocence was quite beyond question.

LEONORE. But did not the hearing bring to light the identity of the person who wrote the letters whereby two unsuspecting families were brought to ruin?

RÜDIGER. No. They were unable to discover it. But I have come here to tell you.

LEONORE. (with foreboding) Do not speak! In God's name, I implore you not to go on! I have not the strength to hear the dreadful news!

RÜDIGER. I wrote the letters!

LEONORE. No, no! That is not true!

RÜDIGER. Do I strike you as incapable of it?

LEONORE. (staring at him with all her eyes) Yes – you could have done it!

RÜDIGER. And now – I ask you to be my wife.

LEONORE. I – saw that – coming.

RÜDIGER. For five whole years, day after day, night after night, my mind's eye has envisaged no other goal. When I first met you five years ago, one look at you was enough to convince me that a nature with your ardour and depth of soul was not to be met with but once in a lifetime. *One* victory this day has already brought me the endorsement of my conviction. You are in truth the woman for whom I have fought these past five years. Now I am no longer afraid to answer for my actions. The victims did not die in vain.

LEONORE. – Leave my house.

RÜDIGER. What is the good of saying that now? You underestimate the importance of the occasion. You underestimate the power you have in your own hands. One word from you would suffice to send me to the penitentiary.

LEONORE. Is that true?! – Will you swear that it is true?! – Are you trying to steal my confidence by misrepresentation?

RÜDIGER. Whether it is true or not, your duty at least is quite plain. As the dead man's wife you have the sacred inescapable duty of making public all that you have discovered.

LEONORE. And then?

RÜDIGER. Then I will bear my fate. Why not?!

LEONORE. (making a supreme effort) Go away! Go away! I do not know you! I have not understood a word of what you have been saying. Do you want me to call for help?!

RÜDIGER. Your tone rings false. – Why do you not simply press the bell?

LEONORE. As it is I cannot understand why we have not attracted attention with all the noise we have been making.

RÜDIGER. You have only the choice between fulfilling your sacred duty of denouncing me, or making up your mind to be my wife. Please decide.

LEONORE. Those are no more than empty boats. You cannot intimidate me with bogies! I cannot see any compelling reason why I should choose between two hell-fires.

RÜDIGER. I assure you, there is no third course open to you! However strong-minded you may be, you will not be able to keep my secret. You would give some hint, and your sister-in-law is burning with curiosity. You would be given no peace, you would feel yourself relieved of a terrible burden and I – I would simply have a piece of folly to regret.

LEONORE. You are right! You are entirely right! No one could conceal something so monstrous.

RÜDIGER. No one but my wife! – You have been my accomplice for five years as it is.

LEONORE. I still hope and hope that there may be some sort of black-mail behind your self-accusations.

RÜDIGER. The biggest thing at your disposal!

LEONORE. Then for heaven's sake name a definite sum.

RÜDIGER. You know that I desire you as my wife!

LEONORE. Of course you desire me! Of course! So that the price may be as heavy as possible. But I am anxious to purchase my freedom from you. I offer you – fifty thousand marks!

RÜDIGER. That is too little.

LEONORE. Fifty-five thousand ...

RÜDIGER. Those are empty words.

LEONORE. I have more than that.

RÜDIGER. You cannot possibly give away a tenth of your entire fortune.

LEONORE. What is it you want, then?

RÜDIGER. I want you to be my wife!

LEONORE. You suggest that I should marry my husband's murderer.

RÜDIGER. The man who has made the greatest sacrifices for you.

LEONORE. Such a marriage would be sheer torture.

RÜDIGER. Marriage is never sheer torture. One loves one another, or one parts. Most healthy people make happy couples. Why should we not be a happy couple? Marriage is not a bondage save to those mentally deranged people who regard it as such. If I cannot idolise my wife let her go and hang herself.

LEONORE. Almighty God! The chivalry of a horse-dealer! Am I to belong to you on the strength of this admission?!

RÜDIGER. You are not to belong to me! You belong to yourself! Marriage is made for man, not man for marriage! Your happiness, your freedom to develop yourself shall be the most sacred objects of our life together.

LEONORE. That is a new idea, I must confess! A surprising idea. But what about you! To whom do you belong? Do you not belong to me?!

RÜDIGER. At least to a greater extent than you belong to me. Have you already forgotten?

LEONORE. If only all this is true! – That is what I keep asking myself over and over again. Or are you boasting of outrages committed by others?

RÜDIGER. Now you need only ask whether I am marrying you for your money.

LEONORE. (quickly) Heaven forbid! No, no! I have no desire to hurt your feelings. Nothing is further from my mind. – But suppose it turns out after our marriage that you were nothing but a betrayed husband after all ...?

RÜDIGER. Madame must excuse me if I take leave.

LEONORE. You have forgotten where you are going!

RÜDIGER. Does that concern you?

LEONORE. Stay here!

RÜDIGER. Only against a deposit!

LEONORE. What do you mean?

RÜDIGER. Only against a reliable security.

LEONORE. What are you asking?

RÜDIGER. If I have to ask for it first there isn't much worth winning here.

LEONORE. Help yourself!

RÜDIGER. (turns towards the door) I am not going to force myself on anyone.

LEONORE. (flinging her arms round his neck) Here I am! Here I am!

RÜDIGER. (kissing her) I hold the prize for five years' struggle in my arms!

LEONORE. Are you not afraid of a woman who lets herself be kissed by her husband's murderer?

RÜDIGER. (with a smile) Am I less to be feared than you? We are a match for each other. Neither has the advantage.

LEONORE. But suppose a woman crosses your path who embodies all the charms and virtues you have ever prized in a woman, will you not betray me with her?

RÜDIGER. No, no, my child, you need not anticipate such follies from me.

LEONORE. In what way follies? When I asked my first husband about it he shrugged his shoulders and more or less gave me to understand that he was prepared to do it at any moment. I always used privately to thank heaven that it had not yet come to that. But the slip for which he paid with his life was the first and only one during our marriage; I would put my hand into the fire for that, even now.

RÜDIGER. I am absolutely convinced of it.

LEONORE. And you can tell me after our first kiss, looking me straight in the eye, and with an unconcern which one usually uses only in speaking of historical facts, that you will ever betray me?!

RÜDIGER. If I betray my wife it means that I have a wife who lets herself be betrayed. That is something one cannot joke out of existence. If my wife lets herself be betrayed by me, upon whom she depends for her happiness, then she will undoubtedly be betrayed by the rest of the world as well. When she buys a partridge in the market the woman will cheat her. And then who has the partridge put in front of him? Who has to choke the partridge down? Who pays for the partridge?

LEONORE. Splendid! Now, can you tell me what follows from this deduction if one reverses it – if I betray you?

RÜDIGER. It's much of a muchness! – If you betray me then at all events you will have married a man who lets himself be betrayed. And by a woman at that. My business acquaintances won't need to be told twice. They will take you as a shining example. In the shortest possible time I will have been cheated of all I possess and you, unless you want to go begging, will have every reason to look about you for another life partner.

LEONORE. (clapping her hands) Bravo! You are the first person on God's earth that I have heard speak a single worthwhile word on this dangerous subject! (Kissing him) Either dirty jokes or quotations from the Bible, that is all one hears in our circles on these subjects.

RÜDIGER. Human emotions speak such an infernal thieves' Latin. Anyone who trusts their nonsense finds himself most grievously sold and betrayed.

LEONORE. Do you really think that a woman has the same right to be unfaithful as a man has?

RÜDIGER. I think no such thing. I merely believe that a woman has the same right to be unfaithful as her husband's mistress has. Of course, a man has an incomparably greater right to be unfaithful than a woman, that is an incontestable fact. But under no circumstances has he a greater right to be unfaithful than his wife's lover.

LEONORE. That is a remarkable revelation! I should never in my life have dreamed that life was so simply arranged! Where do you get all these pieces of wisdom from?

RÜDIGER. From my own experience. I have always found that mutual infidelity, openly committed, conduces to the most comfortable and pleasant parting. Only naturally both sides forfeit all the benefit of what they have expended hitherto. They dig one hole to fill in another.

LEONORE. What do you mean by that?

RÜDIGER. One shakes off one burden, only in order to shoulder another.

LEONORE. Oh, I see!

RÜDIGER. What did you think I meant?

LEONORE. I thought you meant it personally.

RÜDIGER. You can interpret my words as you please. The important thing is that they remain true.

LEONORE. (embraces and kisses him) Marvellous! Marvellous! One can forgive a person anything, allow them anything, if they can say things like that.

RÜDIGER. Be mine!

LEONORE. Here I am! Take me! (Prolonged ringing is heard in the vestibule) What is that? Who can be ringing so rudely?

RÜDIGER. Are we quite alone in the house?

LEONORE. (smiling) The major!

RÜDIGER. What did I tell you? You are doing him wrong.

LEONORE. I am? – In what way?

RÜDIGER. We should let him rest in peace.

LEONORE. (listening) I think the maid has gone to the door.

RÜDIGER. After all, he has done us no harm.

LEONORE. I suddenly feel so strange here – as if the whole house were going to pieces.

Scene Three

EFFIE. (hurries in, dressed in hat and coat, and throws herself on her mother's neck) Mother, Mother! I'm engaged to be married!

LEONORE. You too? But you are still far too young!

EFFIE. But you told me I must get married as quickly as ... (Noticing RÜDIGER) Heavens above! A ghost! On the day of my betrothal!

LEONORE. (introducing RÜDIGER) Rüdiger von Wetterstein, my future husband.

RÜDIGER. My dear young lady, you have not the slightest reason to recoil from me. Until you are married of course the engagement between your mother and me shall remain a secret.

EFFIE. Mother, Mother?! – I don't know – am I still alive – am I dreaming?

LEONORE. All girls of fifteen feel as you do.

EFFIE. Is it true, Mother?

RÜDIGER. As you are engaged yourself you would have parted from your mother soon in any case.

LEONORE. To whom are you engaged?

EFFIE. I can't bring myself to say it ...

RÜDIGER. You can be sure, my dear young lady, that I regret your father's death as much as if it had been my own father I had killed. But having already lost your father, young lady, do you want to lose your mother too? If your mother does not like the man you have just chosen would you send him packing? Do you think you can expect your mother to dismiss the man she has chosen, for your sake?

EFFIE. (kisses her mother's hand) I wish you luck, Mother dearest. I understand. You cannot do otherwise. You are the one who must get on with him.

LEONORE. And what about you, child?

EFFIE. (exultant) The handsomest man in the world!

RÜDIGER. Of course, that was to be expected! What is more, he is one of the richest.

LEONORE. (to EFFIE) Really? Count d'Armont?

EFFIE. I met him down under the plane trees. I asked him if he really believed the Pope would come to Berlin for the Crown Prince's accession to the throne. Whereupon he said: It is no longer possible for me to think of life as endurable without you. I told him quite frankly that as far as I was concerned it was more or less a matter of indifference to me whom I married. The only thing was that I could not guarantee that I was particularly suited to marriage at all. Then he asked me if he may pay us a call. 'On your own responsibility', I said. If he has not got here by lunch-time tomorrow it will be entirely the old countess's fault, who maintains that I am flighty.

RÜDIGER. I know their family doctor. He will have to get her out of the way for a week or two.

LEONORE. How is he going to do that?

RÜDIGER. He will tell her that her heart is weak. Then she will retire into a sanatorium.

EFFIE. You are good at everything.

LEONORE. Effie!

EFFIE. What is the matter, Mother? I have heard the expression often enough from you.

LEONORE. Do not be angry with me for that, child. But I must ask you to be more respectful.

EFFIE. (kissing her) You are right, Mother. I am afraid it will not come very easy, but I will do my best to say 'Father'. We women must stand together.

RÜDIGER. Our emotional life consists of our overrating the importance of human relationships. No one is really irreplaceable.

ACT TWO

Scene One

(Opulently and tastefully furnished room in the Hotel Beau Rivage, Ouchy, on the Lake of Geneva. In the background a door opening onto a balcony with a view onto the lake. It is evening – the lamps are lit)

LUCKNER. (walking about the room) That fine husband of yours, Rüdiger Baron Wetterstein has in the course of the past year misappropriated diamonds to the value of two million. (He bursts into a booming laugh) Holy cannon fodder! If the ape had at least buried the diamonds underground somewhere! But he has been chucking the stones into the jaws of every shady dealer in both hemispheres, as if they were rotten bananas.

LEONORE. I find you positively provocative, but in exactly the opposite sense to what you think. You need not hope you can regard Rüdiger and me as your prospective victims.

LUCKNER. Almighty Panama Canal! (He laughs) Take a lesson from me. The pleasure is costing me a cool two million. Mighty Brahmaputra! (He laughs) Has Wetterstein never sung our priceless Latin school song for your benefit?

'Oh the girl had such a fright,
She couldn't even sit upright
And would have fallen off her chair
If she hadn't held on tight.'

LEONORE. Thank God! At least the monster is completely drunk!

LUCKNER. Me drunk! (He laughs) Don't you know me better than that? No, my heavenly victim. Though my father may have created the most magnificent brewery in the whole Palatinate a thousand times over! But since my earliest youth I have vied with our strongest draysmen in lifting beer casks. That turns every muscle in one's body into bullet-proof armour-plating.

LEONORE. Rüdiger has no idea what has been going on around him. Even today Rüdiger does not in the least realise what a monster he is up against in you.

LUCKNER. Well, well! The first time we were in the mines together, you and he and I, that time in Africa, I could have squeezed your entire fortune out of the fellow in the twinkling of an eye. But you stood at his side, you gaped up at him like a tortoise at a telegraph pole. And I said to myself: Such splendid specimens of womanhood are only to be caught through the men who are loved by them. And he stared at me like a bloated capitalist dismissing a newspaper boy. Good Lord! Good Lord! No, Rüdiger von Wetterstein, I said to myself, we shan't part from each other so very quietly! A woman like this, I said to myself, is only born once every hundred years. Anyone who fails to take her where he finds her, even if it costs him two million ...

LEONORE. Do you think you could allow one to talk sensibly to you for a moment?

LUCKNER. (with a laugh) I'm the sort of man, you know ... really, I am an extraordinary chap! Exceptional! For one thing, I'd like you to feel my head! Posemuckel and Sumatra! Have you ever in your life seen such an excrescence on a human body?

LEONORE. If Rüdiger remains joint owner of our mines in Jagersfontein, as he has a perfect right to do, then he can restore every single diamond to you down to the very tiniest one in the course of the next five years.

LUCKNER. (bursts into a booming laugh) Just like me with my head, you see! It's my weak spot. An historical fact, known all over the world, respected by every boxer and wrestler on the face of the earth. Sailors, butchers' assistants who don't give a damn for the police or providence, any more than people of our sort do for a picture gallery, when we fight together they never lay a finger on my head. Up here, do you see, where my hair is curliest, you can fell me with a wooden spoon, but otherwise, heavenly hail-stones! ... And as for you!

Pestilence and destruction! Your unfathomable emerald green eyes! It's only out of spite that you're not letting them shine now. And then, your hair! Holy hound of Hell! Enough to break one's heart! Sacred Bimbam! I saw you in a dream coming up as a glowing cannon-ball, spitting and sizzling, so that I was scattered to all the winds of Heaven. And your hand! Your hand! Infernal sulphurous pit, your hand! And then, your walk! Blood and thunder! As to that, I've been a reliable judge of horseflesh from my youth up. I'd size up a horse with the same eyes that I'd use to pick myself a woman. The most hidden flaw stares at me magnified a million times. And talking of millions! If Wetterstein and I hadn't gone in for diamond washing I'd have made just as many millions as a horse dealer in the American luxury trade.

LEONORE. (still seated in her chair, wringing her hands) God in heaven! Oh God, show me how I can convince this repulsive monster of my boundless disgust!

LUCKNER. (with a wild laugh) Oh, my poor broken lily! You poor little fool, you, do you think I expect you to love me? Blessed alpine artillery! You're welcome to save your love for that sugar-boy of yours. Almighty fool's paradise! To me there is nothing more frightful than for a woman to find *me* attractive. My personal affairs are no concern of hers.

LEONORE. In any case, I would put a bullet through my head first.

LUCKNER. Then hurry up about it! Your husband, that thirty-carat rhinoceros, is seriously in need of being taken energetically in hand. Five years away from the world will be a re-birth to him. As soon as he is on solid ground he will begin the most glorious period of his career. In six months he will be principal secretary and the director's right-hand man. (Listening) Sacred world parliament! I hear his foot-steps!

Scene Two

(Enter RÜDIGER VON WETTERSTEIN, hurriedly)

RÜDIGER. (catching sight of LUCKNER) What are you doing here?

LUCKNER. We'll light ourselves a cigarette if you have no objection (He does so)

RÜDIGER. Will you kindly get out of here! (He goes for his throat and tries to eject him from the room. They struggle together)

LUCKNER. (hurls RÜDIGER into an armchair and lights himself another cigarette) You poor diamond washerwoman, you! Your legs ought at least to be as big as our arms! Death and Divorce Courts! (He laughs) You had the colossal idiocy to found the dynasty of Wetterstein. Hamurabi, Caesar, Bonaparte, Wetterstein! You ass beyond compare, you would-be Napoleon, you block-head of the first water. You wanted to be the fifth most important man in the world, Rockefeller, Morgan, Krupp, Carnegie and Wetterstein. (He laughs)

RÜDIGER. (in the armchair) I can't possibly put my mind to anything at the moment. Give me till tomorrow.

LUCKNER. Not for the whole of Chicago! Not even if it rains manure! We've been waiting two years already! – In half an hour we shall be quits. It is all so divinely, unspeakably well arranged: when the female resists, the man's strength becomes superhuman. The more desperate the resistance, the more skilfully the man deals with it. But if the man resists – well – I hope you enjoy your dinner!

LEONORE. (coming right up to LUCKNER, with great determination) Aren't you afraid I might throttle you with my two hands?

LUCKNER. Not in the least! We await you in our sitting-room. We shall stay in the hotel till ten o'clock. (Exit)

Scene Three

RÜDIGER. (rising) I am leaving you alone, Leonore. Luckner has notified the police. I do not wish my fate to overtake me in your presence.

LEONORE. Then I go with you.

RÜDIGER. In that case there is no point in my going away. We might just as well stay here.

LEONORE. Do you want to put an end to your life?

RÜDIGER. No! I did want to, I suppose. But I know quite well I have not the strength.

LEONORE. Would it not be far the best for us both quietly to remove ourselves from the world?

RÜDIGER. What for? When I am gone no one can have anything against you.

LEONORE. When you are gone? – What good will it do me for no one to have anything against me?

RÜDIGER. You were happy before you met me. You will find that happiness again.

LEONORE. Those are just words – you don't believe in them yourself. I never knew what happiness was till we met.

RÜDIGER. So much the worse for you. I am always at odds with myself. I was an unhappy child in my parents' house, in my first marriage an unhappy man. I made you unspeakably unhappy when I destroyed your happiness. And since we have been together I have not felt a whit happier than before.

LEONORE. (crying out with pain) Oh! Oh! To hear that now!

RÜDIGER. Forgive me, forgive me. – I am simply not a consistent personality. Since my childhood two enemy races have fought a fight to the death within me.

LEONORE. At this moment your whole life looks just as dark to you as in happier times it looks brilliantly sunlit.

RÜDIGER. If we two were only not chained together!

LEONORE. What chains us together? Tell me, what?

RÜDIGER. What chains us? What chains us? Yes, yes, that is what I am always asking myself!

LEONORE. (after a pause, with a groan) I think, Rüdiger, I know what welds us together.

RÜDIGER. The crime that we committed together; my having driven your husband into the arms of my wife, my using that as an excuse for kicking my wife out, getting your husband out of the way by means of a trumped up duel, our subsequent marriage and our desire to make a life for ourselves the glory of which was to justify the monstrous sacrifices with which it was purchased.

LEONORE. That is morbid delicacy of feeling, empty superstition, bogies that you never knew of as long as you were happy.

RÜDIGER. (with a groan) Then give a name to the terrible fetter which prevents us from separating!

LEONORE. It is perfectly simple. Whenever you wanted us to part I did everything in my power to prevent it. And when I wanted us to part you did everything you could to keep us together.

RÜDIGER. But why?! Tell me why we did so? Why were we always so irrational?

LEONORE. As to that I know no more than you do. But one thing I do know – it is no use probing the mystery now.

RÜDIGER. Unfortunately not! Unfortunately that is what we always told ourselves every time misfortune paralysed our reason.

LEONORE. Unfortunately – you say? I say – thank God! – – You do not reply? – You struggle with yourself?! Rüdiger – we have not much more time. Shall we not quickly make an end of it all?

RÜDIGER. That is easily said.

LEONORE. And quickly done!

RÜDIGER. Here you are. (He lays a revolver on the table) Go on!

LEONORE. Can you not do it yourself? (Reaching for the weapon) I know you can't.

RÜDIGER. (seizing her by the arm and restraining her) Leonore, for God's sake!

LEONORE. We have both asked too much of life if we lack the necessary courage now!

RÜDIGER. (convulsively) I love you!

LEONORE. It is the first time I have heard that suspicious word from you!

RÜDIGER. What do you think it will be like for us both to make an end of ourselves?

LEONORE. I am incapable of thinking. That is all over. From the first day of our marriage we no longer belonged to good society.

RÜDIGER. That was an unforeseen blow for us. Good society is the society in which one does good business.

LEONORE. You direct your entire personality to the task of belonging to the great world.

RÜDIGER. That reproach is late in coming!

LEONORE. (pleading) Not 'reproach'! No, Rüdiger, how could I?

RÜDIGER. The great world is the world in which great deals are made.

LEONORE. As yet no one has threatened our bare existence.

RÜDIGER. Only we ourselves.

LEONORE. But why?

RÜDIGER. Why? Isn't it obvious? Because ofur human dignity is threatened.

LEONORE. Human dignity? Nonsense! Does it preserve a man's dignity for him to spend five years as a hangman's apprentice?

RÜDIGER. Hangman's apprentice? So you are heaping all the responsibility on me?!

LEONORE. How did you arrive at the unholy suspicion? Did you ever have a secret from me?

RÜDIGER. You always knew as much about what I was doing as I did myself. – Jesus Christ in his time discovered the attitude to life proper to that army of rejected ones who in these days spend their lives in prisons or in lunatic asylums.

LEONORE. And what has he to say of us women?

RÜDIGER. (with a scream) Leonore! How can you voice such a ques-

tion? (More calmly) Do what you like, and I will do what I like. –
Human dignity is not something to put on and take off at will.
Human dignity is breath, nourishment, light. Human dignity grows
out of the parents' marriage and is the basis for the marriages of the
children.

LEONORE. (reaches for the revolver) Here is our human dignity!

RÜDIGER. So you want to kill me? (Drawing himself up and looking
her in the eye) Try it, if you can!

LEONORE. If you don't want me to ...

RÜDIGER. I do! ... But be quick!

LEONORE. (withdraws her hand) Where shall I find the strength to do
it!

RÜDIGER. Of course, I am to blame again!

LEONORE. (throws herself on his bosom) No, no! I am to blame! I am
to blame!

RÜDIGER. That is why Christianity conquered the world. No one can be
certain he may not one day find himself in prison or in a madhouse.

LEONORE. And let him who thinks himself blameless cast the first stone
at them.

RÜDIGER. (his voice rising to a scream of pain) Be quiet, I tell you! Be
quiet! Have you gone mad?!

LEONORE. A dreadful agony! Yes! A dreadful fate, God knows! – But
why should I bear this infernal torment alone!

RÜDIGER. (beside himself with horror) Leonore? – The union of our
flesh ... you could ...

LEONORE. I am ready to go to any lengths! I will kill myself on the spot
if it will help you!

RÜDIGER. Kill yourself! Yes, yes! ... but ... no! The very thought ...
that you should think of it ...

LEONORE. You really think it is easier to kill oneself?

RÜDIGER. Easier or not, it does no good!

LEONORE. I will do what you tell me to do.

RÜDIGER. When I have to tell you what your duty to me is, I will long since have lost any reason for doing so.

LEONORE. (staring at him) I don't know the answer to that! It is amazing how little we human beings understand about this life of ours which is forever sending us into transports of delight or horror!

RÜDIGER. To the woman who goes her own way it is not my place to sanction, to ordain, or to forbid anything. Even the chastest woman does not feel it an underestimation if she is bought for two million. God be praised. Then I shall be free!

LEONORE. If they arrest you I shall shoot myself.

RÜDIGER. So shall I, if it should come to that. Of that I am quite certain.

Scene Four

EFFIE. (enters briskly) But Mother, Mother, what are you getting so excited about? I can hear your conversation up in my room. Is that energetic man from overseas still not satisfied? Actually, you know, you had a feeling from the first that you might one day fall into his devilish clutches.

RÜDIGER. The moment one feels oneself bound by something stronger than one's own free will the whole execrable horror of marriage is revealed.

LEONORE. Can we expect no help from your husband?

EFFIE. Do you mean money? – No, Mother dearest. My husband has nothing left but debts. The 200,000 francs which I gambled away last week in Monte Carlo did not for the most part proceed from him. When I left he was turning over a plan to found a railway company in Australia. At any rate he was under the impression that there are no railways in Australia yet.

LEONORE. What are you going to live on?

EFFIE. Something will turn up. In the first six months we would have drowned ourselves from boredom if my adventures had not provided interesting entertainment.

RÜDIGER. Then what is to prevent us from living in peace and turning our back on our misdeeds?

LEONORE. Human dignity prevents us! The simple dignity which the poorest child inherits from the loyal union of its parents. The dignity of which the poorest of human creatures builds his life's happiness!

RÜDIGER. Five minutes ago you were stoutly maintaining the opposite point of view.

LEONORE. What about you? Weren't you maintaining the opposite point of view five minutes ago too?

RÜDIGER. I have overcome my discouragement. I have recovered my composure.

LEONORE. Then why did we not agree five minutes ago? Why do we not agree now? Must I say it? – I know my child and I know you ...

RÜDIGER. You are so upset that you do not know what you are saying, Leonore.

EFFIE. If I were married to the most jealous man in the world I would be willing to help him out of a trap like this, and without prejudicing my fidelity to him, either.

LEONORE. What do you mean by that?

EFFIE. I should act as if I were resigning myself to my fate, go like a lamb to the slaughter. Suddenly I catch fire, become ecstatic – in love. But all this in such an exaggerated, insincere way that the tyrant loses all desire, his hair stands on end, his flesh creeps, so that he does not know where to look. And the problem is solved: Potiphar's wife and Joseph. When he is sober the brute's one desire is that no one should get to hear of it.

LEONORE. Child, my child, to the edge of what abysses have we come?

RÜDIGER. Viewed dispassionately, is our position really so desperate! – (To LEONORE) In the three years I have quadrupled the 400,000 marks which you received from your father as a bride. That money is secure. If we can survive this day no one in the world will have any claims on us. Then we are free and can embark with easy minds on the paths we have mapped out for ourselves. Then I will show people that I was justified in overstepping their boundaries. Then the world will bear the mark of my activities for a hundred years.

LEONORE. And I, poor creature that I am, will do what I can to facilitate your triumphal progress. Have I any other *raison d'être?* I hold you back and hinder you enough.

RÜDIGER. Do you believe that the great fortunes of the world were ever made by more innocent means? The first return that any property yields is the proud advantage that one need no longer concern oneself with where it came from.

EFFIE. I shall not be able to put up with life much longer! I come specially to Ouchy from Monte Carlo to see my parents once more and find them in a mood that makes me want to bury my head. Nothing but difficulties from morning till night. I can't sit all by myself in my room all day reading Dante! You are mortally afraid your marriage might break up, Mother. That is a childish delusion! I know nothing in the world more indestructible than marriage. And I am not thinking of my own marriage, either. My marriage is so resilient, so elastic that one could span the world with it! But I know people who have quarrelled every day for twenty-five years without once being unfaithful to each other. And I know people who have been unfaithful to each other every day for twenty-five years without once having quarrelled! No one would believe what a really proper marriage can stand. And, after all, it is not in the least necessary for people both to be fond of each other. If only one is fond of the other, that is good enough for half a lifetime.

LEONORE. Perhaps I am unequal to the force of events. But I feel myself so crushed by our position. I have the feeling of someone placing their foot upon my head to grind my face in the dirt.

EFFIE. That is known as hypochondria, Mother dear.

LEONORE. Rüdiger, do you remember how I came back from Hamburg, in the first three months of our marriage? You waited for me on the station at Hanover. Hardly were we alone when you told me that you had come to the station an hour too early and had walked up and down on the platform asking yourself which you would prefer – that I had let a man touch me with his foot under the table in Hamburg, or that I should perish in a railway accident on the way home. You said then with absolute conviction that you would prefer my death.

RÜDIGER. If you were to ask me I should say exactly the same today.

LEONORE. For a moment I was bewildered. Then I thanked my creator that we were both exalted enough to be able to look the realities of life fearlessly in the eye.

RÜDIGER. Well? And so ...?

LEONORE. And now?! ... And now ...?!

RÜDIGER. There are intimate thoughts which should never be voiced even between married people. Once their belonging together is called in question they confront each other immediately as mortal enemies.

EFFIE. As far as I am concerned the only people worth considering are the exceptions for whom the impossible becomes the possible.

LEONORE. The impossible, Effie?! It is impossible to give oneself to the murderer of someone whom one loved. I gave myself to him. It is impossible to make sure of a man by destroying oneself. I am prepared to do so. But to wipe oneself off the face of the earth for a man who may no longer even belong to one ...

A WAITER. (enters hurriedly) Je demande pardon. Il y a là bas un indi-vidu qui prétend que Monsieur sera menacé par la gendarmerie.

LEONORE. Now let the whole universe fall in around me! (She rushes out)

THE WAITER. (looks round enquiringly. As he receives no answer he leaves the room, closing the door behind him)

Scene Five

EFFIE. (after a pause) Do you really belong to the old nobility?

RÜDIGER. (sits at a table with his head in his hands, groaning) I am completely shattered. I am no more than a horrible distortion of what I used to be.

EFFIE. In a hundred years' time no one will be able to believe there could be such a fuss over such a harmless trick.

RÜDIGER. (rises and pulls himself together) My mother was a Goldstaub from Budapest.

EFFIE. I know an ancient prayer. It has been handed down from the time when two people could be punished with lifelong slavery if they were caught secretly embracing. The prayer ends with the words:

You should not love in weakness
But from strength
From self-reliance!
Love not in the darkness
But in the light.
Woe to the love
Which vanishes before the glances
Of the multitude,
For as your love is
So will be your children.
He who in darkness loves
In darkness lives.

RÜDIGER. Where did you read that?

EFFIE. The prayer begins with the words – 'I, whom am I'. That is the part I always like best.

RÜDIGER. How does it go on?

EFFIE.

I, the hidden One
Who summoned you to life
For my enjoyment.

... But there are signs and wonders coming to pass. I know an American demagogue. He is devoting his entire life to liberating the relationship between men and women from its mediaeval fetters.

RÜDIGER. I know whom you mean. I know the magic power of his oratory.

EFFIE. And what a bore as a lover! But *my* indestructibility! I have never met its match among any of my sisters! To myself I am an explicable miracle of nature. One moonlit night in the Colosseum in Rome I suddenly realised in what times I really ought to have lived; either in Athens at the time of Pericles, better still in Corinth; or in Rome under Commodus or Caracalla.

RÜDIGER. You are so superhumanly proud of your profession. I have never known even a diplomat to pride himself more on his irresponsibility.

EFFIE. To us surrender is a philosophy of life. I thought about it for two years, till one morning it was as if scales fell from my eyes. It was on a lonely mountain in Upper Austria. Quite alone I was waiting for the sun to rise. As the steel-blue screen was pricked by the first sparks I asked myself – What is the greatest triumph sought by a woman who has no children? – Sensuality!

RÜDIGER. You may have miscalculated. Do you remember Goethe's verse?

The man remains desirable till death,
Woman withers before she learns to use her reason.

EFFIE. (sings)

I know a most delightful child,
A child such as one seldom finds,
Black of eyes and black of hair,
In build and bearing more than fair
Not too large and not too small
Not too fat and not too thin
Sings, laughs, dances, cuts her capers:
Men go crazy for her favours.

And then, there is that other song of Goethe's (She sings and dances)

If the muscles are taut
Shoes and stockings in order
Then begin
Right in the middle

A queen from top to toe
Dance as no woman danced before
Cut every caper that you know
Left leg
Nimble leg
The right leg must be even nimbler.

And do you know what classic author wrote this song by any chance?

The pretty little girl
Has pretty legs
Real miracles
Real paragons.

And best of all
She was good at dancing.
Danced with nimble feet
Straight into my heart.

RÜDIGER. You sing charmingly! I am waiting for your answer.

EFFIE. Patience, patience. Our adventures call for both intelligence and adroitness. A fortnight ago in Monte Carlo I had supper simultaneously with three different men in the same hotel without one of them having the slightest inkling of the presence of the other two. There is emotional gymnastics for you! I had to calculate in seconds. I invented excuses for my disappearances and for keeping them waiting so that my brain buzzed like a mechanical spinning-mill. Each of the three called for me at our house. Each one ordered a different dinner of five courses of which I did not let a single one go untasted. Each one brought me back to the house in his car. It was a hodge-podge of delicious mouthfuls, popping corks, journeys in motor-cars, largesse-scattering ... The waiters had a grandstand view of the whole business. I have never been treated so respectfully and ceremoniously in any other hotel. What a strain it was next day, sorting all the events, contretemps and surprises into their proper categories. I had a slight fog of champagne on the brain, otherwise I would have drawn up a statistical table.

RÜDIGER. (has entirely recovered his composure) After that *tour de force* did you not feel your life was in danger?

EFFIE. What do I care about that? But just listen to the sequel. Next day towards evening the three gentlemen go to the Casino as usual. Each one tells a large circle of friends which they carefully collect around them that at eleven o'clock the previous evening he had supper tête-à-tête with the celebrated Comtess d'Armont, or Little Monkey, as they call me, in the Hotel Méditéranée. The gentlemen furthest away from the narrators heard all three accounts. For quite a long time they keep their amusement to themselves. Suddenly the whole room bursts into a roar of laughter. Naturally my three admirers have always hated each other like poison anyhow. At first they are as if struck by lightning. All at once there comes a shout from three directions at once – 'You liars! You liars!' – Each one challenges the other two to a duel with pistols. Finally there is a tremendous scrimmage. Which was what I had been waiting for. While the bloody heads were being cooled with ice-water I permitted myself to be escorted through the rooms by the Duke of Eurasburg. No one made a single remark about me. I said to myself: how wretchedly small the great world looks when it lies at one's feet.

RÜDIGER. (at her side) There is a sort of moist gleam in your black eye. I have never seen it in any other woman to so fascinating a degree.

EFFIE. I will give you one night ...

RÜDIGER. I am not up for sale.

EFFIE. One single night ...

RÜDIGER. But I have no desire to come to blows with waiters!

EFFIE. Not tonight ...

RÜDIGER. What a pity!

EFFIE. I can't say which at the moment ...

RÜDIGER. I am my own master.

EFFIE. But when the night does come, I will kiss you so that you will remember me all your life!

(A shot is heard from the floor below)

RÜDIGER. (trembling with shock) What was that?

EFFIE. A revolver – what else could it be?

RÜDIGER. There has been a disaster!

EFFIE. Why should there have been?

RÜDIGER. Can you still ask? (Exit)

EFFIE. (alone) Disasters don't happen as easily as all that! And what if there has been one! It will have its good sides as well as its bad. How terrified people are of disaster! As far as I am concerned there can be a disaster every day. When have I myself ever been safe from sheer murder! Just one thrill more! – – Fate, how grateful I am to you for having so prodigally endowed me for this career! No flagging or failing! No inhibitions! No compulsions! No hangovers!

Scene Six

(RÜDIGER brings in LEONORE, who is holding herself upright with an effort)

EFFIE. (with a shrill scream) Mother! (She rushes to her) Merciful heavens, how dreadful you look!

LEONORE. Effie? – Are you still alive?

RÜDIGER. (trembling with anxiety, lowers LEONORE into a chair) Pull yourself together, for God's sake. And go and lie down!

LEONORE. Up the stairs as far as here! The stairs! There was no end to them! One wall after another!

EFFIE. What was it? What happened?

LEONORE. He shot himself.

EFFIE. (kneeling at her mother's side) Shot himself? In your presence?

LEONORE. It was you who put the idea into my head, Effie.

RÜDIGER. Forget that! You should not hear a human voice for a week!

EFFIE. I was boasting, Mother. Showing off to you with childish fantasies.

LEONORE. I stagger down, each step an impassable wall. (With a scream) The way he is lying there!

RÜDIGER. Come to your senses! You will kill yourself if you think back about it.

EFFIE. Shall I call the doctor, Mother? Can I get you a restorative?

RÜDIGER. (stroking her, anxiously) What is done is done. Remember, you must bear up for our sakes. You look as if you had not a drop of blood left in your body.

LEONORE. But your freedom has been bought with blood. You should be proud, Rüdiger! Put yourself side by side with crowned heads! Your freedom has been bought with two human lives!

RÜDIGER. God in heaven! With two!

LEONORE. Do you count mine as nothing? – That made you jump! Does not my life count for anything! What is left of me? No. You had not suffered at all!

EFFIE. What man ever entered a woman's room in such despair as this? And all because we women do not know our own power.

LEONORE. Child! Child! God preserve us from that power! He was at the window, whistling a tune. Oh, the horrible fear that the brute might throw himself on me. I go at him as hard as I can. I see you lost! Myself lost! He is rooted in front of the mirror, purposely tangled up in his tie! Now for the final effort. I force myself to laugh – I laugh – laugh – (She breaks out into wild laughter) I want you! I order – command! Swear to enjoy you! Now you may – love me – to your heart's content!

RÜDIGER. (beating his temples with his fists) Is this torture never coming to an end?

LEONORE. Ah, that wipes the insolence off his face quick enough! His brutality disappears! His exultation fades away! And his laughter rattles in his throat before it breaks off. And then ...

RÜDIGER. Be quick, Leonore! Must the story of my rescue rob me of my reason?

LEONORE. He chokes on his own curses. White as chalk, grinds his
teeth. And I? Let me be cut in pieces, exterminated! Exterminated!
(She has sunk down into another chair, her face in her hands)

EFFIE. (in an undertone, but decisively, to RÜDIGER) You will be crimi-
nally inhuman if you torment this woman further at this moment!

RÜDIGER. Would it be more amiable of me to listen with indifference?

LEONORE. (her face streaming with tears) Did I do anything so terrible?
I kissed him, so that he might stamp me underfoot. But then ...
(Suddenly composed, staring first at RÜDIGER, then at EFFIE) ... he
pulls both hands back over his own head – I can feel his fists burning
against my cheeks – then – there was a jerk – he had shot himself
from above in the back of the head! (Pointing to the crown of her
own head) Just there, he had shot himself. (Staggering back) He falls
against my knees, so that I fall back against the chimney-piece – and
lies motionless. (A pause)

Scene Seven

(VAN ZEETER, manager of the hotel, enters rapidly)

VAN ZEETER. I need not tell you how indescribably awkward this is.
But I must ask the ladies and gentlemen most emphatically to make
as little disturbance as possible. I have put our private automobile at
your immediate disposal. I can do no more. The car is waiting in the
second courtyard, by the back stairs. (He opens the door and calls)
*Vite, vite, Monsieur Duvoisin, finissons! Nous n'allons pas faire trôp de
tapage!* (He admits MONSIEUR DUVOISIN and two GENDARMES.
Pointing to LEONORE) *Voilà la dame en question.*

DUVOISIN. (to LEONORE) *Madame, je suis prefect de police de la
commune d'Ouchy. C'est vous Madame Wetterstein? n'est-ce-pas,
Madame? – Madame, vous êtes arrêté. Suivez-moi!*

EFFIE. What does this mean?

VAN ZEETER. (to EFFIE) The death-sentence is no longer carried out in
this canton. The lady has no need to worry unduly. But please be
good enough to leave as quickly as possible. We are having a big
concert here this evening, with Catalini from Paris.

EFFIE. You realise that it is a case of suicide, of course?

VAN ZEETER. Excuse me, Madame. I realise nothing. (To DUVOISIN)
Eh bien, Monsieur Duvoisin, fermons cette affaire!

DUVOISIN. Madame, vous êtes obligé de me suivre à la préfecture de
police. Dépêchez-vous, Madame!

RÜDIGER. (to LEONORE) They will release you at once, there can be no
question about that.

LEONORE.
I, Effie, go to Prison? Effie, is this
Then your work also? Help me, Almighty God,
Help me to find a way to overcome
This woman's frightful power. No, Rüdiger,
Poor as I am, I have more self-respect
Than to force myself on you. Love each other!
The poorest man no longer pities me,
Why should the child have pity for its mother,
Or why the husband pity for his wife!
Love one another. Perhaps in time to come
People will gaze more mildly on my crime.
Bloodstained I cannot force myself upon you.
Do not touch me. Now let me go to prison.

(Exit rapidly)

ACT THREE

Scene One

(A low, yet spacious apartment with snow white panelling and a white wooden ceiling. Downstage right, as seen from the audience, is the main door; in the centre of the back wall is a door hung with white curtains which have a pattern of pink flowers on them; downstage left, scarcely noticeable in the white panelling, is a small arched doorway. In both side walls, between the side doors and the back wall is a line of wide, low windows very close together. Through the windows in the right hand wall one glimpses the sunlit interior of a large mediaeval court-yard; through those on the left slender tree-tops are visible, the summit of a small watch-tower and above it the deep blue sky. The windows giving onto the courtyard are closed, while those opposite are wide open. The furniture of the apartment consists of three small tables surrounded by light chairs, all dazzlingly white. There is neither rocking-chair, sofa, nor divan. The tables are laid for tea. On the centre table is the tea-kettle. When the curtains over the centre door are raised, one can see, without being able to distinguish details, into a room lit by a dull red glow.

HEIRI WIPF, in shirt sleeves, wearing a green apron and an enormous rush hat with a red band, is filling the fruit bowls which stand on the tables with fresh fruit from a rough willow-basket)

HEIRI WIPF. (sings)
  Oh the plums were so blue!
  Oh the plums were so blue!

PROFESSOR SCHARLACH. (opens the door downstage right and calls
    through it)
  You miscreant, do finally stop that wretched

Ear-splitting ditty!

HEIRI WIPF. (with a laugh) That would be something new! (He
    advances on SCHARLACH with raised fist) You perjured heretic!
    Why shouldn't I sing here?!

SCHARLACH.
    Be quiet! The young mistress is not well.

HEIRI WIPF. What's that? – The young mistress? – Our dear young
    mistress? Has she a pain anywhere?

SCHARLACH.
    Of course she has a pain! That's why she cries.

HEIRI WIPF. She's crying? Merciful heavens! Our young mistress
    crying! Why in the devil's name didn't you tell me that at once? You
    crazy fool! If the young mistress is crying it must be something really
    bad.

SCHARLACH.
    And so it is! And now, get out of here!

HEIRI WIPF. There's no need to talk so uncivilly to me, not by a long
    chalk. You damned perishing heretic! Just you tell the little lady Heiri
    Wipf hopes she'll be better soon!

(Exit HEIRI WIPF downstage right, followed by PROFESSOR SCHAR-
LACH)

Scene Two

(PROFESSOR SCHARLACH leads EFFIE in. She is in full evening dress
and wearing a tiara. Her face is bathed in tears and she is shaken by
violent sobbing. He guides her over to one of the open windows, where
she sinks weeping into a chair)

SCHARLACH. (with a sigh)
    Oh dear, oh dear, oh dear, oh dear,
    What a wretched lout I am! Who would have
    Expected this? Carried away
    By my medical discovery, I pierce,
    Without dreaming of what I'm doing,

My guinea pig to the heart
With my murderous scientific theory.

EFFIE. (howling)
I built a *Weltanschauung* for myself,
Oh God, Oh God, what now remains to me
Of my absurd and childish *Weltanschauung*!

(She cries heartbreakingly)

SCHARLACH.
My child, it's not good for your health that you
Should give full rein to so much agitation.

EFFIE. (howling)
My pride, my arrogance, my self-amusement,
My life as an adventuress, my freedom,
For all of these, I thank my *Weltanschauung*.
For every look with which I got a man,
For every night of riot, conscientiously
I've given to myself a true account,
Exactly as if I had been manageress
Of property entrusted to me. And now I'm told,
It's all disease, my lust is a disease,
My eyes disease, my colour a disease.

SCHARLACH. (with a sigh)
The room which I am living in up here
Is certainly the sunniest, the cosiest
In the whole castle. That, Effie, is a thing I owe
To you. Each morning when the maid
Brings me my breakfast up, I ask myself
Whether I'm not a child dreaming a child's dream.
Right underneath my windows I hear murmurings
From rabbit hutches. And opposite
Flattered by sunlight and the ivy tendrils,
The reddish-brown square masonry of the keep.
Don't show yourself ungrateful, Effie,
For such a magic kingdom. Absolute mistress,
You reign enthroned over a princely seat,
Humanity has not known for centuries.

EFFIE. (drying her tears)
That this should be brought home to me today,

Today of all days, as if planned. My mood,
My understanding, madness, folly, and
My *Weltanschauung*, I need more today
Than ever before. And yet today
Everything collapses, crushing me.

SCHARLACH.
Who knows, my child, perhaps there is
A sign from heaven in this. The whole week long
Only my respect for you has prevented
Me speaking frankly. All of us
Who surround you here like satellites
For once are of the same opinion . . .

EFFIE. (calmly and decisively)
Enough, enough. It is impossible
That I should talk of this with you. Moreover
It's not a matter for general opinion.
But now please tell me, briefly and clearly,
What, through shock, I only half was able
To hear. You said, if I understood correctly,
That the strength of my desire was due
To digestive disturbances?

SCHARLACH. (with a shrug)
Probably you laced yourself too tightly
When you were still a child.

EFFIE.
And for this gleaming
Of my eyes which promises a man
Heaven knows what, I am indebted to
Some affection of the liver?

SCHARLACH.
Effie, you know yourself how ruthlessly
I must pursue my medical problems
Through every net, if anything
Even the smallest catch is to remain
To be evaluated. Twelve years
Already I've been working upon my
Preconditioning of Criminality.
Not that it was solely for that purpose
Of spying on you, that I was your doctor.

> The fee that Dr. Salzmann pays me
> Would have enthused another first class man.
> But is it really so extraordinary
> If in the hubbub of our conversation
> During the midday meal, I should forget
> For one moment that you were the purpose
> Of the Universe, and not science?

EFFIE.
> That my complexion so quickly changes colour
> That my skin is so pale and lifeless,
> All that is the result of gall-stones
> Or possibly an illness of the lungs?

SCHARLACH. (with an affectionate concern)
> Even in the future, Effie, no man
> Will look into your eyes, without his falling
> Your unresisting victim – as truly
> As no one else lives who knows how to flatter you
> As unashamedly as I do.
> Be content! For I can hear already
> Paladins of your kingdom on the staircase.
> Be gay! Let no one see that something's wrong.

EFFIE. (rising)
> Life's glorious flame is quite extinguished,
> And nothing's left but dark and cheerless ashes.
> Expiation through venal love, the whore's
> Sanctification, how shockingly stale it sounds
> To me now. Yet I shan't turn back. Corruption
> Approaches and declines. But they'll find me
> Upright and proud as my good fortune found me.

Scene Three

(RÜDIGER VON WETTERSTEIN opens the door downstage right and puts his head inside)

RÜDIGER.
> May we come in, my child?

EFFIE.
> Please do.

RÜDIGER. (in the open doorway, to someone outside)

Come in, dear heart. We're not disturbing her.

LEONORE VON WETTERSTEIN. (entering)
Dear child, for heaven's sake, have you been weeping?

EFFIE. (with exaggerated cheerfulness)
I have been laughing till the tears
Stood in my eyes. No, dearest mother,
If you had heard the story Hannibal
Just told, it would have laid you howling
On your back, if you had understood it.

LEONORE. (embracing her)
Oh Effie, your gay mood is like a balm
To me. Have you heard then of the princely
Gift you are making us today?

(To RÜDIGER)

May I speak of it?

RÜDIGER.
It's not my business to dictate
To the sharer of my fate. I give no orders,
Forbid her nothing, since I scattered
Her fortune to the four walls and myself
Grew bald with the great effort of it.

LEONORE.
And like a young girl you are still
Snatching at flatteries. My white hairs
Are not due to feverish activity.
The first post this morning brought us
A completed settlement assuring
A regular income certain all our lives.
From today Rüdiger and I receive each year ...

(To RÜDIGER)

May I name the sum?

RÜDIGER.
Eight thousand marks! Professor Scharlach
Has already gained our daughter's confidence.

LEONORE. (to EFFIE)
Child, child, what must it have cost you?

EFFIE.
A conjuring trick!

LEONORE.
It's with Karl Salzmann
As if supernatural powers were helping him.

RÜDIGER.
Dear, good Salzmann! Yes, I never would
have dreamed that I would one day be
A guest in my ancestral castle.

LEONORE.
In Castle Wetterstein! Rüdiger
von Wetterstein at Wetterstein! That has a ring!

RÜDIGER.
Pension Salzmann at Schloss Wetterstein
Sounds on the other hand more up to date.

SCHARLACH.
If Manager Salzmann perhaps shows himself
Without much scruple in his methods
The gift of being an organiser must be
Accorded to him in the first degree.

RÜDIGER.
A paragon of business. It's incredible
The many inspirations that he has.

LEONORE. (to EFFIE)
And what a lovely, touching home he has
Created for your father and myself
In 'Bergfried'. Two hidden steps
Lead secretly as to an upper world
Into our bower. Far to the North
The dark heights of the Schwarzwald, and our windows

Open onto the court above the gateway
Dating from the year sixteen hundred and thirty-two.
Incredible – but here he is in person!

Scene Four

(KARL SALZMANN, WALDEMAR UHLHORST, MATTHIAS TAUBERT
and SCHIGABEK enter. SCHIGABEK has his hair dressed à la madness
and wears a stand-up collar, a bow-tie and wrist-frills; as well as a blue
tail-coat, a gold-trimmed waistcoat, purple velvet breeches, silver-grey
stockings and buckled shoes with red heels. He carries a troubadour-lute
under his arm)

SALZMANN.
Say, let's all have some coffee. Everyone
Feels more at home here than at his own home.

(To EFFIE, as the others enter)

At Yokohama the World Exhibition
Opens in May. And yet I ask myself
If we'd not better go to the South Pole.
Effie, I have a feeling that this summer
Everyone who's anyone, without exception,
Will meet each other down at the South Pole.

EFFIE.
I'm for doing first the Exhibition,
And for going afterwards to the South Pole.

SALZMANN.
Thank you, my treasure!

EFFIE.
In what part
Of the castle will Mr. Tschamper take
Up residence?

SALZMANN.
In the old armoury, South West.
From the court it gets the morning sun. At evening
He'll see the sun behind the furthest peaks
Sink.

EFFIE.
　　And if at noon he should go up
　　To the old bastion, then the glacial brow
　　Of Jungfrau gleams upon him from
　　Eternal snows.

SALZMANN.
　　Fanfares of trumpets will
　　Announce to us Mr. Tschamper's entry
　　Through the gateway of the outer courtyard.
　　In the gallery we have installed
　　The hunting horns. Then in the central courtyard
　　Schigabek will make his speech of welcome.

SCHIGABEK.
　　On the understanding of course, that my tour
　　Of Argentina is contrived
　　By Mr. Tschamper. People say there are
　　Brilliant openings for us humorists
　　In South America just now.

EFFIE. (clapping her hands)
　　Now Schigabek shall sing us a new song!

SCHIGABEK.
　　A Song? When we may find at any moment
　　This thousand year old pile of stones
　　Blown into the air, and ourselves with it?

EFFIE.
　　The time will run on all the faster
　　Till Mr. Tschamper comes.

RÜDIGER.
　　Up here the time
　　Flies with such alarming speed
　　Without explosions even, that night and day
　　I fear the earth may leap out of its orbit.

LEONORE.
　　For God's sake, Rüdiger, don't joke
　　So lightly about this old globe.

RÜDIGER.
  But, darling, there'd be the advantage
  That we could leave this life together.

LEONORE.
  The only boon I still have to beg God.

TAUBERT.
  Piles of stones? Explosions? Is the castle
  In danger of being blown up?

UHLHORST.
  In the anarchist
  Laboratory installed in the basement
  By me, early this morning I rigged up
  A bomb, to test its efficacy.
  If it explodes spontaneously and blows
  Us up, it's absolutely useless.
  But if its violence can be locked up
  Till the word's given, then humanity
  No more needs to fear armies. Earthquakes
  And floods are to be had to order, and
  No criminal with thundering cannon
  Need any longer go unpunished.

SCHIGABEK. (sings to his lute)
  Secretly in catcombs
  We are manufacturing bombs,
  As the ancient curse foretold:
  Heavenly blast and thunderbolt.

EFFIE.
  I have never had a vocal acrobat
  As lover, who knew how to sing
  Coloraturas with the mastery
  Of Schigabek!

UHLHORST. (in an armchair, one leg over the other)
  We three, you, Effie, Matthias Taubert
  And I, are in the same position of being
  At odds with the highly praised social order.
  You, Effie, bayadere, courtesan,
  Matthias Taubert: Metaphysician
  Supported by man's indolence of mind.

And I who'd put my life upon the highest
Stakes, simply to be rid of it
Without dishonour.

EFFIE.
Now let Schigabek
Sing us another song.

LEONORE. (kissing her forehead)
Don't let us
Disturb you, dearest child. Your father
And I are going to take our ease.

RÜDIGER.
In the mulberry tree
Outside our window, thrushes chirp
A lullaby.

UHLHORST.
You heard them as a child!
Isn't Castle Wetterstein your home?

RÜDIGER.
Oh no! I was born in Berlin
Number forty-six Steglitzerstrasse.
From there to the military academy.
Not since the Thirteenth Century has the castle
Been in my family possession.
Forgive me, gentlemen, I am the only
Victim of marriage in the castle.

LEONORE.
But what storms and trials our marriage
Has stood against. And how happily
And indestructibly it holds together.

RÜDIGER.
Only because at last you've realised
What things in life have any lasting value.

LEONORE.
To drink one's coffee in the afternoon
With eyes half-closed and not to think of anything!

SALZMANN. (to RÜDIGER)
 If you will allow me, baron, may I
 Have dinner served for her ladyship
 And you in the seclusion of
 The honeysuckle arbour?

LEONORE. (pressing his hand)
 How good he is!

SALZMANN.
 I wish you an enjoyable siesta.

 (Exeunt RÜDIGER and LEONORE, downstage right)

EFFIE. (clapping her hands)
 Now Schigabek shall sing us a new song!

SCHIGABEK. (sings to his lute)
 On the steamer
 It smells of camphor.
 Who smells of camphor?
 The rich lord, of course.

SALZMANN.
 That song will go down brilliantly
 In the Argentine! When Mr. Tschamper hears you
 He will have to take you. He'll tear you away
 Even if you and Europe have grown together.

TAUBERT. (in an armchair)
 A strange pleasure came to me
 Here unawares. The torture chamber
 In which I work at my *Kingdom of the Sun*
 Is so cut off from the courtyard, on its
 Rugged isolated cray that only
 The Southwards view there keeps me company.
 Then a sensation of happiness overcomes me
 At the thought of unspeakable agonies
 Suffered in that narrow room in bygone
 Times. I scarcely hold myself for ecstasy.

EFFIE.
 I once knew a man who sprinkled
 Glass-splinters in his bed, for fear

That unexpectedly in sleep he might
Die of boredom.

UHLHORST.
When in the year
Eleven hundred and fifty, Barbarossa
Rode up this way, to break his rival
Count Uhlrich on the wheel, historically
Anarchism then was at its fullest
Height of flowering. I mention this
Having in mind the fact that the moral
Order of that time, so parallels
The propagation of action today,
That we might pride ourselves on being heroes.

EFFIE.
Who else but I in this ancient seat
Of princes has the right to boast of real
Contact with princely personages?
Are you, Matthias, since the Holy See's
Excommunication made you famous
At last, in touch with it even by letter?
As for you, Waldemar, floods and earthquakes,
Wait, so they say, upon your word.
But that brings you no closer to the great ones.
At best you'll meet death fighting like a hero
Before the police, and in a trial by jury.
When I think of the wild enthusiasm,
The shouts of joy from a thousand thousand hearts,
When my beloved one with a smile rides out
From his residence to the people's festival,
I count myself as happier than those women
Who groan imprisoned in their families.

TAUBERT.
Come! Uhlhorst, Scharlach, Schigabek,
And Salzmann! Let us slit our stomachs.
Idle, ignoble wretches that we were
Not to have found ourselves with princely blood
Set here within God's world.

EFFIE.
God in heaven, what a handsome fellow!
Withal, no fool. And with such regal

Freedom of self-expression. You all call me
By pet names. Schigabek calls me
'My little Monkey'. You, Salzmann, of course,
'My treasure'. Uhlhorst says to me: 'My pony',
'Epiphania', Matthias Taubert calls me,
And Scharlach has named me his 'Guinea-pig'.
When my prince saw me at the races
Driving my black mares with their white eyes
And flesh-coloured genitals, he cried aloud,
To his adjutant: By the Holy Cross
See how the horses suit that pair of eyes!

SCHIGABEK.
How is it, Monkey, that your prince has never
Employed me as his humorist?

SCHARLACH.
And me
As his physician?

TAUBERT.
Me as confessor?

SALZMANN.
Me
As finance minister?

UHLHORST.
Me as chancellor?

EFFIE.
Because my beloved simply and solely
Must love me for my own sake, for my own
Sake alone. Because I do not wish
To be beholden to your intellects
In any way where he's concerned. No, not
To you nor any earthly power. To me,
Alone, I owe his love, here where I stand.
The prince, in order to prevent a world war
Married. But to me he brings his yet
Unexpended passion. A man who when
He sits upon his horse – women in droves
The loveliest, throw themselves under the hooves.
To this man I am the world's pinnacle.

After our first meeting he gave me
The golden goblet out of which we'd drunk.
My most precious possession. Till today
I've not had time to decipher the inscription.

(She takes the goblet out of a small box which she has fetched from a cupboard and gives it to UHLHORST)

UHLHORST. (slowly deciphers inscription)

Come – what – may
All – things – pass – away.

(To EFFIE)

But what thinks his Royal Highness of
Your *Weltanschauung*? After all,
Your prince must feel rather uneasy
If in the midst of sensual delirium,
He has to fly hither and thither after
A pack of new ideas!

EFFIE.
Consider, Waldemar
A man like him. A sovereign without fault
Immaculate from head to toe. Achilles!
I chatter as I will, the maddest jokes
Cannot dislodge him from his majesty.
He listens too, without batting an eyelash,
When I rave of the rite of the embrace
As if for the royal libertine, there were no
Trace of blasphemy in the expression.
My game of hide and seek makes him so happy,
With which a woman holds a man imprisoned.

TAUBERT.
It's hardly possibly that you've betrayed
To the prince our scale of love.

EFFIE.
Sometimes when deep asleep, he murmurs
Our litany of love. When a ship was launched
At the destroyer station, and he could not read
The speech which had been pressed into his hand,

He said, without reflecting long upon it:
>First in the darkness, then in the lamp-light
>Servile brood in painfullest plight.

UHLHORST.
>Third in daylight, fourth in the open,
>Pleasures we don't regret in death even!

SALZMANN.
>Fifth in nakedness, sixth before mirrors
>Ah, how the storm gives wings to our senses.

TAUBERT.
>Seventh in pearls decked, eighth in gold costumes,
>Sins of slavery are now long-banned customs.

EFFIE.
>Ninth in context, tenth as sacrifice,
>So that our godhead may never depart from us.

SCHIGABEK. (tuning his lute)
>I've parodied our litany of love
>So as to make your sides split. You'll all be
>In contortions, when you hear my verses.

(A solemn fanfare of hunting horns, interspersed by strident sounding
of a motor horn, are heard outside)

SALZMANN.
>Those are the horns of Mr. Chagnaral!
>Let's all together in the courtyard bid
>Chagnaral Tschamper come from Atakama
>Welcome to Castle Wetterstein.

SCHIGABEK.
>I beg you after the address of welcome,
>To recommend me to him for Argentina.

SALZMANN.
>It shall be done. Let us prepare
>For Mr. Tschamper entering the hall
>A welcome such as since Barbarossa
>No world benefactor ever had.

(All except EFFIE and TAUBERT leave the room)

Scene Five

EFFIE.
> Why don't you go along with them to welcome
> Mr. Tschamper?

TAUBERT.
> I have no wish to see him.
> I leave today. How long will he be staying?

EFFIE.
> He's taken rooms with us to stay a month.

TAUBERT.
> Epiphania! Be on your guard against
> This queer fellow! He's murdered three or four
> Prostitutes already.

EFFIE. (laughs)
> Newspaper stories!
> If even one were true, he wouldn't be
> Going free today.

TAUBERT.
> The story goes, the girls
> Committed suicide.

EFFIE.
> The more fools they.,
> But you yourself can see that he
> Did not kill them.

TAUBERT.
> What does he pay for his fun?

EFFIE.
> A hundred thousand dollars.

TAUBERT.
> My respects.

EFFIE.
> It is the highest price anyone yet
> Has paid for me.

TAUBERT.
> You'd better not take it.
> Epiphania, better not.

EFFIE.
> How can I not. The Kaiser interdicts
> My prince if he can't pay his debts again.
> And the provincial chamber will appropriate
> His principalities, setting aside
> The regency, and add them to
> The Empire as imperial territory.
> A deputy will be appointed, and
> The dynasty which ruled a thousand years
> Will rule no longer.

TAUBERT.
> To be ruled by you!
> Then at last you will have him to yourself.

EFFIE.
> No, quite the contrary. I'm sunk if he
> Renounces the succession. Then he'll live
> Only for the sake of wife and children.

TAUBERT.
> Is he so sober then about the affair?

EFFIE.
> He's not free, like the rest of you. The princess
> Wrote this to me herself. And what is more
> He only gets two hundred thousand marks.
> Karl Salzmann sticks into his pocket
> A hundred thousand for making the agreement
> With Mister Tschamper so watertight, my fee
> Can never be reclaimed, not under
> Any circumstances whatever. In our
> Business that's always the worst problem.

TAUBERT.
> A hundred thousand marks are left for you?

EFFIE.
>Provided I fulfil the stipulated
>Obligations – else I get nothing. I
>Needed a larger sum, in order to
>Secure my parents an annuity.
>Karl Salzmann took upon himself the purchase
>Of the annuity, with so much understanding
>My father goes in raptures speaking of it.

TAUBERT
>It's a matter of historic fact that two
>Girls ended their lives under his eyes.

EFFIE.
>The man from Argentina has one wish –
>To die lying in a woman's arms.
>After all that's not astonishing.
>A hundred men would never have had strength
>To kill themselves, if first they hadn't found
>The disgust with life that's necessary
>For such an act, through their affairs with women.

TAUBERT.
>It only strikes me as suspicious that
>Till now his efforts haven't been successful.

EFFIE.
>In our profession there are thousands of
>Pitiful creatures, who can't bring themselves
>To be the witnesses of a man's death.
>They simply have no inkling of the power
>That has been given us over men's fate.

TAUBERT.
>You've seen how many dead?

EFFIE.
>Upon my bosom.
>My husband shot himself.

TAUBERT.
>Epiphania
>Aphrodisiaca! Whenever you
>Enter a graveyard, coffin lids

Lift themselves up. However, be on your guard.

EFFIE. (laughs)
  What do I have to fear? Only last summer
  On the Mondsee I was shut up with
  The mad Prince of Afghanistan. It
  Was a summer holiday like others.
  We played like children.

TAUBERT.
  Epiphania
  Aphrodisiaca! There's nothing you don't know
  And yet ...

EFFIE.
  I knew a gentleman
  Who would let fly a stream of bullets
  If one but tweaked a single one of the
  White hairs upon his chest. Hark! Heiri's singing.

HEIRI WIPF. (on a plum tree outside the window)
  Oh the plums were so blue!
  Oh the plums were so blue!

TAUBERT.
  Ah! That voice! It goes right through me!

EFFIE. (opens the window and calls)
  Leave for the moment your plum-gathering
  Dearest Heiri!

TAUBERT. (at one of the windows)
  Isn't that an indescribably
  Beautiful panorama. Just to think
  How quickly all this beauty will be only
  For other human beings to enjoy.

EFFIE.
  Why, here he comes himself, plum-gathering Heiri!

HEIRI WIPF. (a sack on his shoulders, kneels on the window-ledge) A
  damned pretty song, that one about the plums. One works from
  morning to night like a navvy, but one can't for the life of one get
  the song out of one's head.

EFFIE.

Then sing to us! Come Heiri, climb right in
With your sack full of plums, and sing!

HEIRI WIPF. (climbs into the room) A surprisingly pretty song. It comes
from High Germany. The jester ought to sing it to the princess every
morning. I don't sing High German well.

(He sings)

Oh the plums were so blue, so blue!
Oh the plums were so blue!
Then the peasants come and they crush
The plums in a horrible mush.
They crush the plums so blue, so blue!
They crush the plums so blue!

TAUBERT.

The oaf! Don't let me suffer it, Effie!

HEIRI WIPF. Oaf am I? (With raised fist he goes for TAUBERT) That's
new to me. (As TAUBERT hastily removes himself) I'm filth. You're
filth. And the mistress is – of the finest quality that's made. We'd all
be better off if we were oafs.

EFFIE.

Bravo, Heiri! You're a prophet. Go now
Into the garden. Pick a basketful
Of large fresh pears for us to eat tonight.

HEIRI WIPF. For tonight. Right you are. Pears for the mistress. The
night is such a damned hot time of day.

(Exit downstage right)

EFFIE.

This is a man indeed!

TAUBERT.

Epiphania
Aphrodisiaca!

EFFIE.

Well, my sweet one?

TAUBERT.

> On other occasions you have always followed
> My advice when you got entangled. Aren't we
> Accomplices? For daily we do traffic
> In goods which are unsaleable to those
> Who make use of them daily like dear bread.
> You with flesh, I with spirit. Humans
> Put up with both of us with inward rage
> Because they can't dispense with either of us.
> Epiphania, as Hercules did once,
> You stand at crossroads. Woman buys
> For love all her life's happiness. If that
> Doesn't come off, love's poison. Let go the loved one,
> And give a wide berth to the raging beast.

EFFIE.

> You are a coward like all of those who've thrown
> Their priestly cassocks from them in a rage.
> I find my life simply intolerable
> Unless there's an adventure waiting for me
> Of which no one can guess the outcome.

TAUBERT.

> But just today I recognised no sign
> Of confidence in your voluptuous eyes.
> You looked almost as if an illusionist
> Had crossed your path.

EFFIE. (bursts into tears)

> Don't torture me!
> O stop tormenting me. I cannot live
> Unless I'm loved.

TAUBERT.

> Sooner than with Mr. Tschamper
> I'd even try it with a little child.

Scene Six

(Enter KARL SALZMANN hastily, downstage right, followed by SCHIGABEK)

SALZMANN. (at sight of EFFIE)
  What does this mean? Tears? Now? Why, who on earth's
  Responsible for this?

  (To TAUBERT)

  You clumsy fool
  Get out! Away with you, I say!

SCHIGABEK. (walking up and down excitedly, to SALZMANN)
  You left me on one side as if I were
  A valet! One doesn't keep a waiter more
  Carefully at a distance from one on
  Festive occasions. For you my title is
  Bernburg Ducal Court Opera Singer.
  Please make a note of it. You've absolutely
  No right to treat me as an underling.

SALZMANN. (to EFFIE)
  Tonight there will be a great gala banquet
  Yonder in the hall of Knights. The way
  Across the courtyard from the gallery hall
  To the Knights' hall, will be lit by
  Torches blazing as on a candelabra.
  In the lime trees on the old bastion
  Will burn three hundred paper lanterns,
  And yet you have the boldness to make red
  Your eyes, with weeping.

EFFIE. (gaily)
  Simply and solely
  By way of contrast ... Just as raindrops
  Through which the sun shines, smile more merrily.

SALZMANN.
  The basis of my handling your affairs
  Is that you should be a fille de joie.
  If you are the whining, moaning type
  Then find yourself another entrepreneur.

TAUBERT.
Epiphania, now my apprehensions
Seem to me myself almost absurd.

SALZMANN.
Apprehensions? If one knows the game
There is no reason to be apprehensive.

(To TAUBERT and SCHIGABEK)

But now you two, get yourselves out of here.

SCHIGABEK.
You churlish fellow, you don't have to count
On my recommendations if the Press
Over there should want to know about you.

SALZMANN. (thrusts SCHIGABEK and TAUBERT towards the door
downstage right)
For all the world, please do not recommend me
To anyone. I must entreat you not to.
We have our hands completely full already.
The more the reservations the less careful
Our work becomes.

(Calling through the door to them)

Good merchandise, good prices.
That is my motto.

(He crosses the room diagonally, opens the door in the background
and calls)

Kindly step this way, sir.

(He admits MR. TSCHAMPER and disappears into the room beyond)

Scene Seven

(TSCHAMPER, a gigantic figure, beardless, with cropped grey hair, enters, removing his top hat)

TSCHAMPER.
You know, my child, that it is my intention
To die.

EFFIE.
Is it to be today?

TSCHAMPER.
As soon as possible.

EFFIE.
Good, then I'll go
At once and get my clothes off.

TSCHAMPER.
That is quite
Unnecessary.

EFFIE.
Please excuse me, but
According to the contract you wanted
To die at the sight of a naked woman.

TSCHAMPER.
How could you so misunderstand! The soul
Was to be naked. Since how long have you sold yourself?

EFFIE.
Five years. My calling suits me very well.
Since how long have you bought from us?

TSCHAMPER.
I've been
Your faithfullest customer since the world began.

EFFIE.
So old and still so enterprising.
As anxious as a student for applause.
I'm very glad we got to know each other.

TSCHAMPER.
  Mine is the pleasure, says the Lord. I'd never
  Pay such large sums otherwise for my amusement.

EFFIE.
  Certainly
  It was hasty of you. You'd no idea
  Of what I like. Is then my love your loss?

TSCHAMPER.
  With me you're doing business. I do not wish
  The form of the transaction to be altered.

EFFIE.
  Man is always business for the woman.
  In the best marriages, that is no different.

TSCHAMPER.
  Yet in marriage one doesn't, as a rule,
  Make contracts like the one Karl Salzmann made.

EFFIE.
  One doesn't find it easy to shake off
  Its chains, nevertheless.

TSCHAMPER.
  With superstitions
  Like that fools drug themselves who drag with lust
  The chains of marriage with them all their lives.

EFFIE.
  Do you believe there are such crazy people?

TSCHAMPER.
  Most are like this; in having no idea
  That each one keeps his freedom in his marriage
  And daily does and leaves undone what pleases
  Him most.

EFFIE.
  That sounds intoxicating. But
  In the reality each person asks
  If marriage stems from Heaven or from Hell.

TSCHAMPER.
Because this powerful struggle between Heaven
And Hell is needed by our stomachs.

EFFIE.
But can't the pact that Salzmann made between us
Also be used to the same purpose?

TSCHAMPER.
No.
Impossible. No devil could sustain
Comparison with Salzmann.

EFFIE.
Then I'm bound
To you more closely than in marriage?

TSCHAMPER.
I hope so. For the price I paid for you
Two thirds of the world's marriages
Would let themselves be torn in pieces.

EFFIE.
Then do with me what your heart most lusts after.

TSCHAMPER.
That cannot be avoided. Death is what
I'm after.

EFFIE.
Gladly I'll exert my arts
To ease your parting.

TSCHAMPER.
As you know you're paid
To do that.

EFFIE.
None has ever known me break
A contract. I'm too proud of my vocation.

TSCHAMPER. (sitting down at the table)
I take into account the favoured chance
That suddenly my suicide might come off

Without assistance; to this end I keep
A little vial of prussic acid with me.
If you permit I'll pour a drop or two
Into this goblet here.

(He pours a few drops from the vial into the golden cup that stands
on the table)

EFFIE.
And you forbid me still to take my clothes off?
That isn't courteous: for a fille de joie
Wounded in her vanity is helpless,
Stupid and slow and clumsy as a child.

TSCHAMPER.
That's how I need you – helpless.

EFFIE.
Please allow me
To dilute your drink a little bit.

(She fills the cup with water and hurls the contents out of the
window)

TSCHAMPER.
You also have been married?

EFFIE.
Two years I stood it.
The necessary balance of emotions
Did not appear.

TSCHAMPER. (taking the goblet from her)
Where did you get this goblet?

EFFIE.
My lover gave it to me.

TSCHAMPER. (pours a few drops of prussic acid into the cup and adds
water)
Myself I'll add the necessary water.

(He holds the goblet in his hand)

EFFIE. (decisively)
    Then I shall show myself.

TSCHAMPER.
    I forbid you.
    Nerves taut with spiritual torment give me
    Strength. Don't keep on boasting of yourself.

EFFIE.
    You never will achieve the longed for hatred
    Of the world by measures such as these.

TSCHAMPER.
    The flesh has its own spirit. As soon as some
    Living beings' nerves are stretched so far
    That I can feel myself a man, I'll empty
    This cup. And then the world will be rid of me.

EFFIE. (approaches him cautiously, stroking him gently)
    And yet I'll wager that you scarcely know
    The ten-tone scale?

TSCHAMPER.
    Is that a patent?

EFFIE.
    I'll
    Recite them to you.

TSCHAMPER.
    What is the bottom step?

EFFIE.
    First in the darkness, then in the lamplight,
    Servile brood in painfullest plight.

TSCHAMPER.
    There I have never been. The topmost step!

EFFIE.
    Ninth in contest, tenth as sacrifice,
    So that our godhead never shall leave us.

TSCHAMPER.
    In contest! Wonderful! The thing for me!
    Instead of poetry, now reality.
    Tell me the saddest thing in your whole life.

EFFIE.
    I can't. Impossible. Already I
    Tremble in every limb.

TSCHAMPER. (rises, the goblet in his hand and presses an electric
    button by the centre door)
    To swindle me
    Out of a hundred thousand dollars, is no child's play.

EFFIE.
    It never was my calling to communicate
    Unhappiness. Pleasure is all my service.

TSCHAMPER.
    How wrong one can be!

    (To SALZMANN, who enters from the centre door)

    Open bankruptcy proceedings.
    This creature is unwilling to relate
    The unhappiest event in her whole life.

SALZMANN. (goes right up to EFFIE with an urgent look)
    Must I drive your lover from his kingdom
    With shame and contumely tomorrow
    Show him the door?

    (As he leaves the room, to TSCHAMPER)

    She'll tell what is to tell.

    (Exit into room beyond)

EFFIE. (trembling, to TSCHAMPER)
    Which story then?

TSCHAMPER.
    The saddest one
    In your whole life.

EFFIE.
>The first time that I broke
>My marriage vow, that was the saddest.

TSCHAMPER.
>Incredible! How did it happen? Say!

EFFIE. (approaches TSCHAMPER confidingly)
>Wouldn't you do better, if you used
>The favourable chance, and did become
>Instead of an unhappy beast, the happiest
>Guest in all the world at the great feast?

TSCHAMPER.
>Where is this opportunity?

EFFIE.
>Not far for those who see!
>The unnatural is a labyrinth
>Which many have escaped in thousands.
>One must laugh and dance too.
>In all misfortunes there are two.
>The most refractory of eccentrics
>Declared insane in the statistics
>Did you ever hear of one
>That I could not bring back to reason.
>He was only suffering
>Torments of love before
>Afterwards he's sometimes laughing
>At his acting against nature.
>Harmlessly engrossed in pleasure
>He fights his way through all life's torture.

TSCHAMPER.
>Tell me of your first adultery!

EFFIE. (begins to tremble)
>Boredom was our cursed fatality.
>No girl had ever planned
>Greater happiness
>He the handsomest lieutenant
>From the riding school.
>And since the first kiss
>Each had one thought

To love the other with all his might
As love we must.
But powerful as was our desire
Our boredom grew cruelly.
Then he counselled me
Lest our harmony grow dim
To be unfaithful to him.
I, like one possessed, began,
To provide stuff for conversation,
To throw his money about.
He could not make it out,
Could not forget his dream
Could never stop urging me
To betray him with the next best dandy
For the amusement that would come.

TSCHAMPER. (sets the goblet down again on the table)
   Wasn't that a pleasure?

EFFIE.
   What a year-long
   In me was strong,
   In one night
   Was lost to sight.
   Barren wilderness, barren heart.
   Of reluctance
   No experience.
   Everywhere
   Did appear
   Unsubtle obviousness.
   Desolate, I looked back:
   You threw away your luck
   In order to revive
   Your slackening nerve.

TSCHAMPER.
   You've told that to a hundred men already.

EFFIE.
   As if I had no merrier tales to tell!

TSCHAMPER.
   The man had one idea – to get rid of you.

EFFIE.
>Just the opposite his purpose.
>He threw me to those others
>To heighten his own pleasures.
>Each time I had been unfaithful
>He found me twice as beautiful,
>And of regret not a sign.
>Till finally I took any man
>Who came across my path.
>Always surrounded by admirers
>Lest my body spoil
>While my soul died of hunger.
>The last remains of love
>Then fled away.
>I bore with him as one may
>With some luckless relative
>Whom one can't allow to die.
>I threw his money to the wind
>Always hoping in the end
>He must come to hate you so
>He will flee from you like sin.
>But he sticks like a burr
>Till destitution threatens
>Then shoots himself dead
>Fearing poverty, on my bed.

TSCHAMPER.
>That didn't worry you three days on end.
>How should that steel me for my suicide?
>Give me heart-cries! Are your parents alive?

EFFIE.
>Only my mother.

TSCHAMPER.
>Then, how did your father die?

EFFIE. (starting up in horror)
>No, I can't speak of that!

TSCHAMPER.
>How did he die?
>Relate to me your father's death!

EFFIE.
I can't.

TSCHAMPER.
Tell.

EFFIE. (throws her arms round his neck)
Come with me! Don't let us stay here!
Later you'll no more ask after my father's death
Than about my husband's suicide.

TSCHAMPER.
Who's paying,
I or you?

EFFIE.
You! You're paying.

TSCHAMPER.
I!
Then tell me now about your father's death.

EFFIE. (with increasing agitation)
On New Year's morning, it had been snowing.
Chief Medical Officer Korff, Major von Falkenstein,
Come into us from the garden.
And here am I in my short frock going
To meet them: just look, the gentlemen,
Even-tempered as ever had mislaid
My father: they mutely sign
To me to step aside.
Then my mother comes out of the breakfast room
Major von Falkenstein observes dully:
'Compose yourself, good madame ...
He who trusts God's doom ...'
Tears roll down his cheeks:
Mother shrieks:
He lives! He's still alive.
But the Major shuddered.
No word!

TSCHAMPER.
While with someone of your way of living,
Did he have a stroke?

EFFIE. (screaming)
　He fell in a duel!

TSCHAMPER.
　How genuine and full emotions flourish
　In this old world still. Not America
　Nor all the British Empire could produce
　Such intense feeling. Yet once more must I
　Enjoy the spectacle. What is your earliest
　Memory of your parents? Tell me quickly!

EFFIE.
　On the green bank by the oleander
　Mother and father sat together.
　And standing there upon their knees
　I saw them suddenly embrace.
　I throw my arms around them, seeing
　Their kisses as the joy of my own being.
　Cried out that we must stay this way for ever
　And they continue kissing one another.

TSCHAMPER.
　Can't you still remember how your parents
　Quarrelled, fought and swore at one another?

EFFIE.
　That isn't true! I never saw it happen
　I can't – I can't control myself! Childhood,
　My parents' house. If you had not existed
　Life would be madness, torment, muddle, horror.

　(She is seized and shaken by spasms of weeping)

TSCHAMPER.
　Put that handkerchief away! Stand up! Are these
　Overstrained nerves?

　(He overthrows the chairs and kicks them against the walls)

　Now listen to your father!
　Give answer to your father, speak to him.
　Say to your father, what you've done, since he
　Lay in his coffin on a New Year's morning.

EFFIE.
Leave my father out of this. My father
Is dead.

(She throws herself on TSCHAMPER's breast and kisses him wildly)

But were you ever kissed like this?
And this? And this?

TSCHAMPER.
Yes, for one dollar!
Earn the hundred thousand I am paying!
Earn them! Or do I have to show the way?

(He seizes the goblet and appears to drink from it)

EFFIE. (with an involuntary cry)
No! You must live!

TSCHAMPER.
Feeble creature!
Can't bear to see a man die. Not even you!

EFFIE. (passionately)
Because I love you! Did ever man and woman
Find one another better matched
Than you and I? For the first time, existence
No longer grins at me with hollow eyes.

TSCHAMPER. (apparently tired)
And as for me, a memory stalks me
As if I'd died within these walls before.

(Looking out of the window)

The wide view out on green-surrounded roofs,
The crenulated wall, which from the bastion
Leads to the watchtower. And the plum trees ...
My death is child's play, when its content
Outweighs the content of my life.

EFFIE. (pressing tenderly against him)
Beloved, accept your life, you have not lived
Till now ...

TSCHAMPER.
Neither have you.

EFFIE.
I wouldn't
Have been a whore if I had had a tamer
Who tames like you ...

TSCHAMPER.
Did you look for me?
A person who has courage finds her tamer.

EFFIE. (embraces him. In passionate tones)
You need a woman who gives all to you.
I lack a man to whom to give myself.

TSCHAMPER.
And you, my child, believe yourself this woman?

EFFIE.
Since I am proud, as answer if you doubt it,
I'll drink this cup.

TSCHAMPER.
I doubt it.

(EFFIE quickly seizes the cup, drinks hastily and lets it fall. Then she raises her arms soundlessly, bends convulsively backwards and falls to the floor. Lying on her back, her arms and legs bent backwards as far as possible, she throws herself without a sound from one side to the other until her body, resting on her hands and feet, suddenly rears up. Then spasms set in and subside gradually until she remains lying motionless)

(In an armchair)
Ah, how beautiful! Ah what wonder!
Thank you, my child. None other was so sweet.

(Rises, looks out of window)

This glorious piece of earth. Oh, did the knights
Dream ever of the contests that would rage
Today within the walls of their old castles?
How strange it is that a prostitute never

– As children with their parents otherwise –
Feels herself superior to her parents!
Your fate is that of many.

(He opens the door to the room beyond)

My motor.

Scene Eight

SALZMANN. (enters)

It seems that once more you have failed.

TSCHAMPER.
    I hoped that I had reached the goal, when she
    Drank the poison right under my nose.

SALZMANN.
    Too tiresome!
    The cars are waiting at the central gate.

TSCHAMPER.
    We were chattering harmlessly
    About her childhood home. How does it happen
    That no whore ever can stand that? I and
    The world – we don't see eye to eye. The world
    Must become different.

SALZMANN.
    Certainly. It changes
    As quickly as it can. However, meanwhile
    How to make good my loss?

TSCHAMPER.
    Well, you will come
    To manage my affairs in Atakama.

SALZMANN.
    I'm father of a family. Adventures
    Don't suit me.

TSCHAMPER.

I offer you a salary
Of fifty thousand dollars and guarantee
An annual profit of a hundred thousand.

SALZMANN.
I might consider this.

(Opening the small arched door on the left)

Let us descend
The tower staircase. A cleft in the rocks
Leads as a secret way to the middle gate.

TSCHAMPER. (picking the goblet up from the floor)
This I take with me as a souvenir.

(He walks out, SALZMANN follows him)

HEIRI WIPF. (invisible outside the window)
Oh the plums were so blue!